KW-240-104

EDUCATING FOR
A PEACEFUL FUTURE

David C. Smith

McGill University

Terrance R. Carson

University of Alberta

KAGAN AND WOO LIMITED, TORONTO

CANADIAN CATALOGUING IN PUBLICATION DATA

Smith, David C. (David Charles), 1935–
    Educating for a peaceful future

Includes bibliographical references and index.
ISBN 0-921-099-07-X

1. Peace—Studying and teaching.   I. Carson,
Terrance R. (Terrance Ronald) 1944–   . II. Title.

JZ5534.S64 1998   327.1'72'071   C98-930728-X

Copyright ©1998 by Kagan and Woo Limited
253 College Street, Unit 393, Toronto, Ontario M5T 1R5

ALL RIGHTS RESERVED

No part of this book may be reproduced in any form without
permission in writing from the publisher, with the exception
of pages marked **P**, which may be photocopied for classroom
use.

Design and layout: Joseph Chin
Printed by Coach House Printing
1 2 3   CH   00   99   98

UNIVERSITY OF PLYMOUTH

9007998990

Permissions

Every effort has been made to contact copyright holders of
extracts and artwork reproduced in this text. The publishers
would be pleased to have any errors or omissions brought to
their attention.

Figure 7–1 (page 102), "The steady-state economic vision",
is taken from *Planet Under Stress: The Challenge of Global
Change* by Constance Mungall and Digby McLaren.
Copyright ©the Royal Society of Canada. Reprinted by
permission of Oxford University Press Canada.

90 0799899 0

WITHDRAWN
FROM
UNIVERSITY OF PLYMOUTH
LIBRARY SERVICES

EDUCATING FOR
A PEACEFUL FUTURE

7 Day

University of Plymouth Library
Subject to status this item may be renewed
via your Voyager account
http://voyager.plymouth.ac.uk
Exeter tel: (01392) 475049
Exmouth tel: (01395) 255331
Plymouth tel: (01752) 232323

WITHDRAWN

Contents

Preface

The eminent historian Sir Isaiah Berlin termed the twentieth century one of the most violent in recorded history[1]. Certainly, in terms of the sheer scale of misery and suffering engendered by violent conflict, the twentieth century was without parallel. The industrial and technological change that improved the material circumstances of life for so many also created the technology necessary for waging total war and developing weapons of mass destruction. More people died in the wars of the twentieth century than at any other time in history. These were not only military deaths. The past one hundred years ushered in the phenomenon of unrestricted warfare, which included the massive aerial bombings of civilian populations and the attempted extermination of entire races of people. It was also an age marked by the triumph of ideology over humanity, in which many millions died in the name of radical totalitarian social and political experiments in the Soviet Union, Nazi Germany and elsewhere.

The disastrous consequences of unchecked violence in the twentieth century are clear enough, but the way ahead to an alternative, non-violent future remains cloudy. For many of us who grew up in the West and in the shadow of the nuclear threat, the superpower rivalry between NATO and the Warsaw Pact once appeared to be the major stumbling block to a peaceful future. The end of the Cold War, however, put an end to any such naive views of the causes of conflict. It is

apparent from subsequent events that nuclear weapons did not just cast a shadow over our future survival, they also prevented the recognition of many other issues—issues like environmental damage, equitable development, human rights, and intercultural understanding, all of which have an enormous influence on people's experiences of peace and security. Recognizing these issues, as we now do, suggests that there will be a major task ahead for educators. It will quite simply be the work of learning from the hard lessons of the past in order to open up possibilities for a non-violent future.

An education for peace as defined in this book is an exploration of the way teachers and students might unfold a possibility of teaching for a non-violent future. We are proposing a new form of education because, as Maria Montesorri suggested, the historical record has shown that schools have been far more competent at educating for conflict than they have been at educating for peace. In our view, educating for peace will require "remembering forward". Søren Kierkegaard, the Danish philosopher, coined this phrase in distinguishing between two ways of comprehending change: recollection and repetition. Recollection understands change only as a recovery of the past, in the sense that new possibilities can only be realized in terms of what has been previously defined and understood. Repetition is quite different; it means the unfolding of a new circumstance that is already present in existing possibilities. Repetition, or remembering forward, applies to peace education because we are not yet able to propose a detailed plan for peace that

---

[1] *New York Review of Books,* January, 1995

is based upon a recollection of the past. The past mainly supplies us with the experience of an absence of peace. To educate for peace will require the enactment of a new possibility that has not yet existed, but might be realized through an education that is animated by critical reflection and the development of relationships of respect and mutual understanding.

We might begin unfolding this new possibility of educating for peace by bringing our attention to particular images or events that exemplify the absence of peace and show the necessity of finding new directions. One of the most singular events of human history occurred in Hiroshima on August 6, 1945. It was then that the first atomic bomb was dropped on a civilian population. In retrospect we can see that the destruction of Hiroshima marked a change in the field of human possibilities: a weapon now existed that could put an end to human civilization. Father Pedro Arrupe, a Jesuit priest who had been living not far from Hiroshima in 1945, recognized the meaning of this event. Writing some years later, he recalled noticing a clock on the wall that had stopped precisely at 8:15 a.m., the exact moment of the explosion. He wrote: "For me, that silent and motionless clock has become a symbol.... [It is] a parahistorical phenomenon. It is not a memory, it is a perpetual experience, outside history which does not pass with the ticking of the clock. The pendulum stopped and Hiroshima has remained engraved on my mind."[2] The perpetual experience to which Father Arrupe refers is the enduring knowledge that technological ingenuity can destroy us. We are left with a choice of how to use our technological power, and with the fearful consequences of making the wrong choices.

A second exemplary image is the destruction of the forests. In Canada we have witnessed vast tracts of clear-cutting in the West-Coast forest. In South-East Asia the smoke from burning forests and brush hangs over the region for weeks. In Brazil bare reddish earth is replacing the towering trees and rich undergrowth that were once the tropical rainforest. Concerns have been raised that this destruction of the forests both seriously depletes the rich variety of the biological gene pool and causes great harm to the earth's atmosphere. Biologists tell us that, although the rainforests cover only about seven percent of the earth's landmass, they are home to nearly fifty percent of the living species. We are aware, too, that trees are a vital source of oxygen, and that the destruction of forests, coupled with the increased use of fossil fuels, is adding dangerously to the levels of carbon dioxide in the earth's atmosphere. Rising levels of carbon dioxide lead to global warming which harms agriculture, threatens coastal communities, and portends unpredictable climate change. The image of the damaged forests suggests a need to reform relationships with the natural world, to reconsider the place of humanity as inhabitants of a fragile planet also inhabited by other living species.

A third image is that of the debt crisis. During the 1960s and into the 1980s many countries of the South, or so-called "Third-World" nations, borrowed heavily to finance economic development projects. By 1980 the indebtedness of these nations had reached $750 billion. In order to recover this debt, the International Monetary Fund (IMF) imposed harsh terms upon these countries. These

---

[2] Quoted in *Educating for Peace: Explorations and Proposals* (1986), a report to the Curriculum Development Council by the Melbourne Catholic Education Office and the New South Wales Department of Education, p.16.

terms required structural readjustments to the economies of the debtor nations, which had to cut back drastically on government spending in order to pay back loans to the industrialized countries of the North. Structural readjustment has not reduced indebtedness. According to 1990 figures, the debt has nearly doubled while the level of spending on education, health care and subsidies for basic food and shelter has continued to decline in many of the poorest countries. Moreover, in many cases, economic development has resulted in the flow of capital from poor nations to rich nations and a declining quality of life for the least advantaged.

This book is animated by the belief that schools might become active participants in a movement that will reverse some of the existing trends that threaten peace and security. In so doing, it seeks to both outline a comprehensive framework that guides an understanding of peace education and offer a number of suggestions as to how teachers and school communities might develop appropriate practices. The book is divided into three sections. The first section provides a historical and conceptual sketch of peace education. The second section takes up the theme of how peace education might be infused into various school subject areas and into teaching practices generally. The final section looks at the complex question of introducing peace education practices into the culture and organization of the school.

The book begins with a retrospective on past efforts to educate for peace in the twentieth century. Looking at the violent history of this century might lead one to suspect that there had been little effort to promote peace in schools in the past. In fact, the record shows this not to be the case. Especially before the First World War, peace education

enjoyed considerable official support. Nowhere was this more true than in the United States. But the intention to educate for peace in schools ultimately failed, mainly because educators did not appreciate the powerful effects of the dominant curriculum which promoted national feeling and competitive individualism. The failure to reflect critically on the effects of the dominant curriculum continues to this day. The second chapter attempts to go some way in correcting this tendency by outlining a critically reflective framework for peace education. It is a framework that seeks to take account of multiple perspectives and various experiences of violence that affect people's lives. This chapter concludes by outlining seven dimensions of peace education that guide the formulation of peace education in this book. The final chapter in the introductory section discusses the problem of linking thought and action in peace education. Drawing on the example of Mahatma Gandhi's "experiments with truth", we suggest that practices of non-violent action will inform an understanding of peace just as much as conceptual frameworks can. Gandhi provides this insight as a basic precept of peace practice: The way is the goal.

The second part of the book takes up the practice of peace education in terms of teaching. Each of the first eight chapters in the section is devoted to a different school subject area. Beginning with literature and then moving on through second languages, history and civic education, geography and economics, mathematics, science and technology, music, and finally art education, the chapters discuss how peace education might be infused into these particular subject areas. A ninth chapter in this section, which has been contributed by Graham Pike and David Selby, offers a number of specific teaching suggestions for developing peace education in the classroom. This chapter is organized around the seven dimensions of peace education outlined in Chapter 2.

In the final section we return to the school community as the location of peace education practice. The section begins with a chapter reflecting on the life of the school, considering how an ethos of peace and non-violence might be fostered through the formal curriculum and the informal life of the school. What is taught and learned in school does not simply reflect the intentions of the teacher and the curriculum. The school community, the media, popular culture, and the way in which the school relates to wider culture and the world beyond all have important implications for peace education. Building cultures of peace in the twenty-first century will be a complex matter for educators, but not impossible. The final chapter, on school change, begins with the example of one school that has succeeded in building peace within its local and wider community. Moving from this example, the question of school change is taken up from the perspective of the school's interaction with personal development, the school community and national and global development.

Discovering the way of peace is the insistent question of our time. The violence of unrestricted warfare, colonialism, ethnic cleansing, and environmental damage have all been legacies of the twentieth century, but so too has incredible progress in education, human rights and relief from poverty. According to the 1997 United Nations Human Development Report, poverty has declined more in the past fifty years than in the previous five hundred.[3] Material progress has been impressive, as have been developments in communications and information technologies that bring the peoples and the cultures of the world more closely together. The question now underpinning the activities of all peace educators is this: Can we go forward together, living in harmony on this fragile planet?

---

[3] UNDP, *Human Development Report*, 1997, Oxford: Oxford University Press, 1997.

Acknowledgements

This book was developed in two Canadian universities—McGill University in Montreal and the University of Alberta in Edmonton. There have been close links between these two institutions reaching back to the inception of the University of Alberta in 1908. We have been pleased to contribute to the strengthening of these ties through the collaboration and friendship that developed in the writing of this book.

We would like to express our gratitude to our many colleagues and students who have generously shared and discussed ideas related to peace education, and to those who read and commented on earlier versions of the manuscript. At McGill, we wish especially to acknowledge the following colleagues: Patricia Gordon, John Gradwell, William Lawlor, Cathrine Le Maitre, Christopher Milligan, Claudia Mitchell, Georges Terroux, Lorraine Thibeault, James Watling and John Wolforth. Special thanks to Mark Smith for his valuable suggestions and constructive feedback on certain parts of the manuscript. At the University of Alberta, we gratefully acknowledge the contribution of Wytze Brouwer, Virginia Floresca-Cawagas, Yee Wah Cheng, Ingrid Johnston, Douglas Roche, Hans Smits, and Toh Swee-Hin. Thanks go to the Edmonton Collaborative Action Research in Peace Education (CARPE) group which has played an influential role in exploring peace education practice. We are grateful to our colleagues at the University of Toronto, Graham Pike and David Selby, for contributing the chapter on teaching activities.

We would also like to thank those who gave permission for us to reproduce extracts, illustrations or other copyrighted material in this book: Takashi Hiraoka, Mayor of Hiroshima, for the 1991 Peace Declaration (pages 79–80); Oxford University Press for the diagram of the steady-state economic vision (Figure 7–1; page 102); The Protestant School Board of Greater Montreal for the poem "War...Peace" (page 55); UNESCO for passages from *The Arts and Man* (pages 53, 55, 61); Eric Wesselow for the photograph of his stained glass window "Ruth and Boaz" from "Scroll of Ruth", Sanctuary of Temple Sinai, Toronto (Figure 11–3).

We would like to acknowledge the support of a research award from the Canadian Institute for International Peace and Security which provided important assistance in the early stages of this book project.

Thanks to our families, Rillah, Richard and Sarah Carson and Cecilia Jayme Smith, for their patience and understanding during the many days we devoted to research and writing over the years since the project was first conceived.

Finally our sincere thanks to Elynor Kagan and Terry Woo. Without their continued support and belief in the project, this book could never have been completed.

David C. Smith
Terrance R. Carson
June, 1998

EDUCATING FOR
A PEACEFUL FUTURE

PART 1

The Background to Peace Education

What Can a Teacher Do?
A Century of Educating for Peace

THE DECEMBER 1923 *edition of the* Alberta Teachers Association Magazine *contained a lead article entitled "The Need for Teaching Peace Ideals". The author was Mrs. William Carson, a school board trustee of the city of Calgary. In the article, she asked teachers not to forget the agonies of the recently ended 1914–1918 war which, she said, "had brought civilization to the abyss". In her view, the war was the result of the mis-education of youth, who were encouraged to make heroic sacrifices in the name of racial and national patriotism. The hard lesson, made clear by the experience of the Great War, was the requirement to reject nationalism and to shift the focus of patriotism to a new patriotism of common humanity. She urged a cross-curricular effort by all teachers: "Music and literature must be used to enthuse for peace, art must portray the beauty of concord ...[and] science [must be] devoted to the conservation of human life" (Carson, 1923).*

An event of the kind that really forces a fundamental redirection in life is often the result of negative experience.[1] This is an important point to consider in a historical interpretation of the development of peace education in the twentieth century. There have been many attempts to confront educationally the problem of violence in the twentieth century, a century that the British historian Isaiah Berlin (1993) called "one of the most violent in recorded history". Given that this was the time when mass public education was introduced and when we saw the rapid expansion of universal public schooling, we might be forced to conclude that education for peace has been either neglected or singularly ineffective. Despite hopes to the contrary, the end of the twentieth century has not brought a sense of progress and peaceful, democratic pluralism. Rather, it has given us what appears to be a descent into a new international disorder of frightening ethnic violence and renewed nationalist conflict.

What, in fact, has been the history of peace education in the twentieth century? Has it, indeed, been ineffective, or is it unfair to expect education to turn the tide of national and international events? This chapter will examine the idea of peace education and how it has been practised over the past century. The intention is to understand better the relationship between peace and education.

The Idea of Peace Education

Education for peace could be regarded as being part of the progressive education tradition. Progressivism is the philosophy which holds that students, as members of a democratic society, can actively participate in the improvement of that society. And, in many ways, peace education has been consistent with the idea of an education for social reconstruction as promoted by George S. Counts, Theodore Brameld and others. This view was often at odds with more conservative positions that saw the main goals of schooling as cultural reproduction or vocational preparation. But peace education itself also has quite conservative antecedents. It might be surprising to learn that, especially prior to the First World War, peace education enjoyed wide support from conservative civic leaders and members

---

[1] The German philosopher Hans-George Gadamer (1989) terms this the "essential negativity of experience". Experience is negative in the sense that it originates in a realization that things are not as we had assumed them to be.

of the business elite, such as the Boston book publisher Edwin Ginn and the Scottish-born steel magnate Andrew Carnegie.

In some ways, the history of peace education has transcended ideology. A willingness to confront what is violent, unjust and destructive in life is not necessarily either politically progressive or conservative. Rather, what is common in peace education is a desire to understand the nature of violence and discord, and to seek out alternative ways of relating to one another.[2]

Our examination of the twentieth century experience of peace education begins with a story of the School Peace League. This was an international organization led by decent, civic-minded people who were to underestimate tragically the power and passions of nationalism in the years immediately prior to the First World War.

Joining the March of Progress: The School Peace League

The idea of peace education enjoyed considerable popularity in the early 1900s. One of the most important groups advocating peace education was the School Peace League, which had branches both in Britain and America. The School Peace League was inspired by an idea that was beginning to be widely held among enlightened cosmopolitans of the time. This idea was that humanity had outgrown the need for violent conflict to settle disputes. It was felt that a new world order was dawning in which rational structures and procedures for the resolution of disputes were being put into place. In 1899, a permanent world court

of arbitration was established at the Hague in the Netherlands. There were great hopes that this court would lead to an institutionalization of peaceful dispute resolution.

However, there were darkening clouds on the horizon. This was a time of rising international tensions. Forces of nationalism, fuelled by the success of Italy and Germany in establishing their ethnically based states in 1867 and 1871, were threatening the integrity of the weakening multinational empires of Austria-Hungary and Ottoman Turkey. Moreover, many European nations were aggressively adding to their colonial empires. Nationalism and colonial expansion and consolidation were providing fertile ground for international conflict that was being made ever more dangerous by a growing arms race among the great powers. There was, in the words of H.G. Wells, "a race between education and disaster".

In 1907, a motion was passed to establish the American School Peace League at a National Arbitration and Peace Conference in Philadelphia. Many dignitaries attended this conference, including members of the United States government cabinet, two former presidential candidates, ten senators, four justices of the Supreme Court, as well as a number of state governors, mayors, college and university presidents, church and labour leaders, and prominent members of the business community. The School Peace League began its work in the fall of 1908 with the object of "promoting through the schools…, the interests of international justice and fraternity" (Scanlon, 1959: 107). By 1912, it had branches in nearly every state and was active in providing guest speakers and books for school libraries and helping to organize student peace groups. In the same year, the National Education Association held its annual meeting in conjunction with the

---

[2] The historian Ronald Aronson (1983) has suggested that the search for an education for peace follows the logic of dialectical thinking.

School Peace League, passing a resolution praising the League's activities.

The American School Peace League owed part of its success to the efforts of its general secretary Fannie Fern Andrews. She edited a highly popular pamphlet, *Peace Day*, which was distributed throughout the country by the United States Bureau of Education. This pamphlet contained many suggestions for ways in which teachers and their classes might observe May 18, which had been set aside as "International Peace Day". This date had been chosen for the commemoration because it marked the anniversary of the first Hague Convention.

The year 1912 turned out to be the high watermark for the American School Peace League. For the next two years, Fannie Fern Andrews tried to put into action the League's ideal of achieving peace through international understanding by organizing an international council on education. Despite her unceasing efforts between 1912 and 1914, she was unable to convene the international organizational conference necessary to found the council. She had the moral support of the US State Department as well as the support of a number of individual ministries of education in Europe. But, in practice, most countries were very reluctant to allow external interference in their schools. Although it was yet unrealized, the idea of peace through international understanding was already beginning to collide directly with the forces of nationalism in education.

In retrospect, it is surprising that members of the American School Peace League were so unsuspecting of the outbreak of the First World War in 1914. When war broke out, the American peace advocates were genuinely shocked and disoriented. In fact, a number of them had arrived in Europe in July 1914, fully expecting to attend various scheduled summer peace conferences. To their dismay, they found themselves in the middle of the so-called "July Crisis" and the military mobilization of the Great Powers that followed the assassination of Archduke Franz Ferdinand by a Bosnian Serb in Sarajevo on June 28 of that year.

Understandably, the First World War was to shatter the peace advocates' confidence in the progress of a civilizing movement towards international understanding and arbitration. In fact, the peace movement and the School Peace League were among the casualties of the war. Some of the members were left literally physically and mentally broken. Those who remained in the American School Peace League were divided as to what their response to the war should be. Some favoured an activist course, continuing resolutely to promote mediation and the peace cause among the belligerents. More, including Fannie Fern Andrews, counselled withdrawing from activism altogether, believing there was little that could be done while the combatants were at war. Their preference was to make plans for a postwar peaceful world order that would set in place binding legal mechanisms for the avoidance of future wars.

Lessons of the School Peace League

What might be learned from the experience of the American School Peace League? Why does it seem, in retrospect, to have had so little influence on the events and the attitudes leading to war? Is it the case that peace educators, like Fannie Fern Andrews, so were naïve as to fail to understand the realities of aggression and conflict? Were they stuck in some idealized version of peace? Or is it possible that what schools were actually teaching, despite the efforts of the School Peace League, had very little to do with the aims of an education for peace? In order to answer some of these questions, it is helpful to turn to an investigation of what some of the prewar understandings of peace and education were.

Internationalism and Nationalism

In examining the history of peace education, it is wise to discern the links between research, peace activism and peace education. In the era before the First World War, nationalism was a potent rallying force throughout Europe and the Americas. Schools were very much caught up in this nationalism, particularly in view of the establishment of national systems of education which had begun in the nineteenth century. Since the school was regarded as a key instrument of nation-building, a good deal of its curriculum and teaching supported nationalist goals, at the expense of international understanding. Jean-Jacques Rousseau had expressed the philosophical basis of nationalism in education in the eighteenth century when he wrote:

> Education ought to give national form to the soul of the people, and guide their opinions and tastes in such a way that they will become patriots through inclination, through passion, through necessity. (Quoted in Snyder, 1964: 107)

Consumed by idealism and a faith in progress, the founders of the American School Peace League failed to appreciate the inconsistency between their hopes for international understanding and the powerful feelings of these emergent nationalisms being fostered by state education systems. But peace advocates were not necessarily naïve. Their beliefs did have some basis in fact. For some years there had been a growing development of international communications and commercial links. The permanent Court of Arbitration had been

established at the Hague for the express purpose of providing a forum for the peaceful resolution of conflicts based upon international law. The view that the modern age had rendered warfare obsolete was held widely, and was given expression by Norman Angell in an immensely popular book of the time, *The Great Illusion* (1910). Angell, a British economist, argued convincingly that war had become an anachronism in the twentieth century, because the economies of the mature, most advanced capitalist states, such as Germany and Britain, were now so interdependent as to make waging war completely unprofitable for both victor and loser alike.

The confidence that the early peace educators had in arbitration and international understanding reflected the beliefs of civic leaders who were also active in the peace movement. The committee of the Norwegian parliament that was responsible for awarding the Nobel Peace Prizes, which had been inaugurated in 1901, held a similar conviction about international conventions. Nobel prize winners between 1901 and 1914 were all either organizers of peace conferences, advocates of international law, or long-time pacifists (Gray, 1976: 69).

It was relatively easy for American educators of the time to translate this belief into part of the mission of the school, since great store was now being placed in the power of education to shape the future (Tyack and Hansot, 1981: 3). But these educators uncritically assumed that their vision should become the world's vision. Theirs was an uncomplicated notion of education, based upon their right and responsibility for the moral uplift of the community. In the case of peace education, they simply extended their idea of community to include everyone else in the world. Many fancied themselves as "realists" who understood that war was the natural primitive state of humankind, but they were supremely confident that it could be contained. As Elihu Root, the former Secretary of State under Theodore Roosevelt and the winner of the Nobel Peace Prize for 1912, stated:

> War was the avenue to all man desired. Food, wives, a place in the sun, freedom from restraint and oppression, wealth of comfort, wealth of luxury, respect, honor, power, control over others, were sought and attained by fighting.... (Gray, 1976: 112)

Despite the military build-up and arms race in Europe prior to the First World War, there was also a reasonably well-developed movement in Europe promoting an education for peace. Like their American counterparts, the Europeans also saw peace in the fairly limited terms of an increased international understanding. But even more than the Americans, the Europeans were running counter to the prevailing policies of their own governments, which were avidly stressing nationalism and military preparedness. In the face of this emphasis, educators such as Lebonnois in France, Kemeny in Switzerland and Peeters in Belgium were working to facilitate international communication among educators.

There is also some evidence that certain educators in Europe were willing to go beyond simply advocating internationalism, and were prepared to enter into a critical examination of existing attitudes and practices. Kemeny's investigations, in particular, have a contemporary ring to them: he identified issues such as human rights, chauvinism in textbooks and racial prejudice as being matters of concern for peace educators (Scanlon, 1959: 217). Herman Molkenboer, a Dutch educator working in Germany, was also critical of the ultranational-

ist drift and its militarist consequences. Because he believed that militaristic attitudes were the product of past mis-education, he concluded that little could be done with the adults. For children, however, he advocated the particular importance of peace education, arguing that a peaceful future for the world depended upon educating members of the next generation to love their neighbours.

What might we deduce about the possibilities for peace education from the experiences preceding the First World War? Prior to 1914, the meaning of peace was confined mainly to international relations. Thus, the priorities for peace action centred on replacing institutions of war with structures necessary for the peaceful arbitration of differences between nations. Little attention was given to peace on a personal or intercultural level. For the most part, the active members of the peace movement were good, law abiding, upper middle-class citizens of their respective countries. Just as the rule of law kept internal order within their own countries and communities, so—they felt certain—the development of international structures such the Court of Arbitration would make recourse to war between nations unnecessary in the future.

Peace education at the time reflected the middle-class and ethnocentric assumptions that there was basically no difference between good citizenship at home and good citizenship internationally. Unfortunately, international understanding, with just a few exceptions, did not extend to the critical reflection of nationalist assumptions within their own education systems. Relations between nation states remained their focus of concern, and the nation state was to emerge as their unit of ultimate loyalty. Internationalism proved to be a thin gloss of rhetoric laid on top of this solid base of national pride and feeling. Nevertheless, some peace educators did recognize the dangers of national pride as it became increasingly manifested in militarism and the arms race. Some also resisted the militarization of schools, as was evidenced, for example, by the fierce debate that took place in Britain over the introduction of marching drill and other kinds of bellicose activities in British schools during the Boer War (Young, 1987).

What ought to strike us most forcibly about the pre-World War I peace educators is their certainty of purpose. They did not question the civilizing influence of the school, nor did they doubt the correctness of their view of peace. To them, it seemed to be only a matter of time before education and the establishment of appropriate international judicial structures would create a warless world. In this context, we cannot help but appreciate the shattering effect that the 1914–1918 war had on peace educators and peace activists alike.

The Interwar Years: Education and An Uneasy Peace

What had come to be called "the Great War" went on for over four years. Nine million soldiers were killed and four empires collapsed. An entire generation who had come of age in 1914 had been traumatized by the unprecedented ferocity of the conflict. But the wish to avoid future wars was to be compromised by the peace treaties. Germany had agreed to an armistice in 1918 on the understanding that the treaty of peace would be based on US President Woodrow Wilson's "Fourteen Points", which outlined the principles for a peaceful world order. Instead, The Treaty of Versailles forced the Germans to shoulder the entire guilt for starting the war and imposed punishing reparations payments on them. The peace itself showed an ambivalence between reconciliation and punishment of the vanquished. A famous cartoon of the time portrayed the next generation as a crying child standing behind the elder statesmen of the Allied powers as they affixed their signatures to the Treaty of Versailles.

If the experience of the Great War dashed the confidence that a better world was coming through the civilizing influence of education, the horrors that had been experienced also brought home a collective revulsion against mass conflict. Conventional wisdom would have it that peace movements grow in proportion to the fear of war. But in the interwar years the opposite seemed to be true. The peace movement, which had been so large before the war, was considerably reduced in size by the 1920s (Osborne, 1987). However, hope for international understanding was given new impetus with the formation of the League of Nations as an arbiter between countries. Organizations to support the League developed in a number of different nations and these formed the focus for a rather broadly based peace movement. For the most part, the meanings of peace continued to be limited to liberal ideologies of international understanding and cooperation. But, in contrast to the prewar situation, there was also a growing critical awareness of the destructive power of nationalism and the role it had played in the previous conflict (J.F. Scott, 1926, and others).

To be sure, educating about the League of Nations was a relatively uncontroversial form of peace education. Many member countries supported the ideals and aims of the League and encouraged teachers by providing teaching suggestions. They also saw the League as a forum for international discussion of educational questions, although they were unsuccessful in getting a permanent education commission established under League auspices.

Individual nations were again unwilling to allow international scrutiny in so jealously-guarded a domain of national interest as education. But there was a growing critical edge as well. The International Committee for Intellectual Cooperation passed a resolution in 1925 calling upon League members to lessen prejudice, stereotyping and ethnocentrism in school texts. If the textbook was one culprit responsible for what Aldous Huxley (1934: 47) called the "nationalistic conditioning of all the worst passions", the curriculum itself was another. The history curriculum, in particular, was singled out as the worst offender. As early as 1918 a women teachers' organization in France began a magazine called *Haissez La Guerre* that called for the abolition of history teaching, because it was little more than nationalist propaganda (Osborne, 1987: 17). Unfortunately, efforts at curriculum and text-book reform had scant overall effect on the ethnocentric content of schooling during the interwar years. Ethnocentrism is evident in the following passage, taken from the teacher's introduction to a widely used world history text from Canada:

> To understand the significance of our own national history, we must study it, in its setting, as part of the history of mankind in general and of the British nations in particular. Especially do the young people in our high schools need to know the essentials of world history, with the emphasis on Europe. For decades to come that Continent seems likely to remain the centre of culture of the world. As for the Western and Southern hemispheres, they represent the expansion of Europe, while the "awakening of Asia" results from the Europeanization of Asia. (West and Eastman, 1945: iii)

During the 1920s and 1930s, however, there was also a growing awareness of a unique-ly pedagogical task for peace education beyond curriculum content. The Italian educator Maria Montessori advanced this pedagogical focus in her work. Montessori felt that education held the key to a peaceful future. She claimed that "establishing a lasting peace is the work of education; all politics can do is keep us out of war" (1949). Montessori was critical of simplistic practices of anti-war indoctrination, such as forbidding war toys and teaching about the horrors of mass conflict. For her, the deep-er question of peace was how to deal with the "moral chaos" facing humankind in the twentieth century. We have, Montessori argued, become well advanced in our knowledge of the physical world, but we know very little of the inner world of the developing person.

As evidence of our moral chaos, Montessori pointed to the fact that we seem quite competent in educating for war, but do not seem to have any idea about how to go about educating for peace. She laid much of the blame for moral chaos on the process of formal schooling. She noted how schooling creates a sense of inferiority in a child by constantly imposing the will of an adult and opening up the young person for disapproval. Domination of children by adults fosters a dependency and it arrests their development, making individuals into unquestioning followers of public leaders. Montessori argued that this effective education for war is consolidated by an over-emphasis on examinations, which encourage competition among students and reward those who better their classmates. Montessori wrote:

> Education...encourages individuals to go their own way and pursue their own personal interests. School children are taught not to help one another, not to prompt

their classmates who don't know the answers, but to concern themselves only with getting promoted at the end of the year and to win prizes in competition with fellow pupils. And these poor selfish little creatures, who experimental psychology has proved are mentally exhausted, find themselves in later life like separate grains of sand in the desert; each one is isolated from his neighbour, and all of them are barren. If a storm comes up, these little human particles, possessed of no life-giving spirituality, are caught up in the gusts and form a deadly whirlwind. (1937: 34)

Montessori taught that the way forward towards an education for peace was to attend to the child and allow him or her to be our guide as to what education should be. She expressed the task as follows: "[There is] a new world to conquer—the world of the human spirit."

Reflections on the Interwar Period

What might be said of peace education in the interwar period? The First World War had been a humbling experience for peace activists and peace educators alike. In spite of their predictions of the unfolding impossibility of war in a world becoming steadily more united by webs of commerce and international cooperation, Europe had been caught up in a maelstrom that was beyond the power of either diplomats or people of goodwill to control. Mass armies enthusiastically marched off to battle, confident that they would be home by Christmas. The war dragged on for over four years of bloody fighting in the trenches.

It was clear to most educators during the interwar years that the meaning and scale of warfare had now changed. But the lessons of the war were seldom translated into the general school curriculum or into pedagogical prac-

tices. International understanding was still a distant ideal to which people paid lip-service. At most, it was simply added on to the regular curriculum as some form of League of Nations education. The central beliefs and tenets of schooling remained unchanged. Nationalism continued to permeate the pages of textbooks. The values of pride and obedience to the national ideal were inculcated in the children, as before.

The Second World War and After

The second of the two great wars of the twentieth century lasted from 1939 to 1945. The Second World War was even more destructive than the First, both in scope and in the numbers of people it affected.[3] Total war raged throughout Europe and the North Atlantic, East Asia and the Pacific, the Mediterranean and North Africa. Unlike the First World War, this war involved millions of civilian casualties. London, Coventry and Rotterdam were bombed by Germany. Bombing raids on cities to terrorize populations and destroy strategic targets became common practice on both sides. These raids escalated as the war went on, culminating in the firestorms of Hamburg, Dresden and Tokyo—and finally in the use of atomic bombs to obliterate Hiroshima and Nagasaki in 1945. Another terrifying development was the mass rounding up and extermination of entire populations, the most infamous case being the systematic mass murder of millions of European Jews by the Nazis.

Clearly, the character of warfare had changed during the course of the twentieth

---

[3] Estimates of combined military and civilian deaths indicate that World War II was over five times as destructive as World War I. Francis Beer (1981) estimates 52 million deaths in World War II compared with 10 million in World War I.

century. As the historian Ronald Aronson (1983: 12) reported in *Dialectics of Disaster*, "our century's catastrophes have transformed the field of possibilities...we know what the worst is like." The world had come to know the fury of total war in a modern industrial age, and this was to have a profound effect on the meaning of peace and how it could be attained.

One response to the terrors of total war was a strengthened conviction that a supranational world organization was necessary for collective security. Such an organization would provide an international forum for nations to debate and, it was hoped, to resolve conflicts peacefully. The United Nations was established in 1945, with more power and more agencies than the failed League of Nations. Among these new UN agencies was one established especially to deal with matters of education, science and culture: UNESCO. Another important response was the drafting of a formal statement of the basic individual and collective rights of all people, in the Universal Declaration of Human Rights (1948).

The usual attitudes of preserving peace through military strength and deterrence also returned following the Second World War. The United States and the USSR emerged from the war as the dominant powers. The Soviet Union built up a ring of buffer states with Communist governments in Eastern Europe, these states eventually joining in a military alliance known as the Warsaw Pact. The United States, Canada, and Western Europe established their own military alliance, the North Atlantic Treaty Organization (NATO) in 1949. There followed other regional military security alliances in other parts of the world.

The political decolonization of the countries of the South after the Second World War was another feature that was to be significant for peace education. Beginning with India, Pakistan and Indonesia in 1947, the European countries divested themselves almost entirely, over the next two decades, of formal political control over their colonies in Africa, Asia and the Caribbean. While the United Nations began with only 45 nations at its founding in 1945, by its 50th anniversary, membership had grown to over 180 independent countries. Many of the new nations had previously been either colonies of European colonial powers or the republics of the former Soviet Empire. Despite gaining political independence, many of the former colonies were relatively underdeveloped industrially and economically, dependent upon trade with the industrialized nations of the northern hemisphere.

The United States emerged from the Second World War as the premier economic power. It launched the Marshall Plan to help rebuild European economies shattered by the war. At his inaugural address in 1949, the American president Harry Truman announced support for a similar program for the development and modernization of agriculture for the "underdeveloped" non-European countries, to be carried out through the FAO (Food and Agricultural Organization of the UN).

Thus, the issues of disarmament, human rights and development were to dominate the peace and security agenda in the decades following the Second World War.

Changing Understandings of Peace Education and Peace Action

History shows that peace education is shaped by prevailing attitudes and understandings of peace. In the post-World War II period, four different periods in the evolution of peace attitudes and concerns can be discerned. The first, beginning in the early 1950s and lasting into the middle 1960s, was governed by a vision of a *warless world*. The second period, from the late 1960s to the late 1970s, was marked by a vision of a *just world*, with special concern for global economic and social justice. The third period, beginning in the late 1970s, was concerned with problems of violence in its many forms, including interpersonal, intercommunity and international violence, as well as violence towards the environment. This period is governed by a vision of a *non-violent world* (Aspeslagh, n.d.). A fourth period emerging from the break up of the Soviet Union and Yugoslavia in the early 1990s may be characterized by a concern for the multiplicity of ethnic nationalisms. We might term this a vision of a *pluralistic world*. The four periods of peace attitudes are described below.

A Warless World: 1950s and early 1960s

PEACE ACTIVISM   The vision of a warless world arose from the wish to prevent mass conflict in the future. Peace activism focussed on ways of increasing international understanding and cooperation. But activism also took the form of protests against the development and deployment of nuclear weapons. During the 1950s, a peace movement began to form around a popular concern for the new and dangerous weapons of mass destruction. In Europe, the Campaign for Nuclear Disarmament (CND) began in 1958. The CND held mass rallies and marches against the atmospheric testing of nuclear weapons. Protests became widespread when Strontium 90 (a radioactive substance deposited by the testing) was found in milk. Mothers concerned that radioactivity was finding its way into their families' diets found an effective form of raising their concerns: they began

mailing their children's baby teeth to government officials and scientists for testing. These protests were influential in the signing of a partial test ban treaty in 1963, in which the USA, the USSR and Britain agreed to stop testing nuclear weapons in the atmosphere. Public concern subsided and governments learned to suppress information about the nature of nuclear war and its effects.

PEACE RESEARCH   At this time, peace research developed as a formal field of study in an effort to bring a cross-disciplinary focus to bear on the discovery and elimination of the causes of war. Prior to the mid 1950s, there had been no field of study known as peace research. In 1959, a handful of social researchers gathered in Norway to form the Peace Research Institute Oslo (PRIO) under the direction of Johan Galtung (Galtung, 1985). Other institutes for peace research were set up in the next few years in Europe and in North America. In Canada, Hannah and Allan Newcombe founded the Peace Research Institute Dundas (PRI-D). In 1964, the International Peace Research Association (IPRA) was founded in London. Its American counterpart, COPRED (Consortium on Peace Research Education and Development), was created at about the same time. Since then, IPRA and COPRED have been important forums for peace research and education, each having their respective journals and annual meetings. Over the years, the interests of peace research have been wide ranging, but in these early days the focus was often restricted to investigating the nature of conflict and exploring the effectiveness of non-violent alternatives for conflict resolution.

PEACE EDUCATION   Peace education in the 1950s and 1960s remained strongly rooted in the traditions of international understanding. As before, such education was often not very controversial. A typical program of that time was UNESCO's Associated Schools Project, which began in 1953. This project was part of a general effort by UNESCO to support international studies (UNESCO, 1959). The concept of universal human rights formed a second focal point for peace educators in the 1950s and early 60s. Here, examination of other cultures was encouraged, with a view to analyzing levels of protection and violation of human rights.

A Just World: The late 1960s and 1970s

During the late 1960s, peace understandings and attitudes turned more towards social criticism, addressing the cultural and historical roots of violence. This critical turn was reflected in activism, research and education.

PEACE ACTIVISM During this period, a growing popular peace movement developed in response to the American involvement in the Vietnam War. By the late 1960s there was a large anti-war movement in the United States and Western Europe. The peace movement joined with other progressive movements in the general social criticism of the time. The thrust linking poverty, racism and human rights with peace came about largely through developments in peace research and education.

PEACE RESEARCH Johan Galtung of the Oslo Peace Research Institute provided a major contribution to the change in thinking about the nature of and conditions for peace . In a paper published in 1969, Galtung made an important distinction between negative peace and positive peace. He noted that the primary focus of peace research until then had been on problems of direct or behavioural violence such as war and the arms race. He urged that attention be given to the underlying structures

of violence—that is, conditions of injustice and inequality that are the root causes of conflict. By analyzing and removing structures of violence, a state of positive peace would be brought into existence. This theory of structural violence immediately related development issues to peace.

A second important contribution made by peace research at this time was the rethinking of the relationship between research and practice. By acknowledging their interest in the promotion of peace, these researchers began openly to question the premise of a value-free social science. They criticized the positivism of normal social science and argued for a new stance of "committed humanism" (Eckhardt, 1972) that made judgments about research based upon peace values.

Yet a third important contribution by peace research was a recognition that the meaning of peace can vary from multiple perspectives. Researchers became especially conscious of the need to listen to views about peace from the countries of the South. The World Order Models Project (WOMP) was initiated in New York in 1970. It consisted of nine groups of scholars from various parts of the world who were asked to develop models for world order and the means for actualizing these models. This project has produced some of the most creative insights on peace, security and development.[4]

---

[4] The work of the World Order Models Project continues from its offices in New York. Much of their research is published in a journal called *Alternatives: A Journal of Social Transformation and Humane Governance* (Lynne Rienner Publishers, Boulder, CO, USA). *Alternatives* is now a joint publication of WOMP, The Centre for Developing Societies (New Delhi, India) and the International Peace Research Institute Meigaku (Japan).

PEACE EDUCATION   Peace education, too, became strongly influenced by concerns with justice and development. The Brazilian educator Paulo Freire (1973) called for a "pedagogy of the oppressed" that aimed at liberating the poor. Freire used an economic metaphor, arguing that traditional forms of education were like deposits of cultural capital made by the dominant groups—local elites and former colonial powers. To become "educated" in traditional forms required withdrawing or borrowing portions of this knowledge. Freire rejected this "banking system of education", arguing that the oppressed could create their own knowledge by learning to "name their world", and in so doing freeing themselves, and their oppressors as well, from relations of domination.

In the early 1970s, peace education began to grow and become more widely accepted among mainstream educational organizations. The 1973 yearbook of the (American) Association for Supervision and Curriculum Development (ASCD) was devoted to peace education (Henderson, 1973). The view of peace in this book was still largely oriented towards the earlier, but still important, tradition of reducing negative peace by developing non-violent alternatives of conflict resolution. Nevertheless, the idea of an education based on the newer concept of peace with justice was also being widely introduced. Betty Reardon, as the coordinator of high school programs for the World Policy Institute, was able to make some of the insights of the World Order Models Project available to teachers in her publications. A new international organization, the World Council for Curriculum and Instruction (WCCI) convened its first conference at Keele, England in 1974 on the theme of "Education for peace: reflection and action". Johan Galtung and Paulo Freire were two of the featured speakers. As the Norwegian peace researcher Magnus Haavelsrud (1975: vi) remarked in his introduction to the conference proceedings, a central question of the meeting was "the role of WCCI in relation to peace values and the overall structure of dominance-dependence, oppressor-oppressed".

A Non-Violent World

Towards the end of the 1970s, a new vision of peace education began to emerge based upon an extended concept of violence. As valuable as the peace with justice view had been, and still is, it presented several difficulties. One problem was the conceptual slipperiness of the notion of "structural violence". This was proving to be a very broad and amorphous term, which was sometimes used as a general label to criticize anything that one happened to be against. A second problem lay in the concept of justice itself, which tended to highlight the conflict between rich and poor, but was not able to move beyond this conflict to discover a common ground for dealing with shared problems.

PEACE ACTION   The emergence of the so-called "new peace movement" was a main feature of this period. In the early 1980s, many more people began to join the peace movement in response to the rapidly escalating arms race between the USSR and the USA. This arms race involved both a qualitative and quantitative increase in weapons, as both sides added to their stockpiles and deployed newer, faster and more accurate instruments of destruction. What frightened the populations in the liberal western democracies most was talk of civil defence and the possibility of surviving nuclear war. In June 1982, over one million people marched for peace in the streets of New York at the opening of the United

Nations Second Special Session on Disarmament. Various professions began to join together to address and speak out on specific aspects of the peace question as it related to their areas of expertise. These groups included Physicians for the Prevention of Nuclear War, who studied and spoke out on the public health aspects of nuclear weapons; Educators for Social Responsibility, who developed teaching guides; and Lawyers for Social Responsibility, who discussed the legal aspects of nuclear weapons. Many of these professional groups developed international networks that were representative of a growing tendency towards "citizen diplomacy", which attempted to sidestep the traditional nation-to-nation diplomacy. New communications technologies facilitated this movement, allowing, for example, electronic town hall meetings between citizens of Seattle and citizens of Moscow.

Concern for the global environment was another factor that shifted the focus of peace action. A new appreciation of environmental limits to growth has encouraged the vision of economic development within the context of sustainable growth. Activist groups such as Greenpeace and Friends of the Earth have helped to raise environmental awareness. The concept of sharing a healthy environment in one world extends to include consideration of responsible stewardship for the planet itself.

The role of women in the new peace movement deserves particular mention. The influence of a feminist consciousness is one of the distinguishing features of peace in this period. One of the best examples of feminist activism was the founding of the women's peace camp in 1981 at Greenham Common in England, the site of an American air force base used for the deployment of cruise missiles. The women of Greenham began an enduring, non-violent protest that consistently placed alternative, feminist values against the patriarchal values of the military. The Greenham Common Peace Camp remained in existence over a number or years; at times there were as many as 300 000 women at the base.

PEACE RESEARCH In the 1980s, peace research became concerned with discerning links among various forms of violence, in the interests of shaping an image of a non-violent world. The question posed by some researchers was "How are we to prepare societies to live together peacefully, disarmed and developed?" (Mushakoji, 1987). Increasingly peace research was linking development, disarmament, human rights, and the environment as four dimensions of a non-violent world.

PEACE EDUCATION Peace education programs have been somewhat slower in developing holistic views of peace. In the early 1980s, there were "activist" curricula responding to the public alarm over the arms race. Nuclear education programs were developed, often produced by concerned groups of educators or interested school jurisdictions. Probably the best known examples were written by the Boston-based Educators for Social Responsibility. Several of their curriculum guides were widely used internationally. A number of local school jurisdictions in Canada, the US, Britain, Australia and elsewhere produced their own nuclear education guides.

There were also programs focusing on other peace education topics such as non-violent conflict resolution, environmental education and human rights. It was the nuclear education curricula, however, that tended to be associated with peace education in the minds of both critics and supporters. These curricula became the topic of public debate that raised many important questions about appropriate ways to approach peace issues and the role teachers should play in the introduction of controversial issues into the classroom.

With debate and reflection on the nuclear issue, peace education programs began to evolve in the direction of making links between various manifestations of violence, and developing a deeper understanding of the sources of violence, helping to shape a future non-violent world. One crucial concern of educators has been to foster hope in young people and to empower them to take an active role in shaping that future.

Towards A Pluralistic World

The world at the end of the twentieth century has changed dramatically. The Cold War, which dominated thinking on peace and security questions for nearly half a century after 1945, is now over. The end of confrontation between the two nuclear armed empires has exposed the contours of a complex world that appears to be moving in two directions at once. On the one side is the globalization of economies and cultures. The free market economy is international in scope and is creating a uniformity of markets and lifestyle. On the other side, there is a resurgence of suppressed nationalisms and a reassertion of religions and cultural particularity. This is not to say the sudden emergence of a perplexing pluralistic world means that a new era of ethnic, cultural and religious violence is inevitably destined to replace the threat of superpower confrontation. Ethnic and religious violence is indeed occurring with some regularity, but it is important to note that the pluralistic world is not new; it was simply hidden beneath the imperial weight of the superpowers. With the end of the Cold War, questions of culture, religion and ethnicity have come forward, together with questions of geopolitics, economics and ideology. In many ways, this is a positive development, because peace questions now cover a much broader range and relate to the rich textures and wholeness of human life.

PEACE ACTION, EDUCATION AND RESEARCH
Two features seem likely to influence peace action, education and research in a pluralistic world. The first of these is an appreciation of wholeness. There is a deeper appreciation of what constitutes violations of peace in human life. We have learned, over the years, that violations of human rights come not just from direct attack or even through structural violence. Violations of peace also take place when traditions and culture are denied. To see human beings as primarily consumers, or simply citizens of the nation state, or any other partial view of people, is a form of violence that diminishes the fullness of their human identity. We see now that threats to culture, religion and ethnicity can produce violent counter-reactions. Unless the dynamics of identity are recognized, prospects for a peaceful future are bleak (Küng, 1990).

A second feature of peace in a pluralistic world is humility. The historical narrative related in this chapter has shown that peace cannot be ordered and controlled from above. Rather, it seems that peace grows from the middle, in the concrete experiences of people's lives and cultures. Douglas Roche (1994), former Canadian Ambassador for Disarmament, noted after many years in international diplomacy that we need to be humble enough to hear the message of the traditions speak to the realities of the present. In a post-modern and post-colonial world, we are beginning to see a new humility at work in the willingness to listen again to traditional cultures, particularly to the cultures of indigenous peoples.

Into the Twenty-First Century: The Task Ahead

The sudden end of the Cold War has presented peace educators with new opportunities, but also with tremendous, perplexing challenges. The brief euphoria occasioned during the largely peaceful disintegration of the Soviet Empire has given way to confusion about how to deal with the chaos and violence that has accompanied the emergence of a vast array of ethnic nationalisms. Michael Ignatieff (1993) characterizes this historic time as "the end of the last age of empire". What has followed after this last age of empire is not the peaceful democratic world order for which many in the West had so fondly hoped, but a new age of violence in which many nation states appear to be on the verge of disintegration and descent into ethnic civil war. The question is now, Where do we go from here?

The story of peace education in the twentieth century began with the apparently straightforward problem of establishing international understanding and resolving disputes among nations non-violently. At the end of the century, the task appears incredibly more complex. Vaclev Havel, the president of the Czech Republic, has characterized this time as a "post-modern world, where everything is possible and almost nothing is certain" (Gwyn, 1994). In a post-modern world, we can no longer count on the certainties of rational control through the accumulation of knowledge and uninterrupted progress. The dimensions of the peace problem are many-faceted. They are military, political, economic, environmental, psychological, ethnic, religious and cultural. There are, in the end, too many dimensions to the peace question for all to be resolved by all-encompassing global solutions.

At one time it was said that war is too important a task to be left to the generals. So, too, in a post-modern world the task of peacemaking cannot be left to the experts, the politicians or the generals. This is an age that has grown sceptical of grand solutions. There may, on the other hand, be more willingness to rely on local knowledge. This shift creates a persuasive new role for peace education. Schools operate on local levels. Pedagogy does not attend to the large scale; rather, it is the work of influencing particular lives in specific communities, slowly and over the long term.

To re-orient ourselves to the new tasks for peace education, to what teachers and students might do on the local level, in classrooms, it is helpful to review the experience of peace education in the twentieth century.

The uncertainty of the post-modern age, and the accompanying loss of unquestioned faith in progress, may not necessarily be a bad thing. Of course, there is the danger that continuing conflict could breed cynicism and resignation. But it could also mark the beginning of wisdom, wherein we more fully appreciate that the "will to dominate" is a problem with many faces. It is manifested in systems of domination over nature, superiority over one's neighbours, control over knowledge. Once we realize that domination is the problem, we can catch a fleeting glimpse of what it is that has been obscured in this will to control. What we have lost sight of is the essential and primary *interrelatedness* of all peoples to the planet and the self organization of the planet as a living system. To understand this is to re-learn what the indigenous peoples of North America, the wisdom traditions of the East, and indeed traditional societies everywhere have always known about relating appropriately to the world—that we are co-inhabitants of the world, and not its controllers.

Recall Isaiah Berlin's characterization of the twentieth century as "one of the most violent in recorded history". We need to formulate the future of peace education against this background. We know that the twentieth century was filled with disasters for peaceful relations among people. We know full well that a reorientation in relations among people will be necessary on some fundamental levels. This is a large task for peace education, but it is one that we can engage with the wisdom gleaned from the stark lessons of this most violent of times.

REFERENCES AND SOURCES

Aronson, R. (1983), *Dialectics of Disaster: A Preface to Hope,* New York: Verso Books.

Aspeslagh, Robert (n.d.), "International Education—a Conceptual Reappraisal", Netherlands Institute of International Relations (unpublished manuscript).

Beer, Francis (1981), *Peace Against War,* San Francisco: W.H. Freeman.

Brock-Une, Brigit (1989), *Feminist Perspectives on Peace and Peace Education,* Toronto, Pergamon Press.

Carson, W. (1923), "The need for teaching peace ideals" in *ATA Magazine,* December, 1923: 18–20.

Eckhardt, William (1972), *Compassion: Toward a Science of Value,* Oakville, Ontario: CPRI Press.

Freire, Paulo (1973), *Pedagogy of the Oppressed,* New York: Herder and Herder.

Gadamer, H. G. (1989), *Truth and Method* (rev. ed., translated by J. Weinsheimer and D. Marshall), New York: Crossroads Publishing.

Galtung, Johan (1969), "Violence, peace, and peace research" in *Journal of Peace Research,* 6: 167–191.

Galtung, Johan (1985), "Twenty-five Years of Peace Research: Ten Challenges and Some Responses" in *Journal of Peace Research,* 22(2): 141–158.

Gray, T. (1976), *Champions of Peace,* London: Paddington Press.

Gwyn, Richard (1994), "Chaotic world forcing people to change or seek refuge in tribalism" in *Edmonton Journal,* July 31.

Haavelsrud, Magnus (1975), "Editors preface" in *Education for Peace: Reflection and Action,* Guildford, England: IPC Science and Technology Press.

Henderson, George (ed.) (1973), *Education for Peace: Focus on Mankind,* Washington: Association for Supervision and Curriculum Development.

Huxley, A (1934), *Beyond The Mexique Bay,* London: Granada.

Ignatieff, M. (1993), *Blood and Belonging: Journeys into the New Nationalism,* Toronto: Viking Press.

Küng, Hans (1990) on *Ideas,* CBC Radio, March 7.

Montessori, M. (1937), "Educate for Peace" in *Education and Peace* (1972) (translated by Helen Lane), Chicago: Henry Regnery.

Montessori, M. (1949), *Educazione e Pace,* Rome: Gartzanti Editore.

Mushakoji, Kinhide (1987), "Preparation of Societies for Life in Peace" in *Bulletin of Peace Proposals* 18(3).

Osborne, K. (1987), "A history of peace education" in Terrance R. Carson and Hendrick D. Gideonge (eds), *Peace Education and the Task of Peace Educators,* Bloomington: World Council for Curriculum and Instruction.

Pierson, Ruth Roach (ed.) (1987), *Women and Peace: Theoretical, Historical and Practical Perspectives,* London, Croom Helm.

Roche, Douglas (1994), "Paths of Nonviolence", a panel at the International Institute for Peace Education, Edmonton: University of Alberta, August 19.

Scanlon, D. (1959) , "The pioneers of international education 1817–1914" in *Teachers College Record,* (4). 214.

Scott, J.F. (1926), *The Menace of Nationalism in Education,* London: Allyn and Unwin.

Snyder, L. (ed.) (1964), *The Dynamics of Nationalism,* New York: Van Nostrand.

Tyack, D. and E. Hansot 1981), *Managers of Virtue: Public School Leadership in America,* 1820–1980, New York: Basic Books.

UNESCO (1959), *Education for International Understanding, Paris: UNESCO.*

West, W.M. (1936), *West's Story of World Progress,* Canadian edition, edited by S. Mack Eastman, Boston: Allyn and Bacon.

Young, N. (1987), "The peace movement, peace research, peace education and peace building: the globalization of the species problem" in *Bulletin of Peace Proposals,* 18(3).

CHAPTER 2

Conceptions of Peace Education

On a cold Sunday afternoon in February 1983, a small group of Canadian teachers met in the staff room of a city high school. It was the height of a renewed Soviet-American nuclear arms race, the likes of which had not been seen since the Cuban Missile Crisis of 1962. These teachers met because they and their students were afraid. Newspaper headlines told of threat and counter threat. A newly released National Film Board film featuring the Australian pediatrician and peace activist Dr. Helen Caldicot described graphic details of the effects of a nuclear blast and radioactive fallout and urged education and action.

These Canadian teachers were not unlike many educators across North America, Europe, and Australasia. Relations between the USSR and the USA, already poor since the beginning of the Reagan presidency, were steadily worsening. New weapons were being deployed. In Europe, the USSR was installing the SS-20, a new generation of medium-range nuclear missiles, while the Americans were preparing to deploy their own new medium-range missile, the Pershing.

Canadian teachers in Alberta had a particular interest in the new arms race because their province was directly involved in weapons testing. The federal government had agreed to test another new missile—the Cruise—over the province as part of Canadian responsibilities to the NATO alliance. The Cruise missile was a slow, comparatively small missile that could carry a deadly nuclear payload. The military argument was the familiar one: the Soviets have them, so "we" must have them too. But peace activists had pointed out that these new weapons were dangerously destabilizing. Unlike other nuclear weapons that were open to surveillance, the Cruise missile was virtually undetectable by radar and satellite observation. Thus, it was a sense of local involvement and urgency that brought these teachers together on that cold winter's afternoon.

The teachers decided to form a grassroots organization called Educators for Peace, and to meet regularly for discussions and to share materials. Educators for Peace acted both as a study group, to inform participants of the issues, and as an advocacy group, to raise awareness about the need to deal with the nuclear issue in the school curriculum. They also began to make contact with other peace education groups in North America.

In the summer of 1984, some members of Educators for Peace travelled to New York to attend a two-week International Institute for Peace Education. Most of the 200 or so educators at the Institute were from the United States, but there were also some representatives from Africa, Europe, Latin America and the Pacific region. Meeting educators from other parts of the world was to change the Canadians' perspectives on peace profoundly. Many were surprised to learn of the intense rivalry that the Americans felt towards the Soviets. But the greater surprise was to learn that the educators from countries of the South were not particularly concerned with nuclear weapons. The Canadian and American teachers assumed that they spoke for everyone when they pointed out the global threat of nuclear weapons. They were definitely taken aback when some of the other educators reminded them that nuclear weapons presented an abstract danger. Many of the nations of the South were experiencing actual violence.

One Ethiopian teacher summarized this view: "Really, why should we be concerned? Nuclear weapons are only a faster way of killing people. In our country conventional arms are responsible for killing many every day. People are shot, blown up, or die of starvation because our lives are being destroyed by civil war."

The Canadian teachers left New York with a renewed view of peace. They now appreciated that they had the "luxury" of being able to focus on only an abstract possibility of unimaginable destruction, rather than having to confront the daily reality of civil war and star- vation. But they also left ready to rethink and to enlarge their concepts of peace.

The Challenge of Differing Conceptions

Many of the educators who gathered in New York had come together with unexamined understandings of peace. These understand- ings were meaningful in their own contexts. The Canadians' concern over nuclear arms, for example, grew out of their situation as citizens of a NATO member country, neighbours to the United States, and consumers of media that presented both news of international affairs and popular cultural images of friends and enemies. The Ethiopian experience was different, shaped by a direct encounter with the violence of a protracted civil war made all the more brutal by the weapons financed by outside powers. This ongoing military conflict had wrecked local agriculture, disrupted trans- portation and communications, and displaced many people from their homes.

Meetings such as the New York conference can expose different conceptions of peace edu- cation. They can challenge assumptions, create dialogue and broaden horizons. It is unlikely that either the Canadians or the Ethiopians would find much reason for questioning or extending their original understandings unless challenged by different views. Understandings of peace will depend very much on personal and cultural experiences within particular con- texts. However, by virtue of living in a global society, we need to have a broad and compre- hensive view of peace, if we are going to move towards a genuine peace culture. This chapter will review various conceptions of peace edu- cation in order to articulate a working defini- tion for the purposes of this book.

Sorting Out Conceptions of Peace Education

Because many peace education programs oper- ate quite comfortably within assumed and par- tial definitions of peace, it is important that we attempt to make these implicit definitions explicit.

We can say at the outset that personal and local definitions of peace are important, because people concerned with peace are often initially responding to experiences of insecurity and violence in their own lives. Because such experiences are different, definitions and meanings will vary across different contexts. There is not one indisputable and universal "best" conception of peace and peace education. This does not mean, however, that we are simply left with a relativity of conceptions of peace. Certain definitions are more comprehensive than others, and all will be value-laden. It is important to probe the various conceptions of peace education to analyze what lies behind them.

A Traditional Conception: Peace As Absence

People have often found it difficult to define what peace is. This is because the idea of peace is, in itself, an obscure concept. Peace is known mainly by its absence; we have little direct experience of it as being something that can be done as a positive quality. That peace is an absent or negative concept can be heard in everyday language. A father, for example, yells at his noisy children, "Give me some peace and quiet!" He wants the children to stop what they are doing so he might concentrate on some work. For this father, peace and quiet is defined as the absence of interference. Peace is defined in a similarly negative way for the UN peacekeeping forces or in the motto of the United States Air Force: "Peace is our profession". In these cases, and in many others like them, peace signals the prevention or the cessation of violence. What peace actually might look like as a positive condition, and how we may go about achieving it, is never indicated by these conventional uses of the word.

The fact that peace is largely a negative concept in ordinary language presents some problems for education. Designing curriculum and developing teaching practices requires some positive idea of what peace might be. Peace education has been somewhat hampered by this difficulty. It was for this reason that, in the 1970s, peace education began to look towards a positive definition of what peace is.

Peace As a Positive Concept

Help in constituting a positive concept of peace has come from the writings of Johan Galtung, the founder of the Oslo Peace Research Institute (PRIO). As an interdisciplinary field of study, peace research is dedicated to discovering the roots of violence and the promotion of peaceful alternatives. Research showed violent conflict was often the result of injustice and inequality within social structures. Galtung coined the term "structural violence" to designate this systemic injustice. Proceeding from this analysis, Galtung held that a positive conception of peace would require identifying how equality and social justice could be produced in particular situations.

Structural violence, it was noted, resides in institutions and conventions that preserve permanent relations of inequality and injustice. Examples of structural violence include the institutionalized racism suffered by indigenous peoples or visible minorities; the gender inequities endured by many women who are not given equal pay for equal work, and whose work is systematically undervalued; social class biases that are reflected in social and educational policies that protect privilege and do nothing to redress economic imbalances. The identification of social justice by Galtung and others as the basis for building peaceful structures gave peace education a socially critical edge. By the early 1980s this perspective had found its way into peace education curricula and teaching.

Emergent Conceptions of Educating for Peace

Conceptions of educating for peace are still in flux. Because education for peace is based upon the hope that we can learn to live in harmony with one another and with nature, beliefs about how we might do this will alter as circumstances change. Nowadays it is the dangerous and threatened state of the planet in the late twentieth century that is providing a new and increasingly comprehensive perspective of the peace problematic.

It seems to be very clear that a peaceful future will have to be rooted in caring for the earth. The global environment is the most urgent issue, because there now exists the threat of ecological disaster brought on by a host of humanly created problems. In peace education terms, these problems have a common source of concern: a sense that there has been a long-term and abiding violence against the earth itself. Sometimes this violence takes the form of overt destruction and wanton damage to the environment through pollution and careless use of natural resources. But there is a growing awareness that this overt environmental damage signals a deeper and more subtle kind of violence that stems from regarding the planet only in narrowly instrumentalist ways.

A regard for the earth as our common home has long been reflected in the traditional teachings of the elders among the First Nations. In western thought, however, technology has changed humanity's relationship with the world. In 1954, in an essay entitled "The Question Concerning Technology", the German philosopher Martin Heidegger introduced the notion that we do not use technology just for specific ends. Rather, he argued, our lives have become so bound up with technological thinking, that we are "enframed" in a technological relationship. This means that we can no longer view the earth in any terms other than "standing in reserve" for the actual or potential use of humanity.

The search for alternative ways of relating to the planet has resulted in a critical reading of the scientific revolution and a questioning of the assumptions behind modern development. Critics who have taken this stance have located the source of contemporary problems in the ethics of aggressive individualism and mechanistic views of the natural world (Borgmann, 1992). As evidence, they refer to the violent language employed by one of the fathers of modern science, Francis Bacon, who in 1627 spoke of "torturing and subjugating nature" to benefit humanity. The same orientation to control and subjugate nature continues to underpin the view that the natural world serves as an instrument for our purposes.

Critics of technical science point out that this view seriously misunderstands nature. Citing new evidence from physics, biology and chemistry, they suggest that nature is best understood not as a mechanism made up of discrete parts, but as an arrangement of intricate living systems. This new view of science, as the study of the relationships of living systems, corresponds with perspectives drawn from indigenous cultures and from eco-feminism. Rather than objectifying the earth as separate from ourselves, we can attempt to relate to the planet on more cooperative and harmonious terms.

One example of this outlook is the "Gaia hypothesis", which suggests a way of understanding the earth as a living system. This idea was first put forward by the British scientist James Lovelock in his studies of biological systems. Lovelock (1987) concluded that, because the earth's atmosphere is so geochemically improbable, planetary life as a whole can only be understood as a self-regulating organism. Such a theory would explain the dynamic balances and interrelationships that make up the earth's environment, and would indicate that these must be respected if the planet is to survive as a nurturing home for humanity and other forms of life. One small change within the organism could lead to unpredictable results that could have an important influence on the environment as a whole. For example, we can point to the reduction in the thickness of the ozone layer in the earth's atmosphere which is leading, on a small scale, to the unexpected bleaching and death of corals in the South Pacific. These kinds of changes are symptomatic of potentially massive changes in the environment that could ultimately affect the quality of life.

Understanding the earth as a living system will cast the net of peace education very wide indeed. This understanding will not translate clearly into a defined set of conceptions about what peace is, but it does provide the basis for an appreciation of the links between the environment, human culture, economic development, and broadly non-violent practices that can contribute to a working definition of peace education.

Dimensions of a Working Definition of Peace Education

In creating a working definition of peace education for this book, we will take account of the links outlined above, which have become more apparent in the closing years of the twentieth century. Their importance suggests that our working definition will have to be comprehensive and multi-dimensional.

Substantively, our comprehensive definition of peace encompasses both a fundamental opposition to violence as well as an understanding of the relationships amongst the underlying causes of violence. There are seven dimensions to this broad definition of peace education: non-violence, human rights, social justice, world mindedness, ecological balance, meaningful participation, and personal peace.

A BASIS OF REFLECTION AND ACTION Before we turn to an examination of each of these dimensions, it is worth noting that peace practice is developed and fostered through a process of reflection and action. Critical reflection is necessary because peace education begins as a response to suffering that is inflicted by violent actions or violent structures. It is a basic human responsibility to construct peaceful alternatives by analyzing and investigating the sources of peacelessness. However, analysis alone is clearly not enough. Positive action is also necessary if we are to work towards more peaceful ways of relating with each other and the world. The task of peace education is ultimately to prepare both children and adults to participate in developing a more peaceful future in a world that is requiring us to rethink former certainties about our knowledge and control of the global environment.

In declaring critical reflection to be central to our working definition of peace education, it is important to recall that it was largely lacking in most of the earlier forms of peace education, as we saw in Chapter 1. Since the 1960s, however, reflection and action have formed an important part of conceptions of peace education. Our working definition takes this into consideration. The seven dimensions of peace education identified below involve both a critical reflection on present situations and positive action for change. This inseparable relationship between thought and action for peace is best summed up in the words of

Mohandas Gandhi who observed that "the way is the goal". The rule of relationship in peace education also bids us to remember that each of the seven aspects of peace education is linked inseparably to the others.

1. NON-VIOLENCE   A state of non-violence should not be confused with a condition of non-conflict. Conflict is the inevitable result of contending interests and differences of viewpoints. Peace education focuses on non-violent alternatives to resolving conflicts. It has two separate kinds of aims, depending upon whether the field of action is global or local.

At the global level the primary aim is to develop knowledge and understanding of non-violence. Conventional historical accounts tend to focus on the dramatic and the violent. Wars form the centrepiece of history courses. A survey conducted in Canada on the 50th anniversary of the beginning of the Second World War showed that Canadians had "an exceptionally good" knowledge of this conflict (*Edmonton Journal*, August 28, 1989). Our daily media diet, like conventional history teaching, is also organized around often violent and dramatic stories. Peace education attempts to provide a more balanced picture, drawing attention both to international problems of violence and to alternative stories of successful non-military and non-violent actions. There is a rich history of non-violence. The Harvard historian Gene Sharp (1973) has collected and recorded over four hundred examples of successful non-violent actions that have been conducted through the ages.

On a local level, peace education draws upon the experiences and techniques of personal peace practice. Here the focus is on the principles of conflict resolution and the considerable body of skills and attitudes that have

developed in this area. Non-violent conflict resolution, like the history of peace, has often been overlooked and undervalued in the dominant view that sees conflict in terms of power and win-lose solutions. The non-violent alternative recognizes the natural inevitability of conflict, but rejects the necessity of resolution through a power struggle. It attempts to create win-win resolutions that respect the rights of the participants and do not leave a residue of anger.

Crucial to a conception of peace is an understanding of structural violence, which preserves relations of inequality. Overcoming structural violence is central to the human rights, social justice, and participatory aspects of our definition of peace education. But it is related to education for non-violence too. Globally, structural violence concentrates resources in the powerful military industrial sector. Although the cold war has ended, the so-called "peace dividend" has failed to materialize, and a large portion of the money spent on scientific research and development is still spent on the military. Locally, structural violence is often evident in hierarchies that impose obedience. The key to overcoming such types of violence at the community and interpersonal level is unrestricted communication.

2. HUMAN RIGHTS   A broad definition of peace education will address human rights. It will be guided by the Universal Declaration of Human Rights (1948) which describes three kinds of human rights: liberty-oriented rights, security-oriented rights, and basic human rights.

Liberty-oriented rights have to do with civil and political rights. They include rights such as freedom of movement and assembly and equality before the law. Security rights describe economic, social and cultural rights.

Rights such as the opportunity to work, to have a decent standard of living, and the right to social security are examples of security-oriented rights. Basic human rights are those that safeguard human dignity, such as freedom from torture and imprisonment.

An education for peace will recognize restrictions of human rights, particularly inequalities suffered by women, children and cultural minorities. It will also take note that human rights are many-dimensional, and that positions taken on human rights are not without ideological biases. Traditionally, most western democracies with capitalist economies have tended to focus on the protection of individual rights, concentrating on liberty-oriented rights, as opposed to security rights. Formerly, the socialist bloc countries gave priority to the security-oriented rights of housing, jobs and social programs at the expense of individual and collective liberties. This distinction is no longer the case in Eastern Europe and the former Soviet Union, where social safety nets have been dismantled as these countries move towards market economies. Nor does the existence of free markets necessarily ensure a respect for liberty-oriented rights. There are numerous examples of countries that practise economic freedom but deny human rights.

3. SOCIAL JUSTICE The concept of social justice particularly addresses structural violence in holding forth the vision of peaceful structures. The global dimension of social justice is closely linked to questions of economic development. There is an unequal distribution of wealth between North and South, where nations of the North, with 25 percent of the population, control 80 percent of global wealth. A socially just international system would attempt to redress this imbalance, in an effort to redistribute wealth more fairly.

Traditionally, the idea of economic development has been associated with modernization based on the model of the industrialized North. Peace education underlines a conviction that there are many routes to development that may not necessarily follow the modern industrialization model. There are many examples of new directions being taken by small-scale development projects that draw upon local expertise and respect indigenous lifestyles. As Toh Swee-Hin indicates, a peaceful paradigm of development is historically specific, embodying the yearning of people for "bread and justice" (1988: 124).

On the local level, the concern with social justice allows us to question the lack of opportunities for certain segments of the population, systemic problems of racism, pay inequities, sexism and so forth. The focus here is on the understandings and the actions that promote relations based on justice and human development, rather than on charity.

4. WORLD MINDEDNESS Because problems of peace are global in scope, developing a "global literacy" is one of the most important aspects of a comprehensive definition of peace education. Curriculum in Canada is provincially or territorially controlled. Walter Werner (1988) notes that, while there is a global education component in most social studies curricula, there is little effort to treat views of the world from the perspectives of other cultures. True global literacy recognizes the necessity for the understanding of others in their own terms, not just as objects of inquiry.

It is also clear that peace education needs to make links between the global and the local. The slogan, "Think globally, act locally" effectively describes an attitude that is central to peace education. Global thinking develops a consciousness of the conditions of structural and direct violence beyond our own communities. Consciousness of these conditions enables us to understand the root problems of peacelessness and to extend the net of our concerns. Some educators have expressed concern that an over-emphasis on global problems will cause students to despair. They argue that, as individuals, we have precious little power to materially alter global conditions by ourselves. In response, it could be said that positive collective action is necessary to maintain hope. Local activities such as boycotts, assistance to refugees, or letters to politicians about national foreign policy questions are some examples of positive expressions of concern through action. It is also important to remember that, in a critically reflective stance on peace education, there is no sharp distinction between thinking and doing. A change in consciousness is, in itself, an important kind of action.

5. ECOLOGICAL BALANCE   As we approach the twenty-first century, there is probably no other aspect of educating for a peaceful future that arouses more concern in Canada and many other countries than the global environment. Global warming, fears about the ozone layer, and the destruction of natural species all indicate the urgent need to learn to live in harmony with the earth.

While the concept of ecological balance is a significant aspect of a more complete definition of peace education, peace education, in turn, provides some interesting and unique insights into environmental questions by linking development, human rights, and the environment (Reardon, 1988: 31). The problem of deforestation is one example. A great deal of deforestation occurs as a result of desperate economic circumstances. Large tracts of good agricultural land are owned by wealthy families and agribusinesses, forcing the poor to live on marginal land in virgin forests. The forests

are cleared by slash-and-burn techniques, and for a few years, people scratch a living on poor tropical soils. However, the soil is soon degraded, the forests gone, the environment depleted. Peace education can allow that further development is an economic necessity, but that it should be environmentally sustainable.

Peace education also reveals how the relationship between development and the environment is linked to political questions of power and control. Poverty is a structural problem, and land ownership determines decisions about cultivation practices and who will benefit from the production.

A peace education perspective on the environment also provides an historical dimension to the present crisis. John Huckle (1988: 197) notes how humanity, for most of its existence on earth, has lived in cooperative communities based on mutual aid. It is only with the development of, first, the warrior class and, second, the rise of modern capitalism that there has been a concentration of power and the control of economic surplus.

6. MEANINGFUL PARTICIPATION   Alienation is a significant cause of peacelessness. The sixth dimension of a broader meaning of peace—meaningful participation—allows us to identify means of reversing the problem of alienation.

People become alienated when they lack power to influence the decisions that affect them. For example, the people who are supposed to benefit from development might be excluded from the processes that decide on the forms the development will take. Their exclusion might be the result of a political process that favours local power elites rather than citizen participation, but it is also often a result of a form of technical reasoning that attempts to replace political decision-making with the laws of science. Decision-making of this kind relies upon expert knowledge, which is assumed to be generalizable to many different situations. Rather than being active subjects, the people involved become objects of manipulation.

The challenge for peace education is to democratize decision-making, particularly at local levels, in order to allow meaningful participation. For this reason, some peace educators and peace researchers are becoming increasingly interested in grassroots organizations, especially those in the countries of the South (Alger, 1987). Grassroots organizations tend to use local expertise, involving their members in participatory research and action plans that meet local needs. This is a new paradigm of development which places human thought and action at the centre. The Brazilian educator Paulo Freire has been very influential in the description and development of this paradigm. According to Freire (1973), the poor must first become aware of their oppression and the peacelessness of their own situation. This first step is *conscientization*. It motivates change that then comes from the analysis and desires of the participants. Closely allied with Freire's conscientization is participatory action research. Action research provides a structure whereby people in communities can simultaneously learn about and improve their situations. There are examples of action research in countries of both the South (Fals-Borda & Rahman, 1991) and the North (Carson, 1992).

7. PERSONAL PEACE   The dimension of personal peace covers a range of human experience that is often neglected or undervalued in many conceptions of peace education. Toh and Cawagas (1987: 27) offer a notable exception to this tendency. They have included personal peace as an important issue in develop-

ing a peace education framework for the Philippines. By including personal peace, they address the problems of personal alienation that result from the world-wide spread of advanced industrial culture. Personal alienation manifests itself in the form of addictions, neuroses, suicide, and family violence. Toh and Cawagas argue that peace educators need to respond by seeking out cultural and religious traditions that support inner harmony. The inner harmony they speak of extends to relationships with nature and with other people; it is hardly possible to achieve inner harmony without harmonious external relationships.

In Canada we are only too familiar with examples of personal alienation. Substance abuse, suicide, family breakdowns, and family violence are not uncommon. Conventional wisdom has tended to regard these forms of alienation as individual problems or pathologies and to treat them accordingly. Peace education urges us to go beyond such limited interpretations and to investigate the sources of alienation in the interrelationships between person and world. This allows for critical reflection; on what we mean by the "good life", for example. Does living the good life mean having a high-paying job to maintain ever-increasing consumption? What kinds of stresses and strains does this "good life" produce on individuals and families?

Personal peace becomes more difficult to achieve as the culture of the market place extends further into public and private life. The values of the market—consumption, production, competition, efficiency and, above all, profit—have begun to take the place of other values. These other values—compassion, loyalty, self-restraint, reverence and public interest—are eroding, shrinking the human spirit and impoverishing the public space. The drift to market values has been subtle, but pervasive. It is vital that we notice the effects of this drift on our relationships with our families, communities and the global environment. Equally vital is recovery of a broader spectrum of values.

Summary and Conclusions

One concept that stands out in educating for peace is *interconnectedness*. There are interconnections among the global, the local, and the personal. At the same time, peace is related to justice and to the environment. The conceptual links we have mapped in this chapter might be consolidated by establishing some map coordinates. Among the seven dimensions of peace described we can discern four thematic areas: peace and conflict, rights and responsibilities, development, and environment (Greig, Pike and Selby, 1987: 38). These four themes mark the content elements of peace. Content forms one axis of the grid for the concept map. The other axis is formed by the person/world relationship. The Norwegian peace educator Magnus Haavelsrud (1987) situates the person-world relationship both spatially and temporally in terms of the individual person's experience. Space includes the person's inner and outer realities. Time includes past, present and future. Outer reality varies, depending upon how close it is to the direct experience of the individual person. Thus, in Haavelrud's scheme, the global dimension forms a distant reality.

We can place the seven dimensions of educating for peace on this conceptual map. Educating for *non-violence* is concerned with the theme of peace and conflict in terms of both the near and distant realities of the individual. Educating for *human rights* also relates to its theme in terms of the near and distant realities. *Social justice* relates to the development theme and requires the individual to make links between personal practices and more distant realities. It also relates to the theme of rights and responsibilities. *World mindedness* attends to all four themes, but it does so in such a way that it brings distant realities closer to personal experience. *Ecological balance* most centrally relates to the theme of the environment. It also attempts to relate near and distant realities, particularly in the sense of developing personal responsibility. Personal responsibility is central to the dimension of *meaningful participation*. Participation relates to all four themes of peace education, but it challenges such education to be meaningful to the experience of the learner. *Personal peace* is the one dimension of peace education that crucially concerns itself with the inner and outer realities of the person.

In conclusion, we offer this caution about the limitations of a conceptual analysis of peace education: Conceptions of peace education are abstractions; they are not what peace education is. To come to a better understanding of what peace education is we must also describe its practices and aspirations.

REFERENCES AND SOURCES

Alger, Chad (1987), "A grassroots approach to life in peace: self-determination in overcoming peacelessness" in *Bulletin of Peace Proposals*, 18(3): 375–392.

Borgmann, Albert (1992), *Crossing the Postmodern Divide*, Chicago: University of Chicago Press.

Carson, Terrance (1992), "Remembering forward: Reflections on educating for peace" in William Pinar and William Reynolds (eds.), *Understanding Curriculum as Phenomenological and Deconstructed texts*, New York: Teachers College Press.

Freire, Paulo (1973), *Pedagogy of the Oppressed*, New York: Herder and Herder.

Galtung, Johan (1992), *The Way Is the Goal: Gandhi Today*, Ahmedabad: Peace Research centre, Gujarat Vidyapith.

Galtung, Johan (1969), "Violence, peace and peace research", *Journal of Peace Research*, 6: 167–191.

Greig, Sue, Graham Pike and David Selby (1987), *Earthrights: Education as if the Planet Really Mattered*, London: Kogan Page.

Haavelsrud, Magnus (1987), "Peace education: the operationalization of the peace concept", *Bulletin of Peace Proposals*, 18(3): 363–374.

Heidegger, Martin (1968), "The question concerning technology" in *Martin Heidegger: Basic Writings*, New York: Harper.

Huckle, John (1988), "Environment" in David Hicks (ed.), *Education for Peace*, London: Routledge.

Lovelock, James (1979), *Gaia*, Oxford: Oxford University Press.

Sharp, Gene (1973), *The Politics of Non-violent Action*, Boston: Porter Sargent.

Toh, Swee-Hin (1988), "Justice and development" in David Hicks, (ed.), *Education for Peace*, London: Routledge.

Toh, Swee-Hin and Virginia Floresca-Cawagas (1987), *Peace Education a Framework for the Philippines*, Quezon City: Phoenix Press.

Werner, Walter (1988), "Curricular content for peace education" in Douglas Ray (ed.), *Peace Education: Canadian and International Perspectives*, London, Ontario: Third Eye Publications.

CHAPTER 3

Teaching for Peace

IN THE EARLY MORNING *hours of March 12, 1930, Mahatma Gandhi set off with 78 followers to walk nearly 400 kilometres from the Sabarmati Ashram to Dandi, a place on the sea coast in western India. On that morning, his party included Hindus, Moslems and Christians. They came from all regions of India and represented both young and old, female and male. What all the participants had in common was their firm commitment to* satyagraha *("truthforce" or non-violent resistance). Gandhi had expressly chosen his most trusted and disciplined* satyagrahi.

The objective of the group, once arriving at the coast, would be to evaporate sea water in shallow pans in order to obtain salt. This would be an act of resistance to British colonial rule, because by making salt for themselves, Gandhi and his followers would be seen to be evading the salt tax that the British rulers had levied on India. To many of Gandhi's friends and enemies alike, this act of civil disobedience seemed rather strange. But making illegal salt would prove to be an immensely powerful gesture.

Practical Action, Comprehensive Understanding

The story of Mahatma Gandhi and the Salt March provides an example of a project that combined practical action with a comprehensive understanding of peace. With further examination, the story will allow us to address the difficulty of orienting ourselves to a comprehensive peace practice.

Gandhi was working for the independence of his country from Britain. He was a member of the All-India Congress. But, unlike many of his compatriots, Gandhi wanted more for Indian home rule (*Hind Swaraj*) than simply a change in rulers. He said, "I don't want to exchange British rule for Indian rule." Gandhi felt that, if the people of India were to become truly free, *swaraj* (self-rule) had to mean that each person achieved inner freedom. In order to reach this state, the people of India had to learn to rule their own passions and greed. Gandhi knew that, unless the materialistic habits and values of the colonizers were rejected, independence would mean nothing more than "English rule, without the English". Thus, Gandhi's aim was not simply political independence, but rather a fundamental spiritual transformation of the people of India; that they might willingly come to embrace a life of simplicity, self-sufficiency and non-violence. To accomplish this goal, Gandhi always insisted that the means and the ends of civil disobedience should never be separated.

Thinking about how to achieve a commonality of ends and means gave birth to the idea of the Salt March. At the start of 1930, the Great Depression was just beginning. Many people in both England and India were feeling the economic pinch. At a New Year's rally, the All India Congress decreed that this would be a good time for a determined campaign for

Indian independence to begin. Gandhi was torn by this call for independence. Of course, he agreed with the need to throw off colonialism, but he worried that the circumstances of the Depression coupled with the daily injustices of colonialism could easily inflame people to violence. He sought a way to support the sentiment for independence and yet teach a lesson in non-violence to both the people of India and their colonizers.

After much soul-searching, Gandhi chose to stage a march against the Salt Tax as a focus for civil disobedience. He began the protest by fully informing his opponents of his intentions, hoping to give them a fair chance to make a peaceful settlement of the grievances. In a long letter to Lord Irwin, the British Viceroy of India, outlining the injustice of the Salt Tax, Gandhi wrote, "The tax…[is] most burdensome on the poor man when it is remembered that salt is the one thing he must eat more than the rich man" (Fischer, 1990: 339). Salt was as necessary as air and water for those who laboured outdoors in India's heat. Gandhi went on to connect the Salt Tax to the inequities of the colonial system. He described how the tax was a concrete expression of a system that permitted the Viceroy himself to be paid five thousand times as much as a peasant who laboured in the fields.

The Viceroy chose not to reply in person to Gandhi's letter. Rather, sensing that there was a dangerous demonstration against British rule in the works, he had his secretary draft a terse note to Gandhi cautioning him against disobeying the law and warning him that there was a strong potential for inciting violence. Citing the rejection of his offer of peaceful settlement, Gandhi continued his plans for the march: "On bended knee I asked for bread and received a stone instead." Thus it was on March 12, with the full knowledge of the

British and a watching international press corps, that Gandhi and his followers set out on their long walk to the sea.

For 24 days they walked, stopping at villages along the way and asking at night only for a clean area to sleep and the simplest of foods. At each stop the *satyagrahi* prayed and preached the message of *swaraj*, while spreading the message of non-violence and non-cooperation by telling of their intention to refuse the tax by making salt from the sea. As they continued on their journey to the sea, the attention of the press and of the nation became riveted on Gandhi and this band of disciplined followers.

By the time they had arrived in Dandi, on April 5, the number of non-violent protesters had swollen to several thousand. On the coast of the Arabian Sea, with his followers watching, Gandhi announced: "Watch me. I am about to give a signal to the nation." He bent down and picked up a pinch of salt between his fingers. Everyone then set to work drying sea water in pans to make salt in contravention to the law.

Many years later, Jawaharlal Nehru, who was to become the first prime minister of India, described the image of Gandhi that came to be held by many:

> Many pictures rise in my mind of this man, whose eyes were often full of laughter and yet were pools of infinite sadness. But the picture that is dominant and most significant is as I saw him marching, staff in hand to Dandi...in 1930. He was the pilgrim on his quest of Truth. Quiet, peaceful, determined and fearless, who would continue that quest and pilgrimage regardless of consequences. (Brown, 1989: 237)

Gandhi did, indeed, give a signal to the nation. Not only at Dandi, but in every village along India's seacoast, villagers went to make salt. The non-violent action spread to challenge other manifestations of colonial rule. Shops that sold foreign cloth were picketed and there were demonstrations in front of liquor stores. For the first time, all classes of people joined in the demonstrations, even members of aristocratic families who would not normally have made common cause with the poor. Indian civil servants, in response to Gandhi's suggestion for non-cooperation, resigned in large numbers from the public administration. The Viceroy reported to London, "[Gandhi] has already achieved a considerable measure of success in undermining the Government" (Brown, 1989: 238). Over the next six months there were as many as 100 000 arrests. Gandhi himself was taken into custody on May 4, 1930.

A few days after Gandhi's own arrest, the most important event of the protest took place. Twenty-five hundred satyagrahi volunteers staged a non-violent demonstration at the government salt works at Dharasana. The salt works had been fortified against demonstrators by ditches and barbed wire and was guarded by the police. As the unarmed volunteers approached the barbed wire they were savagely beaten by the police with heavy sticks. The *satyagrahi* offered no resistance. As each battered and bleeding person was carried off on a stretcher, a new one would come to take his place. This went on throughout the morning. An American journalist witnessing this demonstration was sickened by what he saw. He wrote at the time: "Those struck down fell sprawling, unconscious or writhing with fractured skulls or broken shoulders.... The survivors, without breaking ranks, silently and doggedly marched on until struck down." (Miller, 1936: 192)

The demonstration, no doubt, shocked many observers. When it ended, over 300 had been injured and two lay dead. But this dramatic act of non-violent resistance, a refusal to either retreat or fight the soldier's clubs had a profound effect on the future. It showed there was a different way to combat injustice. The Indian writer and teacher Rabrindranath Tagore wrote in the *Manchester Guardian* that Dandi was "a great moral defeat for Europe.... Even though Asia is still physically weak...she can now look down on Europe where before she looked up." And according to the Gandhi biographer Louis Fischer (1954: 352) the campaign of non-violence against the Salt Tax was a decisive moment, because ultimately "[it] made England weak and India invincible."

Reflecting on the Salt March

Gandhi's non-violent action was undoubtedly successful. In what ways does the story of the Salt March shed some light on the contemporary problem of teaching for peace? There are some significant points to note.

1. There was harmony between non-violent means and peaceful ends.

The Salt March employed non-violent means to counter the violence of the colonial system. Gandhi held to the belief that ends and means could not be separated. Peace with justice could not be attained by violence, but only through disciplined non-violence, in a spirit of loving kindness towards one's opponent. In this way, a lived alternative to violence could be shown.

2. There was a strong link between peace and justice.

The point of protesting the salt tax was not to agitate against the British, but to work in the name of justice for the poor. Gandhi chose salt partly because it symbolized the injustice of colonialism, but also because the salt tax had real effects that weighed most heavily on the poor. Gandhi often said that when he was in doubt about what to do, he would think about what would help the poorest person.

3. There was an effort to work in solidarity.

Gandhi did not blame individual police officers, soldiers or government officials. He acted on the belief that the cause of oppression lay in the colonial system, not in the person of the oppressor. Thus, he made every effort to act in solidarity with "the enemy" in order to "melt their hearts" so that, together, they might remove oppression.

4. There was an effort to expand an understanding of peace.

The Salt March was an experiment that put the belief in non-violence to the test in a practical action. The result on this occasion was largely successful. At other times demonstrations did turn violent and had to be suspended. Gandhi and his followers learned from each of these "experiments with truth" and in so doing, their understandings of peace enlarged over time.

Roots of Gandhi's Practice

Before considering how the story of Gandhi might inform the practice of peace education, it is worthwhile reflecting on some particular aspects of his historical and philosophical roots. Gandhi's comprehensive understanding of peace and his practice of non-violent action had deep spiritual roots. He did not draw upon any one particular religious tradition, but followed a confluence of truths from the wisdom traditions of many religions.

The central truth that summoned Gandhi to the practice of non-violence (*satyagraha*) is the basic precept that all life is sacred. This precept is found in the principle of *ahimsa,* or non-harming. *Ahimsa* has a superficial similarity to the Christian commandment of "Thou shall not kill." However, the concept of *ahimsa*, which is found in the ancient texts and teachings of Hinduism, Jainism and Buddhism, covers much more than direct violence. According to these teachings, *ahimsa* is the fundamental task of being human. It is assumed that the natural state of the world is violent, so the potential for harm exists everywhere. The work of becoming truly human is devoting one's life to removing harm. The work of *ahimsa* is done in two ways: first, by personally avoiding causing direct injury to others; and second, by not allowing a structure or a system that does harm to continue exist. We can see from the example of the Salt March, as well as other non-violent actions, that Gandhi emphasized both aspects of *ahimsa*. As Gandhi saw it, the duty of the *satyagrahi* (the follower of the non-violent way) was to oppose a system of oppression and to replace it with a new social order that projected *ahimsa*.

Two other roots of Gandhi's practice are worth mentioning. These are *swaraj* (self-rule) and *swadeshi* (self-reliance). The concept of *swaraj* explains why self-discipline was such a powerful feature of Gandhi's practice, and why he was cautious in his support for Indian independence. As we have seen, political independence was not the real issue for him. Gandhi (1931: 38) reminded his followers that "*Swaraj* is a sacred word meaning self-rule and self-restraint, and not the freedom from restraint that 'independence' often means."

Related to the self-discipline of *swaraj* is the idea of self-reliance. *Swadeshi* does not mean self-reliance in either a personal or collective sense. Rather, it more properly has to do with the ideas of restraining self-interest and opening up the self to service and recognition of one's interdependence. In its most fundamental, sense *swadeshi* has to do with being of service to those who are closest: family, neighbours and community. The symbol of *swadeshi* is the spinning wheel. Gandhi urged people from all classes—rich and poor—to spin for a certain number of hours each day. By engaging in this practice, people would be reminded of the connection between the land, labour and the products they used. In making this connection, their endless wanting for more riches would be disciplined, and their attention turned from enslaving desires to freeing responsibilities. The basic attitude of *swadeshi* is humility and love. Gandhi envisioned humility and love as the foundation of the Indian state. This state would be organized differently from the traditional centrally governed national state; it would be a country consisting of a multitude of interdependent and self-reliant communities.

Can Gandhi's Example Guide Teaching for Peace?

To what extent can Gandhi's lessons of non-violence inform peace education practices at the present time? To answer this question, we can begin by comparing some of the particular features of Gandhi's India with the situation in the late twentieth century western world. We can then use this comparison to discuss the kind of stance that teachers might take in teaching for peace.

India of the 1920s, '30s and early '40s was a nation ruled by British colonial power and divided by internal differences of religion, class and caste. It was a demoralized country, lacking confidence in its own traditions in the face of the powerful force of European industry and technology. Gandhi introduced an alternative idea of development that forged a new direction for the nation. It was a direction based not upon borrowed models of European modernism, but upon a creative reinterpretation of

Indian traditions that addressed the sources of internal conflict and envisioned a new kind of society inspired by the values of self-reliance and non-violence. This alternative caught the imagination of the people of India and it enjoyed a tremendous moral authority among them.

Gandhi's thinking was fundamentally different from the mainstream in an era of imperialism and nationalism. A convincing argument can be made that we, too, have reached a time when we must do some fundamental rethinking about the meaning of peace and the direction of peace education in an era of globalization.

We have seen in the previous chapters that a major shift in our understanding of peace education has been from a negative conception of peace (an understanding of peace as the absence of violence) to a positive conception of peace (an understanding of peace as the creation of conditions of equality and social justice). Where a negative conception of peace had the advantage of directly addressing experiences of violence, it has been weak in analyzing the underlying sources of that violence. A positive conceptualization of peace has had the advantage of providing a strong analysis, but has tended to be weak on action. In this sense, the two conceptions of peace could be seen as complementary. In reality, however, the two have remained somewhat distant from one another and it has been difficult to connect analysis with action.[1] While peace research has grown and developed as an interdisciplinary field of study, findings about the links among issues of peace, social justice, culture and the environment have not found their way into peace education and action often enough.

Against this backdrop, we now face the problem of how to come to terms with the changed political and social landscape resulting from the the end of the Cold War. In the West, we are having to redefine the terms of a debate that seemed neatly contained within a logic of opposites: defence vs. detente, capitalism vs. socialism, individual liberty vs. social equality, etc. Even if we did not personally think in such terms, we had become deeply influenced by the binary oppositions that formed the alternative positions around which public debate about peace and security had been organized. This framework has left us unready to deal with the post-Cold War world.

If we were to examine the economic and social policies of most governments, we would likely now conclude that the focus of capitalism and individual liberty has triumphed over socialism and equality. Witness the enthusiastic embrace (or the sullen acceptance) of the market economy as the universal economic system. And with this "victory" of the free market, this belief that it is wrong-headed for governments to intervene to any large extent in the economy, has come a related attitude: that it is naïve to assume that other kinds of collective action for social change can bear fruit.

This situation has serious implications for the state of peace education. The move towards a globalized and unfettered market economy means that the inequities at the heart of structural violence will remain and likely worsen.[2] And without some form of governmental and global collective action, violations of human rights, environmental damage, and various forms of direct violence will also con-

---

[1] Theodore Herman (1994) comments on the limitations of connecting analysis to action: "[T]heories do not trigger action...; you must move my heart as well."

[2] According to Erskine Childers (1994), in 1960 the richest fifth of the world's population earned 30 times as much as the poorest fifth; by 1990 the figure was 60 times as much.

tinue. A fundamental redirection in thinking is needed in peace education, because we appear to have reached an impasse where the problems remain, but there is no longer faith that many of the old solutions will work.

Crisis and New Beginnings

Such reflections are not necessarily cause for despair. Indeed, it may be argued that the first step towards new thinking in peace education will come with a recognition of the crisis. The German philosopher Hans-Georg Gadamer (1989) argues for the productive quality of what he calls "the negativity of experience". He points out that we reassess our understandings when we realize that things are not as we had originally supposed them to be. According to Gadamer, this type of reassessment is not just a minor adjustment in thinking. It has far-reaching consequences, altering understandings that we have had about many things. Some recent examples illustrate the far-reaching implications of the negativity of experience with respect to peace education.

The Crisis of Global Conflict Management

The United Nations was set up in 1945, following the end of the Second World War, with great hopes that its various agencies would be able to manage problems of peace and development. In the years since its inception, the UN has often been effective in preventing conflicts from escalating into war and in providing an ongoing forum for discussion for its member states[3]. During the Cold War, however, the UN was continually hampered by the East-West conflict. When the Cold War ended, it was assumed that the UN would

finally be able to take on a much greater role in conflict management. However, this expanded role seems beyond the UN's resources. It is constantly short of money, and its credibility has been badly damaged by its seeming lack of effectiveness in dealing with conflicts in countries such as the former Yugoslavia, Somalia and Rwanda.

A NEW BEGINNING Disappointment in the United Nations invites us to rethink the potential and proper focus of an international association. This focus has changed. In the early years of the UN's existence, the vast majority of conflicts took place between states; today, most are taking place within states.[4] Thus, the focus of conflict management needs to change from dispute resolution between nation states to the protection of human security within states. Peace educators everywhere despair at the sudden and ferocious inter-ethnic violence in countries like the former Yugoslavia and Rwanda. But what these events demonstrate is not so much the weakness of the UN, as miscalculations on the part of the leadership and failure to recognize warning signs of the scale of impending violence.

What we are now beginning to appreciate is the extent of the insecurities that have been unleashed by global changes. We realize, of course, that we have misunderstood the attachments of blood and belonging that had been hidden by the ideological battle of the Cold War. The sudden, tragic violence that erupted is forcing a new understanding of the power of nationalism. But, if we look beyond the headlines and the gruesome television images, we can see that nationalism is also being used to cover other problems. The

---

[3] By its 50th Anniversary in 1995, the number of member nations in the UN had grown from 51 to 184.

[4] Mahbub ul-Haq (1994) indicates that of the 82 conflicts recorded by the UN from 1991–1994, 79 were within nations, and only 3 were between nations.

violence in the former Yugoslavia, at least, is related as much to basic socio-economic factors and the control of resources as it is to historical ethnic animosities.[5] The ethnic conflict there has been stirred up by powerful former communist elites who are fearful of losing control. Moreover, the ethnic seed finds fertile ground among people who are already experiencing the insecurities of globalization and economic retrenchment. Insecurity will continue to accompany globalization and economic restructuring. And as national states continue to weaken, the people who live in them will have a tendency to scapegoat "the other"—the foreigner—just as they will have the tendency to turn to "their own kind" in their search for security in this uncertainty. These are all issues that should form a new focus for international concern.

In order to understand the present situation, it is necessary to analyze the human effects of globalization, or the weakening of the centralized state. Incessant media reports of disasters would have us concentrate on the negative examples of Yugoslavia and Rwanda. By so doing, we miss the many positive examples of growing democratization—in South Africa, in East Europe and in much of Latin America. It is important to note that these new beginnings will need the support of new global structures.[6]

The Crisis of Modernization and Development

During the 1950s and the 1960s there was considerable confidence that modernization would reduce poverty and relieve the disparity between rich and poor nations[7]. At the time, great efforts were made to transfer technology, to provide capital and to encourage educational reforms in order to bring the so-called "underdeveloped world" up to the standards of the "developed" nations. Embedded in this ambitious project was the idea that development is unidimensional, consisting of the pattern of industrialization followed by the nations of the North in their modernization and growth. Industrialization, it was assumed, ought to be the standard to which all others should aspire.

The "modernization paradigm" is now in disarray. Rather than reducing poverty, the decades of development have, in fact, increased the disparity between North and South. At the same time, development has failed to sew the seeds of industrialization. In the process, a staggering debt has been incurred by nations that were already poor. These nations now face a steadily worsening quality of life[8] as the result of the "structural adjustment programs" imposed on them by the International Monetary Fund and the

---

[5] Michael Ignatieff (1993) reports that the ethnic conflicts in the former Yugoslavia have less to do with old hatreds than with the centralizing interests of the communist government which failed to allow a civic political culture to develop. As a result, Ignatieff says, "the fall of [Tito's] regime turned into the collapse of the entire state structure".

[6] A proposal that provides a combination of local and global democracies is articulated by David Held (1993).

[7] In his inaugural address on January 20, 1949, US President Harry Truman announced that "Greater production [among poor nations] is the key to prosperity and peace" (Sachs, 1992).

[8] For example, according to the 1994 UNESCO World Education Report, the average per pupil spending on education in sub-Saharan African countries declined from $83 per year in 1980 to $76 per year in 1990.

World Bank, to ensure that they repay their debts.[9] Thus, in the 1990s, the result of the so-called "decades of development" has been social disruption and a flow of capital, not from rich nations to poor, but the reverse. In addition, it has become clear that the dream of global industrialization is environmentally unsupportable. The industrialized nations already use 80 percent of the world's energy resources. To extend this rate of use equally on a global scale would place an impossible burden on the environment.

A NEW BEGINNING   A worldwide environmental movement took the lead in the mid-1980s in promoting an awareness of the global limits to growth. This movement continues to enjoy wide public support, but runs into opposition when it is confronted by local pressures for development and the jobs that such development will provide. In addition, powerful commercial interests have found it both popular and profitable to climb on the environmental bandwagon, but they have worked to blunt its effectiveness when environmental protection threatens to harm growth and profits. It has been argued that being coopted by the media and the marketplace has become increasingly harmful to the environmental movement and other alternative movements (Rajni Kothari, 1993).

There are some persuasive examples of new thinking about development. One of these is the work of Wolfgang Sachs (1992), of the Institute for Cultural Studies in Germany, who has written an archaeology of the development idea. In this work, Sachs unearths the foundations of many assumptions about global poverty. Poverty was "discovered," he points out, when the gross national product per capita measure was established as a common statistical method for gauging the wealth of nations following the Second World War. Sachs argues that this seemingly neutral measuring device is already biased toward defining development in terms of the cash economies of consumption and production that exist in the industrialized world. He goes on to say that GNP per capita does not, in fact, mean the same thing across different contexts. Poverty may not necessarily exist in a given situation, even when the GNP measure suggests it should. This is because the measure of per capita income does not distinguish between frugality and destitution. A peasant in rural India may, for example, be living frugally and quite well on a small amount of cash income, while the urban dweller in Canada or the United States would be completely destitute having to get by on several times the same amount of money. Given the problems of global development and links between peace, development and the environment, Sachs' distinction between frugality and destitution is a crucial one for peace educators.

The Crisis of Colonialism and Decolonization

The political decolonization that took place throughout Asia and Africa from the late 1940s to the 1960s has not necessarily produced the salutary results expected of independence. In many countries, colonial rulers have simply been replaced by local elites who have been educated abroad and who preserve

---

[9] By 1980 indebtedness of the nations of the South had reached $750 billion. Following ten years of "structural adjustment" imposed by the International Monetary Fund (IMF), the debt had increased to $1355 billion by 1990 (*New Internationalist*, 1994: 6).

the same oppressive relationship with their compatriots as their foreign rulers had.[10]

A colonialist relationship also remains between nations, the difference now being that the direct, formal governmental control by a colonial power over a subject people has been replaced by a new colonialism of capital, education and mass culture. In this neocolonial relationship, the economies and cultural institutions of nation states are progressively being drawn into and integrated within a global marketplace. Much of this marketplace is controlled by transnational corporations that are based in countries of the North, largely beyond the control of national governments.[11] These transnationals have thus been able to create a powerful hegemony of both material production and image production through advertising and media control. This kind of control is more difficult to resist than conventional colonialism, because the "enemy" no longer takes concrete form in the person of the colonial administrator or the soldier. The enemy itself is now far more amorphous. If an enemy can be identified at all, it is the "neocolonial system". But "the system" is far too abstract an idea to rally and focus the attention of the masses. Therefore, resistance is difficult.

A more significant dimension of neocolonialism is an "inner colonialism"—the internalization of subjugation within the psychology of the person. As people become immersed in a monoculture of free market thinking, individualism and consumerism, other ways of being are crowded out, and it becomes more and more difficult to think outside of this existing arrangement. The end result is that many people in the former colonies continue to experience oppression, but are unable to articulate alternative directions. This is a dangerous situation, both because it restricts human development and because it allows anger and submerged violence against to fester.

A NEW BEGINNING Finding a way to think outside the structures of modernization, development and neocolonialism has become the preoccupation of many scholars, particularly those from the former colonies. While it is true that there has been a long tradition among subject peoples of protesting against colonialism, much of the literature of this resistance has rested upon a critique of domination. This critique has been important to the extent that it has raised critical consciousness. However, it is limited because it depends upon oppression for its existence. The challenge is to move beyond purely oppositional thinking, without forgetting the critique. It is being explored by writers from nations of both the North and the South, attempting to understand what it means to be a "post-colonial subject".[12] They often focus on their own subjectivity, acknowledging that a person's identity is made up of a collection of parts. These parts include not only colonial experience, but also traditional culture and the unfolding late modern world. The realm of this identity has been labelled a new "third space"

---

[10] For example, many former British colonies have preserved the elitist aspects of the British secondary education system. Very few students complete their "A" and "O" level school-leaving qualifications. Although many do not succeed, there is resistance to change, because this is the education that has already benefitted the elites.

[11] Joyce Nelson (1987: 117) reports that "[t]he symbiotic growth of American television and global enterprise has made them so interrelated that they cannot be thought of as separate."

[12] These scholars include Homi K. Bhabha (1994), Ashis Nandy (1983); Trinh Minh-ha (1989) and, in Canada, David G. Smith (1994).

(Bhabha, 1994), which is neither oppositional nor colonial. Thinking from this space opens up new and creative possibilities. In this respect, Gandhi's attempts to forge an alternative path of development for India are again becoming of interest.

To Teach for Peace

It is clear that the three crises we have identified—the crisis of global conflict management, the crisis of development and the crisis of neocolonialism—are all related. Each, in some sense, points to a loss of faith in progress. "What to do now?" is the question we must ask. It is the inability to answer adequately that has given rise to the pessimism invading politics and society in the West. This dominant mood has produced a defensive posture of budget cutting, turning back social programs, and toughening up of laws. This reactive stance, aimed at protecting what is left and at redoubling efforts to make old solutions work, is sure to worsen an already deteriorating situation. Violence and human rights violations will continue as various nation states weaken, with some in danger of collapsing altogether. Disparities of economic development will also continue to grow worse, and the very legitimacy of the poorest of the nations will be threatened by their crushing foreign debts. Pessimism will also do nothing to change neocolonial relations between the rich and the poor, the North and the South. All of this, too, will continue unabated.

To educate for peace in these times of failed imagination requires a new vision. Gandhi, quoting the New Testament, said: "Where there is no vision, the people shall perish" (Brown, 1989: 282). Gandhi's vision rejected the West. He was a severe critic of what he saw

to be the dehumanizing industrialism and consumerism that the colonial West brought to the world. He urged, instead, the recognition of the spiritual basis of human existence.

We would argue that a similar kind of vision is required again now. We cannot return to Gandhi, for he was clearly a person of his own time and place. And while Gandhi's analysis of modernity was penetrating, and his alternative vision inspiring, ultimately it did not prevail in India. The vision that prevailed was Nehru's: the modern, national and secular state. What is needed at this time is a new trajectory of action that will ensure quality of life for future generations. What that future world will be like is not for us to say, but it is important that we begin to live now, responsibly, in a manner that will make this future more likely. The task of the peace educator is both critical and creative: to point to those things that are likely to impede the possibility of a peaceful future, and to teach in such a manner as to be consistent with realizing the goal of a just and sustainable world.

We can construct broad outlines of such a world. It includes the following dimensions:

1. Respect for the security of persons

Human security does not mean personal security. In fact, privatized security, in the sense of locks and electronic security systems, actually contributes to a disintegration of community and greater insecurity. Security means fostering those conditions of life that can support a secure existence for all, not just for those who can afford it, or not just for the neighbours we know. It means a secure existence for the stranger. It especially implies a solidarity between North and South, for there can be no genuine security of persons in a global society in which vast disparities of wealth continue to exist.

2. A respect for the integrity of cultures

There are a multiplicity of cultures across the world. Many are under threat from national governments anxious to promote a unitary version of a nation—by assimilating aboriginal peoples, for example. Most now are also under threat from the homogenizing influences of the media and the mass market. Cultures carry within them spirituality, history and diversity. They transcend autonomous individuals, linking generations past, present and future. It is important, of course, not to romanticize culture or to stereotype it in superficial features of diet, dress and decoration. The point is to respect both the difference and the integrity that is present in all cultures. Moreover, in a global environment, all cultures are hybrid (Bhabha). Recognizing this truth will prevent the violence of trying to maintain purity.

3. A respect for the interdependence of environments

The interdependence of human and natural environments has been easily forgotten in the successful exploitation of resources for economic development. New understandings of science have provided fresh insights into the interdependence of living systems (Maturana and Varela, 1992). A systems view indicates that human activity can have far-reaching and unanticipated detrimental effects on a natural environment, because of the interdependence of living organisms. But a new understanding of science as a living, interrelated system also suggests a humility, or "listening" to nature as opposed to trying to dominate it. New science promises a greater harmony with the earth.

Examples of Peace Education Practice

The following examples present concrete suggestions based on these principles for a peaceful world order. They are drawn from the winners of the "Right to Livelihood Award". This award, sometimes called "the alternative Nobel Prize", has been given annually since 1980 to individuals and organizations that have contributed to peace, sustainable development, environmental integrity, social justice and human rights (Seabrook, 1993).

UNITED STATES: INSTITUTE FOR THE ARTS OF DEMOCRACY   In many western countries such as Canada and the United States, cynicism about politicians has damaged faith in democratic institutions. The cynicism is understandable, but also dangerous. There is some justification to the charge that vested interests and the economically powerful control democratic institutions; however, the solution is not to abandon democracy, but to make it work.

Frances Moore Lappé, who won the Right to Livelihood Award in 1987, recognized the connection between equity and democracy as a problem in both the North and the South. In order to revitalize democratic institutions, she set up an Institute for the Arts of Democracy. The basis for the Institute was the work that Lappé did in the 1970s in relation to the politics of food. In this work, she determined that hunger was not a problem of scarcity, but of political and economic decisions that are made without any kind of popular input.

The Institute for the Arts of Democracy has developed a number of initiatives to study the philosophy of democracy, as well as analyzing the sources of social fragmentation that prevent democratic discourse and action. These studies are accompanied by educational projects that bring school students together with community activists and organizations. The point is not to create activism on particular projects, but to develop "a language of democracy" for American society (Seabrook, 1993: 154).

INDIA: LOKAYAN In India there is a movement called Lokayan, which means "dialogue of the people". It is an experiment in popular education and action that aims to build a unity of academics and community grassroots organizations.

Lokayan is based at the Centre for Developing Societies in New Delhi. This is a non-governmental organization known for creative and penetrating research into questions of development and humane governance. One of its major concerns has been the way that modernization has by-passed people in the interests of national economic development. As Smitu Kothari of Lokayan points out, "the modern project of integration, whether into world economic order, the technological market-place, or the global strategic order, has effectively split society into two [the rich and the poor].... [T]he poor are being reduced to being stateless..., displaced from traditional local habitats..., [and] find no place in modern political and social structures." (Seabrook, 1993: 157–158).

Lokayan began work in the early 1980s, making contact with local activist groups in many parts of India. Based on the ethic of self-reliance, Lokayan refuses foreign aid. In so doing, it believes that it is able to centre its practice and thinking on India and South Asia, avoiding "the universalism imposed by the North in its own interpretation of the world". Different priorities are set and different relationships are made that are in tune with local cultures. For example, the environmental question in India becomes not just a question of protection of air, water and land, but an issue of culture and "inter-generational sustainability".

Under the rubric of "dialogue of the people", Lokayan has undertaken a number of practical projects. It has sponsored national gatherings of local groups who are resisting environmentally damaging development projects such as the Narmada Dam and the Singhroli super-thermal plants. They also encourage respect for pluralistic and locally responsive solutions.

The solutions sought by Lokayan harken back to Gandhi's view that "those who speak of separating religion and politics understand neither religion nor politics". Lokayan gives priority to the link between the political and the spiritual. It argues that separation between the political and the spiritual de-legitimizes multiple religious and cultural identities, and marginalizes them, leaving them open to "hi-jacking" by fundamentalists. Repairing this split helps to bring spiritualism back into public life, and liberates religion from communalism.

JAPAN: THE SEIKATSU CLUB Japan has been held out as one of the most successful models of technological and economic development. But within Japan there has grown a grassroots consumer cooperative known as the Seikatsu Club. It began in 1965 with a group of Tokyo housewives who were concerned about the price and availability of milk. The Club has now expanded to become a national organization of some 500 000 members who are trying to change their patterns of consumption and production.

As the Seikatsu Club developed, its members began to discern broader critical social and economic trends that were linked to urbanization and consumerism. For example, they saw that their role in the family was being reduced to that of mere shoppers in supermarkets. They saw that consumers have little real power, because decisions about what to buy are controlled more and more by the concentrated ownership of large corporations. They saw that, with the rapid urbanization of Japan, fewer people are being able to appreciate the link between consumption and the production of goods.

These critical insights have enabled the Seikatsu Club to develop into a powerful grassroots alternative to conventional market forces. Unlike traditional cooperatives who have tended simply to compete with traditional stores, the Seikatsu Club has aimed to use its power as "downstream buyers" to influence the "upstream production" of goods. Their announced aim is a richer life for all. A richer life means that those with wealth will need to minimize consumption and simplify their lives, while those without wealth will be ensured a decent and secure livelihood. As a result, the Seikatsu Club, as a provider of consumer goods, questions the amounts and the sources of the goods required, and endeavours to enter into direct relationships with producer-owned cooperatives and environmentally responsible companies. For example, bananas are purchased directly from a worker-owned cooperative in the Philippines at four times the rate paid by private companies, while coffee is purchased directly from growers in Peru. Cooking oil is supplied by a small plant that purifies old cooking oil in Japan. As Jeremy Seabrook, the author of *Pioneers of Change*, indicates, "Seikatsu is of a piece with many attempts, worldwide, to resist the excesses of capital promoted consumerism, and probably the most successful" (Seabrook, 1993: 198).

Invigorating Peace Education Practice

In the previous chapter we listed seven features of a working definition of peace education. These were non-violent practice, a sensitivity to human rights, social justice, world mindedness, a concern for ecological balance,

meaningful participation of people, and the cultivation of personal peace. These features form the dimensions of a comprehensive understanding of peace. However, they are not achievements in and of themselves; they are only labels that can serve to guide actions. They will take on meaning in our schools and communities only with thoughtful and informed practice.

There is a danger that, in trying to make these concepts a reality, we might slip into a kind of peace evangelism that attempts to inculcate orthodox understandings of non-violence, human rights, social justice and so forth, without regard to the particularities of individual situations. This would be a mistake. The point to remember is that we have recognized these dimensions of peace by their absence, and we cannot make them present by imposing authoritative definitions on others. They can become present only through reflective practice, and in relation to the improvement of the quality of life of those who are directly implicated in that practice.

An example will serve to illustrate how peace education cannot be implemented dogmatically. A group of eight teachers in Edmonton, Alberta, had formed a Collaborative Action Research Project on Peace Education (CARPE). One member of the group, a junior high teacher, was having his class raise money to support an individual foster child in India. The project had been determined by the students, and the teacher supported them. Many social justice arguments could be made against such a practice: it perpetuates charity and it fails to educate students about the structural violence of the global economic system. However, the other members of the action research group supported this teacher's practice, accepting that the students needed to take some sort of positive action to encourage their hope and sense of effectiveness. As the teacher said, "I find my students have a tremendous sadness about the legacy left to them. After writing letters to politicians and making posters, there wasn't much else they could do. They needed something positive" (Carson, 1992).

Practices fill out and deepen understandings of peace. The examples from the United States, India and Japan show not only that thoughtful alternative practices are helping to build a peace culture, but also that rich dimensions to social justice, ecological balance and meaningful participation are being developed. These dimensions are very specific to their context, yet they show a world mindedness. They are a conscious link between thinking globally and acting locally.

REFERENCES AND SOURCES

Bhabha, Homi K. (1994), *The Location of Culture* , London: Routlege.

Brown, Judith (1989), *Gandhi: A Prisoner of Hope*, New Haven: Yale University Press.

Carson, Terrance R. (1992), "Remembering forward: reflections on educating for peace" in William Pinar and William Reynolds (eds.), *Understanding curriculum as phenomenological and deconstructed text* , New York, Teachers College Press.

Childers, Erskine (1994), in *London Review of Books*, August 18.

Fischer, L. (1954), *The Life of Mahatma Gandhi*, New York: Mentor Books.

Fischer, Louis (1990), *The Life of Mahatma Gandhi* , Fifth Edition, Bombay: Bhavan's Book University Press.

Gadamer, Hans-Georg (1989), *Truth and Method* , Revised Edition (translated by Joel Weinsheimer and Donald Marshall), New York: Crossroad Publishing.

Held, David (1993), "Democracy: past, present and possible futures" in *Alternatives: A Journal of Social Transformation and Humane Governance* 18(3): 259–271.

Herman, Theodore, "Adding Gandhi to Galtung for peace work" in *Peace, Environment and Education*, 5(4) (1994): 23–27.

Ignatieff, Michael (1993). *Blood and Belonging: Journeys Into the New Nationalism* , Toronto: Viking Press.

Kothari, Rajni (1993) "The yawning vacuum: a world without alternatives" in *Alternatives: A Journal of Social Transformation and Humane Governance* 18(2): 119–139.

Maturana, Humberto and Francisco Varela (1992), *The Tree of Knowledge: The Biological Roots of Human Understanding* , Revised Edition, Boston: Shambhala.

Miller, Webb (1936), *I Found No Peace*, New York: Simon and Schuster.

Minh-ha, Trinh (1989). *Woman, Native, Other*, Bloomington: Indiana University Press.

Nandy, Ashis (1983), *The Intimate Enemy*, Delhi, Oxford University Press.

Nelson, Joyce, 1987, *The perfect machine: TV in the nuclear age*, Toronto: Between the Lines.

Sachs, W. (1992) *On the archeology of the development idea.*

Sachs, Wolfgang (1992) "Development: a guide to the ruins" in *New Internationalist*, June: 4.

Seabrook, Jeremy (1993), *Pioneers of Change: Experiments in Creating a Humane Society*, Gabriola, B.C.: New Society Publishers.

Smith, David G. (1994), *Pedagon: Meditations on Pedagogy and Culture* , Bragg Creek, AB: Makyo Press.

ul-Huq, Mahbub (1994), Interview with Chris Brazier in *New Internationalist*, December: 20–23.

PART 2

Infusing Education for Peace into the Curriculum

Literature

AMONG THE MANY *books written by Canadian author Gabrielle Roy is a gentle fable entitled* L'espagnole et la pékinoise, *a children's story about a farm cat and dog, both female, who detest each other. Their state of continuous war is due partly to their sense of territoriality and partly to their perceptions of each other.*

The cat has the run of the attic upstairs, where the dog is not permitted to go, and the dog is seethingly jealous that the cat has the nooks, crannies and comforts of a whole floor to herself. For her part, the cat despises the dog for her aggressiveness and for the uncouth way in which she eats her meals.

These differences lead to constant wrangling and name-calling that, on occasion, bring them into physical combat in which the dog mauls the cat and the cat spits and claws at the dog. The perennial solution used by Berthe, their mistress, is to separate the combatants—the dog being sent behind the stove and the cat banished to her quarters upstairs.

Then comes a tender moment in the story in which the cat gives birth to three kittens in the attic. The dog, pressing her luck by climbing the stairs, sees the cat lovingly nursing her young. In her mind, the dog no longer perceives ugliness or spitefulness in the cat's face but, instead, the look of a gentle mother whose eyes are filled with love for her young. The dog is astonished not only by the transformation of the cat, but by her own sudden change of character.

As the days pass, the dog takes advantage of the cat's occasional roamings outside to steal up the stairs and play with the kittens. The Pekinoise, longing for motherhood herself, allows the little ones to romp all over her, as she lies on her back with her feet in the air. It is in this posture that the dog is unexpectedly discovered by the cat returning early to her family. From that point on, their friendship grows. It is strengthened when, together, they hatch and execute a plan to hide the kittens in order to prevent Berthe from giving them away to visiting friends.

The dog and the four cats eventually become virtually a single family. Their mistress, rocking in a verandah chair and watching them play together before the house, muses philosophically that it was the little ones that brought peace, and that one day, perhaps, like her pets, children will join hands the world over and bring an end to strife and war.

It is in such stories as these, that we can see the application of literature to peace education. Why were the cat and dog adversaries? What methods did they use to resolve their differences? How was Berthe involved as a third party? How did the feelings of the dog and cat change towards each other? What caused the relationship between the two fundamentally to alter? How effective is the author's use of a family of pets as a symbol of the human community?

Even a simple fable like L'espagnole et la pékinoise *is rich in opportunities for broaching basic questions about peace. In this chapter we will examine ways in which literature may be used as a powerful means for peace-making and peace-building by promoting and upholding significant values, by developing respect for other cultures, by providing models of interpersonal and inter-group reconciliation, and by stirring in readers a sense of their identity as members of the human community.*

Identifying Values in Literature

All literature, whether in the form of novel, drama or poem, exemplifies positive or negative values. In his essay dealing with a world view of the role and functions of literature in society, André Maurois takes a very positive view: "The really great writers...have always buttressed their work with stable values—goodness, love and friendship. They lead the reader to experience feelings which strengthen him." (1969: 110) Some modern writers have, by contrast, produced novels that display or uphold negative values such as egotism, cruelty and destruction. Hollindale points out that literature has the capacity to "free us from the limitations of our egotistical perspectives of what it means to be human" (1986: 35), and that because of the decline in religious education and religious beliefs, literature is increasingly an important instrument for moral education. Teaching literature for peace requires an examination of the consequences of negative values but, more significantly, it involves identifying and adhering to values that are life-supporting and community-building in their application *on a global scale.*

Some specific examples of values in literature may be helpful at this point. They are particularly useful for teaching at the secondary school level. In schools where the Bible is studied as literature, there are abundant opportunities for considering value questions. The Book of Ruth tells the story of Ruth, a Moabite, who loses her husband. In spite of pressures to return to her mother and father and to disassociate herself from the family into which she has married, Ruth decides to stay and help support her mother-in-law, Naomi, to whom she develops a very strong attachment. When Ruth moves with Naomi from Moab to Judah, she is is an "unprotected" for-eigner in a new country, but she is welcomed as a gleaner of wheat among the Israelites and materially provided for among them. Recognized by the community as a person of noble character, Ruth is eventually married to Boaz. This short story exemplifies a number of values, including Ruth's loyalty and fidelity to Naomi's family; friendship extended by the Judeans to Ruth; industriousness of Ruth in joining the gleaners to support herself and Naomi; and Boaz's generosity and kindness in inviting Naomi to join in the gleaning of his fields.

The parables of the New Testament are also rich for value analysis. The parable of the prodigal son is a compact story about the younger of two sons, who asks his father for the portion of inheritance due to him. Leaving home, he spends all his money on riotous living in a foreign country. Reduced to living on the food of pigs, he comes to his senses and decides to return home. He is welcomed, rather than chastised, by his father. The dominant values in the story are repentance by the son, love and forgiveness of the father, and reconciliation between father and son. The reunification and reintegration of a family triumph over separation and fragmentation.

The novels of Charles Dickens, which are often included in secondary literature syllabuses, also constitute good examples for the teaching of values. All his life, Dickens was haunted by a hard childhood. When his father was imprisoned for debt, he had to take on humble work to help support his family. It brought him into contact with the lower social classes and caused him to identify strongly with children, women and the poor. His experiences are reflected in *David Copperfield, Oliver Twist, Little Nell* and *A Christmas Carol.* In these books we see compassion and pity for the poor and oppressed. In the Christmas tales, especially, we see, as Maurois (1969) points out, the victory of goodness and warmth of human fellowship over selfishness.

Both classical and modern literature generally hold up as heroes people of physical or moral courage who are admired for their bravery and noble deeds. Frequently, they are the winners or losers in armed combat and the concept of hero is interpreted within the arena of war. However, Morgan (1985) has drawn attention to the idea of the peaceful hero in literature, one whose courage and bravery is able to serve humankind without participation in battle itself.

Such a hero, she suggests, is found in Paul Gallico's fictional legend *The Snow Goose*. The hero in this story is a disabled young man, Philip Rhayader, who lives in an abandoned lighthouse off the coast of Essex and has established a sanctuary for wild birds. In winter months, he occupies himself painting canvasses of the surrounding landscape. In spite of his physical disability, he is a powerful man, and becomes a sailor, using his hands and teeth to manage the sails of a small craft. In the story, Rhayader heals and cares for a wounded snow goose, which then chooses to stay within the sanctuary rather than migrate. This episode is paralleled by a loving relationship he develops with Frith, a girl in a nearby village, who also comes to him freely. The climax of the story comes when Rhayader chooses to leave the relative safety of his sanctuary to sail to Dunkirk to assist in the evacuation of soldiers stranded on the beaches in the Second World War. Rhayader's life, in its entirety, advocates peace.

When we reflect upon the values in this story, we are struck by the resourcefulness of a disabled man. He masters sailing. He is a healer of wounded birds. He is creative in the artistic interpretation of his surroundings. He demonstrates remarkable compassion for both

animals and fellow humans, showing that even in relative isolation, he manifests love. Morgan concludes that Rhayader is "a moving, memorable example of the hero who chooses peaceful action in response to some larger strife", and further suggests that the teaching of literature, more generally, should highlight fictional characters "who raise their voices with quiet dignity and nobility when confronted with turmoil and unrest" (1985: 12).

Opportunities for teaching values through literature also present themselves in the study of biographies. Literary accounts of the lives of men and women can help us to focus on values that served to propel them to greatness. Greatness is often measured in terms of the contribution made to humankind. While the lives of such individuals uphold important values in themselves, they also serve as models that inspire "ordinary" people to greater living.

Classes can consider great people and analyze the reasons for their greatness. Alternatively, the teacher can identify important values for peace and ask which lives exemplify those values. In this case, the teacher might include the values of unity in diversity (Simon Bolivar, Wilfrid Laurier); compassion and healing (Florence Nightingale, Henri Dunant); selfless public service (Eleanor Roosevelt, U Thant); philanthropy and peace (Alfred Nobel, Maria Montessori); pacifism and non-violence (Mahatma Gandhi, Emily Pankhurst), international order (Dag Hammarskjold). It is interesting to note that, even in the brief listing given here, the exemplars of peaceful values come from cultures and nations the world over.

The suggestions above offer but a few possibilities by which teachers can explore and develop the discussion of peace-building values in literature. Maurois reminds us that some modern authors offer nothing but despair or hedonism as a response to our contemporary predicament; however, he is quick to point out that there are always minds that are eager to search for positive solutions to the most difficult problems that beset us. "There is every reason to hope," he writes, "that beyond despair and disaffection there will continue to flow an abiding literature which is now becoming world-wide, a current of understanding, of pity and of love." (1969: 115)

Studying Conflict Through Literature

War
noisy, scary
shooting, fighting, crying
struggle, fight, rainbow, dove
singing, strolling, caring
quiet, soft
peace

This short poem, written by Andrea Superstein, a grade four student in Montreal, shows in its beautiful symmetry and simplicity, a transformation of war into peace. In addition, through its associations, it helps us to think about the language of conflict. The idea that peace is a process, and that it is linked to our language and our thinking patterns, is fundamentally important to the study of conflict in literature. In this section, we will consider the place of language in conflict, the structure of conflict in fiction, and some specific examples of conflict in drama and other literary writing.

Language and Conflict

Linguists have helped us to understand the role of language in conflict and peace. Thompson (1985) and Smith (1997) demonstrate how language controls our thinking, guides our behaviour, and affects the way we perceive the world. Drawing upon a study by Lakoff and Johnson, he cites, by way of example, the metaphor, "argument is war" (1985:13):

1. Your claims are *indefensible.*
2. He *attacked every point* in my argument.
3. His criticisms were *right on target.*
4. I *demolished* his argument.
5. I've never *won* an argument with him.
6. You disagree? OK, *shoot.*
7. If you use that strategy, *he'll wipe you out.*
8. He *shot down* all of my arguments.

Thompson identifies three kinds of metaphors that tend to be ingrained in our thinking. The first is the structural metaphor, in which a concept is expressed as something else ("argument is war", "peace is love"). The second is the ontological metaphor, which implies that a concept is a whole and complete entity, excluding other meanings ("peace is costly", "peace is free"). The third is the orientational metaphor, which tends to position an idea or concept ("war is the lowest form of behaviour", "peace is one of our highest ideals"). It is suggested that students adopt a critical approach to the use of metaphors. For example, thinking about peace as an entity—that is, a thing to be achieved—may preclude our thinking of peace as an action, or as a process. In this way, students may develop a more critical interpretation of literature related to conflict and peace, and search for alternative ways of expressing peace in their own creative writing.

Exploring meanings in language can help in the formulation of new concepts of conflict and peace. Thompson points out that peace is often thought of as an entity ("peace is commitment", "peace is freedom"). As such, it is something to be achieved. However, expressing peace as an entity—an end product can constrain our thinking. Thompson suggests that students "unravel" the metaphors, to consider the actions that can be associated with them. For example, in the metaphor "peace is commitment", what precisely are we committed to? To honesty? Fairness? Forgiveness? Equality? Non-violence? Other peace-building values? By studying metaphor in literature and in their own writing, students can come to recognize that their very conceptions of fundamental notions such as peace or conflict are rooted in language.

Narrative Structure and Conflict

Understanding the way in which conflict is represented in literature and drama can help students learn more about the dynamics of conflict and its resolution. Cusac (1985) has described three kinds of narrative in fiction. The first is *episodic structure,* in which events are strung together like beads on a string, but have no causal relationship one to the other. The second kind of narrative has an *events structure,* in which there is a sequence of events having causal relationships. The third type is *thematic structure,* in which there may not be events in the usual sense and no causal relation in the story development. Those stories that have an events structure are more likely to be helpful in studying most kinds of observable conflict.

In fiction with an events structure there are a number of identifiable points that can help us to understand the conflict process. Among the first identified by Cusac is the *defining event,* which pinpoints the situation in which the protagonists find themselves. At this stage, the reader is able to identify the basic conflict that gives thrust to the story and leads by cause and effect to a crisis. In the case of Shakespeare's *Hamlet,* for example, the defining event comes in Act I, Scene v, when Hamlet learns that his father was murdered by

Claudius so that he could become King of Denmark, and Hamlet feels compelled to seek revenge:

The time is out of joint; O cursed spite,
That ever I was born to set it right.

The next identifiable point in the story is the *crisis,* or turning point. In this event, the protagonists are faced with a crucial situation in which they must make a critical decision to resolve the conflict. Hamlet reaches this point in Act III, Scene ii. Having obtained evidence confirming Claudius's guilt, he decides to murder him:

Now I could drink hot blood
And do such bitter business as the day
Would quake to look on.

The result of the decision made in the crisis is the *catastrophe,* or outcome of events. In this case, the immediate outcome is that Hamlet, in a case of mistaken identity, kills Polonius. Through further cause and effect, however, this leads to a later outcome in which Claudius is stabbed to death by Hamlet; the Queen dies from a poisoned drink intended for Hamlet; and Hamlet and Laertes both die from the wounds of a poisoned sword in a fencing match. The outcome reveals the consequences of the cumulative decisions made to resolve the conflict.

The final element in the narrative of events is the *denouement,* which brings the story or drama to a close. In *Hamlet* it consists of only a few lines in which Horatio promises to explain how the tragic sequence of events occurred and announces that Hamlet's body will lie in state. The denouement often provides an account of the sequence of events which the reader may not have been in a position before to understand.

56

Destructive and Constructive Conflict

In discussing the nature of conflict in children's literature, Bond (1984) identifies three different levels of conflict and provides examples from her own fiction for children. In the discussion here, we will focus more on adolescent literature, using as examples Shakespeare's plays *Hamlet* and *As You Like It*. Bond describes, first, what she terms *global conflict*, in which a large number of people are struggling or fighting against each other. In *Hamlet*, the only global conflict is a battle between the armies of Norway and Poland over a small disputed territory in Poland, a conflict that is, in fact, somewhat peripheral to the main story of the play.

The second kind of conflict is *interpersonal*, and arises between different characters in the story. It is this type of conflict that is central in *Hamlet*, since the prince seeks revenge against Claudius. Besides this principal conflict, there are at least three other tensions developed in the play: between Hamlet and his mother, between Hamlet and Ophelia, and between Hamlet and Laertes. Tragically, all these conflicts escalate and end in suicide or murder.

The third kind of conflict is *intrapersonal*, concerning the internal struggles that go on inside the individual characters. In *Hamlet*, we learn a great deal about the internal struggles of the characters through the technique of the soliloquy. We learn that Claudius is torn between a desire to seek divine forgiveness for his crime and a paralyzing sense of guilt that prevents him from doing so. We learn that Hamlet is torn between taking action against Claudius or committing suicide as a way out of his dilemma. Even after he decides to take revenge, his resolution continues to waver.

Two or three levels of conflict are often found in fiction or drama, and they may be cleverly interwoven and related to one another. Of special interest to us in examining the link between literature and peace are the sources of conflict and the way in which conflict at any of the levels is handled in a story. Conflict in itself is always present in life and literature. As Bond (1984: 301) points out, there are a great many things that put a person, or a group, into conflict. It may be misunderstanding, insensitivity, anger, revenge, competition, ambition, greed, and other drives on the dark side of human character. Hamlet, for example, is driven by his desire to avenge the death of his father.

In trying to resolve the conflict, the characters often resort to psychological or physical violence, and the conflict becomes destructive. Psychological violence consists of actions taken by one character to damage the self-esteem, dignity or self-concept of another. Hamlet uses psychological violence by feigning madness, which not only casts a pall over most of his contacts at court, but is a contributing factor to the suicide of Ophelia. Physical violence consists of actions causing physical injury or destruction. In *Hamlet*, as we have seen, all of the main characters meet a physically violent death.

The study of psychological and physical violence in a tragedy can be very instructive, by stimulating discussion about the cause of the catastrophe and possible alternatives that might have been considered by the principal characters to avert it. How might the story be different if the ghost of Hamlet's father had not asked for revenge? If Hamlet had contrived something other than murder for revenge? Or if he had been determined to forgive his uncle and mother for their misdeeds?

When they are handled in a constructive way, conflicts generally lead to personal growth, the healing of interpersonal relationships and group reconciliation. There is a need for such models of constructive conflict to be presented and discussed with students in addition to those that deal with destructive conflict.

As an example, we can contrast the conflicts, and the processes by which they are resolved, in *Hamlet*—a tragedy—and *As You Like It*—a comedy. In *As You Like It*, as in *Hamlet*, the conflict is mainly interpersonal. Frederick, motivated by greed and ambition, has usurped the lands of his brother, the Duke, and has exiled him to the Forest of Arden. At the same time, a subsidiary tension develops between Frederick and Rosalind, the Duke's niece. Rosalind has been allowed to stay behind because of the closeness she has with Celia, Frederick's only daughter, but Frederick

> Hath ta'en displeasure 'gainst his gentle niece;
> Grounded upon no other argument,
> But that the people praise her for her virtues,
> And pity her for her good father's sake.

There are two other minor tensions in the play. One is between Orlando and his eldest brother, Oliver, both sons of the deceased Sir Rowland de Bois. Oliver is supposed to take care of his younger brother, but Orlando is neglected and treated disdainfully. Orlando quickly falls into disfavour with Frederick, and he leaves to join the Duke in the Forest of Arden.

After Celia and Rosalind, together with the court clown, Touchstone, also escape to the forest, the play focuses on the love affairs between Orlando and Rosalind, Silvius and Phebe (Shepherd and Shepherdess), and Touchstone and Audrey, a country woman. However, the tensions in the play heighten as Frederick orders a search for Celia and

Rosalind and demands that Orlando be brought back dead or alive.

The conflict between Oliver and Orlando is resolved when Oliver falls in love with Celia, and decides to live a shepherd's life with her in the forest. Accordingly, he assigns his father's estate to Orlando.

The major conflict between Frederick and his brother is also resolved. Travelling to the forest, Duke Frederick meets an old religious man who successfully persuades him not to kill his brother, and to turn from his worldly ways. The crown is restored to the banished Duke and all lands to their rightful owners. The play ends happily with music and song for the marriage celebrations of Rosalind and Orlando, Oliver and Celia, Touchstone and Audrey, Silvius and Phebe. There is a complete healing and reconciliation of all relationships.

In the conflict between characters in *As You Like It*, we see essentially a conflict of values. On the one hand, Frederick represents the negative values of greed, ambition, jealousy and aggression, while Oliver depicts favouritism, prejudice and vengefulness. On the other hand, the exiled Duke is the epitome of the positive values of gentleness, humility and kindness. Rosalind, as the heroine, represents intelligent resourcefulness, gentleness and patience; while Orlando, as hero, conveys a combination of the values of strength and tenderness, bravery and valour. Through constructive conflict, the play clearly portrays the triumph of positive over negative values.

Conflict and its resolution are, of course, an integral part of most literary writing. Much of contemporary literature for young adults deals with common, specific problems and conflicts experienced by young people now. The way in which these problems are handled in literature can serve to broaden students' understanding and experience of conflict. Two examples of such books are Sarah Pirtle's *An Outbreak of Peace* (1987) and Theresa Nelson's *And One For All* (1989), both suitable for senior elementary or junior high school readers. The first of these stories is set in a closely-knit, multicultural community and has to do with tensions that develop between two families that have previously been close friends. However, conflict arises when it is discovered that the company where one of the parents works supplies computer parts for the manufacture of nuclear weapons. Wanting to restore the relationship, a group of young people take the initiative in organizing an extraordinarily creative, but provocative, arts display for peace and justice. The display and subsequent debate over the issues influence parents and neighbours to work harder for a more caring community and a safer world.

The second book has its setting in the United States during the Vietnam War. It is about three high school students—two boys and a girl—who pledge everlasting friendship to each other. National divisions over the war are manifested also in their families, however, and bring a crisis to the relationship between the three friends. One of the boys volunteers for the US Marine Corps, while the other supports movements for the peaceful withdrawal of US troops from Vietnam. The reader is challenged to reflect upon the complexity of the issues unravelled and the unexpected outcome of the story, as tragedy touches the lives of the respective families involved.

Both classical and contemporary literature can greatly illuminate the nature of conflict: they can help students to identify the sources of conflict, the choices open to different characters, the values inherent in alternative actions, the dynamics of conflict, and the consequences that follow from choices made.

Literature and Inter-Cultural Understanding

Nearly all the large metropolitan centres in the West have experienced tremendous social change in the past 50 years, and are now made up of people who have come from different regions of the world. Moreover, certain rural societies, through waves of immigration, have had long traditions of cultural diversity. Because these various groups must learn to live harmoniously together, there is a need to develop respect for cultural and ethnic differences. Regrettably, the literature taught in our schools does not always take into consideration the reality of cultural diversity. Yet literature (along with geography and history) is one of the most appropriate subjects by which each group can learn about other societies and the people who come from them.

In addition to recognizing the nature of multicultural communities, there is a need for us to understand better the people who live in other countries. The distinction between these two kinds of learning is usually expressed as *multicultural* education and *inter-cultural* education. Multicultural education may be construed as education for living in a pluralistic society. Education for inter-cultural understanding involves the appreciation of cultures that are at a greater distance from us but are often, in this shrinking world, no less influential than those closer to home. In considering their relationship to education for peace, the latter is an extension of the former.

In developing respect for other cultures, teachers of literature are often confronted with two principal problems: one is the cultural bias or stereotyping that is sometimes represented in books for children and adolescents; the other is finding appropriate books that have any representation at all of the culture and reality of other societies. Among the studies that have examined the images of different ethnic groups and cultures in literature books is that of Timm (1988). After examining the text and illustrations of a 167 widely used books, she identified a number of stereotypes of cultural groups. The message that young people get from being exposed to such literature is that some cultural groups are more able than others to perform roles and responsibilities in our society, and that our society does not value equally all of the groups that comprise it. Clearly such implicit teachings are unacceptable.

In reviewing literature for children, Norton (1987: 503) summarizes the value of studying multiethnic literature for both minority and majority cultural groups. For minority groups, it helps individual members improve self-concept and develop a positive cultural identity. It can help them develop a sense of pride in their own heritage and recognize that their own culture makes an important contribution to national and world culture. And when members of a group read about notable accomplishments and efforts to solve problems in their culture, it helps to raise their levels of aspiration.

For members of a majority cultural group, the study of multiethnic literature can help to develop a respect for the values and contributions of others. It can broaden their understanding of the complex nature of society. And it can help them to understand that, while cultural groups have different values, beliefs and customs, all must learn to live together in harmony with one another.

Within Canada and North America, a rich body of multiethnic literature has been developing, particularly for children. It includes a variety of poetry, fiction, legend and biography from First Nations, as well as books representing the experiences of different religious, racial, linguistic and ethnic groups. Anthologies of such literature include, for example, those by Ives and Billeadeux (1982) and Dixon (1986), and recommended representative stories and fiction are included in the writings of Carlson (1972), Fassler and Janis (1983), Norton (1987), Blair (1991), Cai (1992) and Johnston and Mackey (1995). As the title of Carlson's book so aptly describes it, multiethnic literature is a picture of "emerging humanity".

While some literature is based upon the experiences of ethnic groups in their adopted countries, there is really no well-defined boundary between multiethnic literature and literature for inter-cultural understanding: the difference often lies in the context in which books are read and discussed. Literature that comes from Greece, India or the Soviet Union can be used to enrich studies for a pluralistic society in which people having those national origins are now living, or it may be used to understand better the similarities and differences between those societies and our own. One or both of the objectives may be applicable.

Literature and a World Perspective

While the reading of literature from other lands helps us to appreciate cultural similarities and differences, a number of authors believe that reading literature generally, including that produced by our own culture, has important values in another sense: it reveals to us that people the world over have feelings, emotions and needs similar to our own, and that we share with them a common humanity.

André Maurois (1969: 107) points out that, whenever we read a novel, we seek a hero or heroine with whom we can identify. The central figure may contend with any one of a multitude of problems—scorn and criticism; rejection or alienation; a death or broken social relationships; excessive rivalry; injury resulting from accident or assault; displacement through fire, earthquake, war or other disaster; and the like. For the reader, it is reassuring to discover that other people whom we like and admire have experienced similar troubles, similar sadnesses, similar challenges, and perhaps eventually a sense of failure and tragedy or triumph and jubilation. We are not alone in what we have gone through. In one sense, Maurois says, literature humbles us by helping us to recognize that we are not different from other people. At the same time, however, we feel an exaltation: literature "restores our place in the human community from which we thought ourselves excluded."

Other writers have similarly claimed that literature can help to counteract our feelings of anonymity and our sense of isolation in the world. Nancy Bond (1984: 306) states that literature constantly reminds us that we are not faceless, numbered human beings, but that every individual on the planet is one who has a life as complex as our own and who has a right to that life. This constant reminder helps us both to acquire our own identity and to recognize the identities of others in the larger human community.

Marion Bauer (1987) has written about the relationship between isolation and conflict. Her thesis is that isolation is destructive, that "it is our sense of being unique and alone that makes it possible to destroy others" (715). The feeling of isolation, she says, is experienced early in life after an individual is separated from his or her mother's body. At some point, each one of us realizes that we are unique in that no one else can see through our eyes, hear through our ears, feel what we personally experience, know what we know. It is this isolation, she believes that gives us the potential "to kill what we cannot share."

For Bauer, stories and novels help to remove our sense of isolation, because through them we are able to get inside the thoughts and feelings of another person and to see the world through that other person's eyes. When we can share the experiences of another person, our sense of kinship with the rest of humanity opens up. By helping individuals to build connections in this way, literature can make an important contribution to world peace.

Besides the real contribution of good fiction to the development of a sense of our common humanity, fiction that deals more directly with the theme of our membership in the human community also has a role to play. Two novels—one coming out of First World War experiences and the other from the Second World War—deal extremely well with this theme and will be described here for illustrative purposes.

All Quiet on the Western Front by Erich Maria Remarque (1983), originally published in German, describes with terrifying authenticity the experiences of a young soldier, Paul Baumer, fighting in the trenches of the First World War. The climax of the story comes when Baumer, reacting with his training and instincts as an infantryman, stabs an enemy soldier who has accidentally stumbled into a shell-hole in which Baumer has taken temporary refuge from enemy fire. In the hours that follow, Baumer shares the shell hole with the dying man, and there is a gradual transformation in his attitude. Baumer develops a genuine desire to help the man in his agony, then wishes he could undo what has happened, and finally realizes that they share a common humanity:

> Why do they never tell us that you are poor devils like us, that your mothers are just as anxious as ours, and that we have the same fear of death, and the same dying and the same agony—Forgive me, comrade; how could you be my enemy? (91)

The book *Flight to Arras* by Antoine de Saint-Exupery (1942) has a similar message. Originally published in French, it recounts the author's experience as a pilot in the French Air Force, on a reconnaissance flight over German-occupied Arras during May of 1940. Interspersed in the narrative of dramatic action are the pilot's developing observations and reflections. The reader learns, at first, that Saint-Exupery feels one with the officers of his unit at the air force base. During the flight itself, he observes a stream of French refugees fleeing from the advancing German army, as France collapses: "…now that I have come down out of the clouds, I have become one with that mob." (205)

As Saint-Exupery later ponders the meaning of defeat for his country, he experiences a feeling of oneness with all of the people of France and realizes that he is a part of France and France is a part of him. Finally, towards the end of the story, he comes to the realiza-tion that he is one with all humankind:

> Beyond my village I saw my country, and beyond my country all other countries. I came back to a civilization which had chosen Man as the keystone in its arch. (251)

In both stories the central figures move from a limited awareness of their closest social grouping to a consciousness of their membership in humankind as a whole.

Summary

In this chapter, we have considered the importance of identifying dominant values in literary works with a view to determining whether they make for positive inter-relationships between people and the building of community. Because its various genres—poetry, novels, drama and biography—frequently deal with conflict, literature affords a special opportunity for the study of the causes of conflict, how it can be handled, and the consequences that arise when it is resolved in different ways. In this respect, literature is almost like a safe laboratory for the study of destructive and constructive conflict. We have also examined the value of developing inter-cultural understanding through literature and the ways in which the subject can help us to achieve our sense of kinship with all of humankind.

REFERENCES AND SOURCES

Abrahamson, Richard F. and Betty Carter (1987), "Of Survival, School, Wars, and Dreams: Nonfiction that Belongs in English Classes", *English Journal,* 76 (2), February: 104–109.

Barrone, Diane (1993), "The Butter Battle Book: Engaging Children's Thoughts of War", *Children's Literature in Education,* 24 (2): 123–135.

Bauer, Marion Dane (1987), "Peace in Story, Peace in the World", *The Horn Book Magazine,* 63 (6), November/December, 1987: 714–715.

Bell, Wilma (1985), "Great English Teaching Ideas: Peace in the Classroom", *Virginia English Bulletin,* 35 (2), Winter 1985: 23–29.

Blair, Linda (1991), "Developing Student Voices with Multicultural Literature", *English Journal,* 80 (8), December, 1991: 24–28.

Bond, Nancy (1984), "Conflict in Children's Fiction", *The Horn Book Magazine,* Vol 60 (June 3, 1984): 297–306.

Cai, Mingshui (1992), "A Balanced View of Acculturation: Comments on Lawrence Yep's Three Novels", *Children's Literature in Education,* 23 (2): 107–118.

Canadian Children's Book Centre (1989), *Canadian Children's Books on Peace and Conflict Resolution: A Resource Guide,* Toronto: Canadian Children's Book Centre.

Carlson, Ruth Kearney (1972), *Emerging Humanity: Multi-Ethnic Literature for Children and Adolescents,* Dubuque: Brown.

Cline, Ruth K. J. (1985), "Peace Education in the English Classroom," *Virginia English Bulletin,* 35 (2), Winter, 1985: 5–8.

Cusac, Marian H. (1985), "Narrative Structure as a Tool for Discovering Theme in Short Fiction", *Virginia English Bulletin,* 35 (2), Winter, 1985: 53–60.

Day, Bonnie (1984), *Observations on War and Other Poems,* Argenta, British Columbia: Argenta Friends Press.

Dixon, Mary (ed.), (1986), *Pieces: A Multi-cultural Anthology for Young Readers,* Winnipeg: Peguis Publishers Limited.

Dixon, Mary (ed.), (1986), *Of The Jigsaw: A Multicultural Anthology for Young Readers,* Winnipeg: Peguis Publishers Limited.

Dixon, Mary (ed.), (1986), *Puzzle: A Multi-cultural Anthology for Young Readers,* Winnipeg: Peguis Publishers Limited.

Dohrmann, Gail V. (1991), "John Dollar: Marianne Wiggins' Anti-Utopian Novel", *English Journal,* Vol 80 (4): 69–72.

Dougall, Lucy (1982), *War and Peace in Literature: Prose, Drama and Poetry which Illuminate the Problem of War,* Chicago: World Without War Publications.

Eleftheria, Ireni Kai (1987), *The Peace Book,* Montreal: Black Rose Books.

Fassler, Joan and Marjorie Graham Janis (1983), "Books, Children and Peace", *Young Children,* 38, September, 1983: 21–30.

Foster, Frances Smith (1987), "Ethnic Children's Literature in the Schools", Paper presented at the Annual Conference of the Society for the Study of Multi-Ethnic Literature of the United States, April 24–30, 1987. ERIC Document ED 291 842.

Hollindale, Peter (1986), "Values in the Teaching of English and Drama", in Peter Tomlinson and Margret Quinton (eds.), *Values Across the Curriculum,* London: The Falmer Press.

Ives, Jane and Jean-Luc Billeadeux (1982), *Favourite Stories from Around the World,* London: Cathay Books.

Johnston, Ingrid and Margaret Mackey (1995), "Multicultural Books for Readers 10–18", *Emergency Librarian* 23 (2), November–December 1995: 24–30.

Kessler, Kate (1991), "Teaching Holocaust Literature", *English Journal,* 80 (7), November, 1991: 29–32.

Lander, Faye A. (1981), *War and Peace in Adolescent Literature,* M.A. Thesis in Education,

University of Akron, 1981, ERIC Document 248 169.

Maurois, André (1969), "Literature considered as a means of expression", in *The Arts and Man: A world view of the role functions of the arts in society*, Paris: UNESCO.

Mitchell, Paula A. (1985), "War and Peace in Children's Literature", *Virginia English Bulletin*, 35 (2), Winter, 1985: 17–21.

Morgan, Charlotte G. (1985), "The Peaceful Hero", *Virginia English Bulletin*, 35 (2), Winter, 1985: 10–12.

Nelms, Beth and Ben Nelms (1986), "Young Adult Literature: Wars and Rumours of Wars", *English Journal*, 75: 106–108.

Nelson, Theresa (1989), *And One For All*, New York: Bantam Doubleday Dell.

Norris, Margot (1987), "Teaching the Literature of War", *LSA*, 10 (2), Winter 1987: 20, (Journal of the College of Literature, Science and the Arts at the University of Michigan).

Norton, Donna E. (1987), *Through the Eyes of a Child: An Introduction to Children's Literature*, Second Edition, Toronto: Merrill Publishing Company.

O'Reilley, Mary Rose (1984), "The Peaceable Classroom", *College English*, 46 (2): 103–112.

Pirtle, Sarah (1987), *An Outbreak of Peace*, Philadelphia: New Society Publishers.

Prothero, James (1990), "Fantasy, Science Fiction, and the Teaching of Values", *English Journal*, 79 (3), March, 1990: 32–34.

Remarque, Erich Maria, (1983), *All Quiet on the Western Front*, London: Heinemann.

Roy, Gabrielle (1986), *L'espagnole et la pékinoise*, Montreal: Boréal Jeunesse.

Russell, David L. (1993), "The Gammage Cup as Utopian Literature for Children", *Children's Literature in Education*, 24 (4): 241–249.

Saint-Exupery, Antoine de (1942), *Flight to Arras*, Translated from French by Lewis Galantiere, New York: Reynal and Hitchcock.

Sasser, Linda (1992), "Teaching Literature to Language Minority Students", in Patricia A. Richard-Amato and Marguerite Ann Snow, *The Multicultural Classroom: Readings for Content-Area Teachers*, New York: Longmans.

Smith, David C. (1997), "De-Militarizing Language", *Peace Magazine*, July/August 1997: 16–18.

Thompson, Herb (1985), "Understanding the Language of Peace: How Metaphors Control Our Thinking", *Virginia English Bulletin*, 35 (2), Winter, 1985: 13–16.

Timm, Joan S. (1988), "Cultural Bias in Children's Story Books: Implications for Education", Paper presented to the Annual Meeting of the American Educational Research Association, New Orleans, April 5–9, 1988. ERIC Document 294 943.

Tunnicliffe, Stephen (1981), "English and Nuclear War", *The Use of English*, 32 (3): 3–9.

CHAPTER 5

Second Languages

LUDWIG ZAMENHOF *was born in December 1859 in the small town of Bialystock in Russian Poland. As a young boy, Zamenhof developed a keen interest in languages, perhaps because his community was made up of different ethnic groups all of whom spoke principally their own languages, and his father was a school language teacher.*

At home Zamenhof spoke Russian. In secondary school he studied French, German, Latin, Greek and English. At the synagogue he acquired Hebrew, and in his day-to-day activities, he learned to speak Polish fluently. Although he personally loved languages, most people in Bialystock spoke only their own language and they harboured unfriendly feelings towards members of other ethnic groups.

Zamenhof saw a parallel between the linguistic divisions in his own community and those within a Europe of rising nationalisms. He reasoned that the prevalence of so many languages contributed to separation in the human family, and that an absence of communication, or a misunderstanding of what was spoken or read, often divided people and caused conflict among them. If only, he thought, there could be better communication, people would understand their common humanity.

At the age of fifteen, Zamenhof began working on the development of an artificial language, which could be spoken and written. His idea was not to replace existing natural languages, but to create an auxiliary language that all people could quickly acquire and use to communicate effectively with each other. Such a language had to be easy to learn; it had to have relatively simple and logical rules with no exceptions; and it had to be easily convertible into and from other major languages.

After secondary school, Zamenhof interrupted work on his project while he studied medicine at Moscow University. When he returned to Poland to practise medicine, he completed his work, and published it under the title An International Language: Introduction and Complete Manual. *In order to preserve his anonymity, he used a pseudonym, Doktoro Esperanto ("One who hopes"). As a result, the language he formulated became known as Esperanto.*

During this period, interest in artificial languages and their possibilities for humankind grew remarkably. Besides Esperanto, other languages were developed, including Volapuk and Ido; however, by the beginning of the twentieth century, Esperanto had the largest following. Supporting organizations flourished in many countries and an increasing number of books and journals were published in the language (Large, 1985).

After the First World War, interest in Esperanto continued, but to a lesser extent. Today, there are still many organizations that pursue and promote the learning of Esperanto. In some countries, it is still taught as an optional second or third language in secondary schools. However, some writers have observed that English, used increasingly throughout the world, has become a de facto international auxiliary language, and consequently there is less need for artificial languages such as Esperanto.

While artificial languages have not enjoyed the popularity that their creators hoped for, the learning of auxiliary languages (or second languages) is now encouraged in schools throughout the world.

Can the learning of such languages help to change values and our attitudes towards others? In what ways may language learning contribute to peace-making skills and the non-violent resolution of conflict? What role may the learning of languages have to play in building multicultural and inter-cultural understanding?

In this chapter, we will explore the relationship between the learning of second languages and peace: first, by examining modern language teaching as a vehicle for values education; second, by considering opportunities for teaching conflict resolution in language-learning activities; and finally, by considering language learning as it relates to understanding the culture of other people.

Teaching Values in Second Languages

A number of authors have written about the values associated with the teaching of modern languages. An examination of these values shows they are usually very important in that they underpin attitudes that favour peace-making and peace-building behaviours. We will examine the values in three areas: those that are inherent in the second languages as a subject in the school curriculum; those that are learned through the content of language instruction; and those that are taught through the methodology employed in language teaching.

The very inclusion of modern languages in the curriculum itself suggests the desirability for young people to understand the existence of languages and cultures other than their own. A second language is one key to understanding the completeness and integrity of another culture and its study has implicit within it a value for diversity. In this respect, Beattie (1986: 119) asserts that language stud-

ies may contribute to the tolerance of differences, to the lessening of prejudice and to an appreciation of the complexity of the human groups in our world.

Students in a unilingual and relatively closed cultural environment may tend to be ethnocentric and to feel threatened by languages and cultures beyond their neighbourhoods or borders. In a discussion of the relationship between language and cultural pluralism, Morain (1970: 74) suggests that second-language studies may cultivate openness towards other cultures and, in consequence, an appreciation and respect for them. The development of such values can significantly diminish prejudice and national or cultural stereotyping.

Besides conveying values through the subject of second languages in the curriculum, we convey them also through the content of the studies. The literary content of language learning, which may include biographies, stories, plays and poems, will convey significant values. Biographical accounts of outstanding figures in the history of the country studied will normally uphold important values, such as selflessness (as in the case of a leader genuinely dedicated to public service), openness and intellectual adventure (often typical of scientists), and creativity in resolving political or economic conflicts (a necessity for mediators in industrial disputes). The teaching of values in the literature of the second language will be similar to teaching literature in the first language. For this purpose, the reader may wish to refer to Chapter 4.

Reading authorized textbooks, which may constitute a good part of the study materials in second languages, will occupy much class time; however, creative teachers will, by choice, incorporate other sources into their programs, adapting them to the special needs of the class: films, videos, magazines, newspapers, advertising, simulation games, computer programs and other alternatives. In any of these cases, teachers may wish to analyze the materials for their implicit value orientations, and occasionally have explicit discussions in the second language about peace values and their alternatives.

Of special concern to second-language teachers is instructional methodology: the method they choose to employ can also be a vehicle for teaching values that develop peaceful individuals and a peaceful classroom climate. Omaggio (1978) describes a number of games for the second-language classroom that inculcate the values of cooperation and collaboration between the students. The ideas originated with the Jigsaw Puzzle Method, which was designed to develop better relations between students in racially integrated schools in the United States. The method encouraged students to communicate with one other and to serve as resource persons to each other in the solution of problems. In one game, called Jigsaw Reading, analyzed in detail by de Berkeley-Wykes (1983), the sentences and parts of sentences of a short and intriguing story are distributed at random to members of a class whose collective task it is to reconstruct the story in its original sequence. Participatory activity by the entire class emphasizes interdependence and mutual assistance.

Personal values may be articulated and discussed through a variety of values clarification techniques. Writing on values clarification theory and bilingual education, Green (1975) describes a number of activities that simultaneously provide exercises in second-language vocabulary, grammatical structure and creative writing. For example, when students are assigned to write on the topic, "If I were prime minister of Canada I would...", they are given practice in using the conditional tense of verbs and also in eliciting their values concerning national issues. It is quite probable that creative writing of this kind can lead to a consideration of health, education, safety, unity in diversity, social justice and other values essential to a peaceful and ordered society.

The development of values through second-language education need not be a passive process; neither does it have to be contained within the walls of the classroom. In bilingual or multilingual communities, Rivers (1983: 26-27) advocates giving students direct contact with the cultures they are studying. By actively assisting with community projects, they can develop and demonstrate friendship, support and genuine caring, at the same time having opportunities for authentic communication in the second language. Rivers emphasizes that the study and discussion of cultural differences should always be two-way. "The students identify and discuss their own values as well as those of others. The experience becomes one of self-discovery, as well as the penetration of other values and viewpoints."

The discussion of values in second languages, if it is to contribute to peace, needs always to focus on the values that make for inner tranquillity, constructive interpersonal relations, prizing and cherishing differences, community-building and national and international solidarity. Even when such attempts are made, students will inevitably encounter tough questions relating to value conflicts.

Studying Conflict in Second-Language Learning

There has not been a great deal of systematic attention given to the study of conflict in second-language learning; yet it is clear that teachers of languages, drawing as they do upon many different fields of knowledge, are in an especially good position to incorporate the study of conflict into their syllabi. The existing literature suggests that second-language teachers may help students deal with inner tensions, to develop skills in resolving interpersonal conflicts, as well as to understand better and contribute towards the resolution of conflicts at the inter-group, inter-institutional and international levels.

Several writers have suggested that there are special contributions, as well as more general ones, that second-language learning can make to the study and management of conflict. In her essay on cultural pluralism, Morain (1970) stated that when learners of a second language develop the values of openness and sensitivity towards another culture, there is promise of reducing tensions between different cultural groups. Under the right conditions, learners can develop sufficient empathy with another culture to allow them to view its members more objectively in times of conflict.

How cultures, or potential adversaries, perceive each other is often critical in the escala-

tion, or de-escalation, of a conflict. As a result, building positive perceptions of other cultures is important as a means of coping constructively with conflict. Beattie (1986) suggests, for instance, that exchange visits between students from different linguistic and cultural groups can have a dramatic affect upon values and attitudes. Students who participate in such exchanges cross the divide between "us" and "them". They may even go further to discover that to "them", "we" are "them". These kinds of perceptions and perspectives can help to favour the constructive management of inter-group tensions.

Second-language studies also have a special role to play in helping students to understand how tensions develop, and the dynamics of the way in which they may be moderated and resolved. Green (1975) suggests that the study of any culture in the second language can include ways in which that culture handles conflicting values and settles differences between people and among groups. Every society has developed ways of coping with conflict at different levels, including both violent and non-violent means (police or military intervention, judicial proceedings, collective bargaining, mediation techniques and the like). Studies of both historical and current events can help to develop an awareness and knowledge of this facet of a culture.

A variety of practical activities have been suggested in the literature on second-language teaching to relate the subject effectively to conflict. Three specific suggestions, dealing with conflict at different levels, will be described briefly here.

At the level of inner conflict, students may be troubled by tensions within themselves. For example, beginners in language learning may experience intense anxiety over their inability to function adequately in the second language.

Such an anxiety is essentially an inner conflict between the insecurity of the learners who genuinely desire to learn a second language and the security that they have in the proficient use of their first tongue.

In discussing a therapeutic approach to helping students deal with such anxieties, Curran (1983) implies that the teacher needs to become a language "counsellor" who will guide students through various stages of growth, attaining a greater sense of self-worth and wholeness as they increase their knowledge, skill and confidence in the language. In the first stage of growth, the student speaks the first tongue, and is wholly dependent upon the language counsellor who sensitively uses the second language. In the second stage, the students speak and retain words and phrases and gain confidence and courage with the new language. By the third stage, there is a growing independence on the part of the learner in which the counsellor provides immediate correction and tutoring. In the fourth stage, the counsellor reduces involvement by helping only with idioms and subtle language expressions. In the final stage, students have independent and free communication in the second language and have satisfactorily resolved the inner conflicts and anxieties that originally beset them. Curran's schema is entirely built upon the assumption that the educative process itself needs to start by addressing inner anxieties and conflicts that inhibit learning.

Another level of conflict is that which occurs between individuals, and is often referred to as interpersonal conflict. A frequently used technique to help students resolve tensions of this kind is role-playing, or sociodrama. This type of activity is often favoured by second-language teachers because it involves social interaction between students and encourages them to use the new language in spontaneous and improvisational ways. The procedure recommended, for example, by Scarcella (1978) and Zelson (1978b) is for the teacher to prepare a short story that contains a dilemma for the characters involved in it. The story is incomplete; it stops abruptly at the point where the dilemma arises. Students are then asked to assume characters in the story and to role-play the way in the which it might continue. One dilemma cited by Zelson concerns a family watching television. As is often the case, one person wants to view one program, while the rest are intent upon watching something else. At this point, the story stops, and groups of students take turns in role-playing members of the family to find different solutions to the dispute.

Conflict can also occur at another level, between complex groups of people. Green (1975) recommends that social tensions of this kind can be used to study ways in which a society resolves its conflicts. In this case, she has suggested that a teacher may prepare a case study of a current event. The written work, in addition to familiarizing students with cultural content, can provide practice in recognizing and understanding language rules and principles. An alternative way of combining an understanding of conflict resolution with practice in second-language communication is to prepare a simulation game based upon the conflict situation, preferably one in which all members of the class can be involved.

No matter what kind, or level, of conflict teachers incorporate into second-language studies, opportunities may be found for helping students to identify the precise nature of the conflict (often expressed as a value conflict); to understand the different perceptions of adversaries; to develop creative alternative solutions for resolving the conflict; and to understand the consequences that follow from a chosen solution. Conflicts that are resolved through compromise in which both sides "win" usually result in a more durable peace than those which leave one of the parties defeated and resentful.

Second Languages and Multicultural Education

There is a special opportunity for teaching cultural understanding, an important step in overcoming ethnocentrism, when the second language being studied is spoken by a linguistic group in the community. From a pedagogical point of view, learning a language in a multicultural setting has great possibilities because of the immediacy of the use of the language, the meaningfulness of the linguistic and cultural environment, and the potential for authentic communication. In North America, the second language being learned may often be English, French, Spanish, German or Italian, but young people may also be inspired to acquire other widely used languages such as Russian, Arabic, Japanese or Mandarin. The multicultural community is a valuable, but often neglected, resource for language education. It may also be, as a number of authors point out, a beneficiary, whenever language programs lead to better communications between the component groups.

A number of studies, including those summarized by Robinson (1981:25–35) and Cadd (1994), indicate clearly that learning a foreign language does not automatically lead to the development of positive attitudes towards another linguistic group or a reduction in ethnocentrism. Language exercises that are hollow in a personal, cultural or motivational sense do not contribute to improving cultural understanding. Children in a French immersion program, for instance, may not learn as much about French culture by taking mathematics or physical education in the second language as they would by taking the social studies. The cultural goal in language teaching is likely to be attained only when verbal language and extra-verbal behaviours transmit cultural messages to the students.

Both Rivers (1983) and Wallerstein (1983) suggest that the curriculum for learning a second language in a bicultural or multicultural community can be determined, in good part, from the students and the cultural community themselves. In applying the teaching approach of Paulo Freire to second-language learning, Wallerstein proposes a problem-based curriculum. Such a curriculum is developed first through sensitive listening, interaction and observation in the classroom and the community. The teacher needs to become familiar with the traditions, the values and subtleties of the culture and the nature of neighbourhood and family life, particularly any processes involving cultural transmission, preservation and disruption. A significant step in determining curriculum is the identification of the problems and concerns of the community. While Freire's approach is designed more for adult learners, with a view to giving them a sense of empowerment to regain control over the structures that affect their lives, it is applicable to school learning insofar as it sensitizes the school to the specific needs of the culture and adapts learning to present cultural realities.

An essential step in the Freire approach to teaching second languages, according to Wallerstein, is critical thinking and action. Wherever a minority linguistic group has concerns about the human rights of its members and about related questions of social justice, learning the language of the majority, or the language of those who wield political power, becomes an important tool in building a peaceful community. At the same time, other applications of the Freire teaching approach emphasize learning and action beyond the classroom. Rivers, for instance, states that, as their skills in the language improve, students can be encouraged to participate in various community activities, to forge friendships and to help the community in its relationship with one or more other cultural communities. In the same way, Morain (1970) and Beck and Simpson (1993) report that students at more advanced levels of study can go out into cross-cultural situations to serve as teachers, interpreters and other resource persons for more experiential language learning.

It is important for teachers of second languages to recognize that their efforts in this regard need not be in isolation, but can be harmonized with those of other school specialists. Language studies can be connected effectively to the appreciation of the art or music of the linguistic group; to family lifestyles, home design and the preparation of food in home economics or family or consumer studies; to the history and migration of the cultural group in the social studies; and to other subjects. Each school can plan and coordinate its curriculum offerings to suit the special needs of students and its own unique philosophical orientation.

In conclusion, it is evident that second-language teaching has an important part to play in multicultural education, especially when the language being learned is one spoken by a cultural group in the community. Cultural understanding can develop when language instruction is not a hollow exercise, but has real and immediate cultural content. In addition, learning the language of a local linguistic group provides opportunities for genuine communication and interactive involvement in the community. There is some evidence that culture-filled language instruction of this kind can lead to positive attitudes towards the second linguistic group, which may even be generalized to other cultural entities. Education having this quality not only leads to better communication but also contributes to building a stronger sense of a united community.

Second Languages and Intercultural Understanding

Preller (1976) has pointed out that the extent of the teaching and learning of foreign languages appears to be directly associated with, on the one hand, the degree of isolationism of a nation, and on the other hand, the degree of its people's involvement in international affairs. It seems probable that, while government foreign policies may have a decided influence upon enthusiasm for learning modern languages, a predisposition to internationalism among citizens in a democratic society may also have some bearing upon the formulation of attitudes in international affairs. In an age when nations knowingly and willingly have become more dependent upon one another, acquiring intercultural understanding and, beyond that, larger regional and world perspectives has become nationally advantageous.

It is within this context that the goal of second-language teaching to promote intercultural and world understanding has assumed a special significance. Cultural awareness may be developed first in the simpler sense where students are encouraged to understand the culture of the societies that use the second language. A number of different ways of analyzing other cultures have been suggested at various times by various writers (Morain 1970, Stern 1983, Ortuuwriter and Mantle-Bromley

1992). One method is to examine the component aspects of a culture, and then to consider the relationship between the parts as a step towards synthesizing an integrated understanding. The following outline, adapted from Stern (1983) and others might well be used:

(a) **The family unit and the personal sphere**
   - family relationships
   - eating and shopping
   - games, pastimes, recreation and leisure
   - homes and housing

(b) **The social sphere**
   - population and its distribution
   - social structure
   - national sports
   - social customs, traditions and festivals

(c) **The economic sphere**
   - agriculture and rural life
   - business, industry and urban life
   - maritime economy
   - international trading patterns
   - transportation networks

(d) **The environmental sphere**
   - physical and political geography
   - weather and climate
   - natural resources
   - ecology

(e) **The political sphere**
   - government and ideology
   - system of education
   - law and justice
   - military affairs

(f) **The religious and ideological sphere**
   - role of religious institutions
   - folklore and history
   - literature, music and the creative arts

The study of a culture may, of course, be much more focused. Cultural topics may be chosen according to such criteria as the availability of outstanding source materials, accessibility to resource persons, the special interests of the students, or current issues and concerns in the country being studied.

Morain (1970: 73) cites a scheme proposed by Jack Seward for studying Japanese culture, based upon common civilities that one would need to know in order not to offend when visiting that country. They would include customary behaviours in the following circumstances:

- meeting an acquaintance
- entering a home
- as a guest, before eating
- as a guest, after eating
- as a host, serving guests
- returning home
- parting
- expressing appreciation
- asking pardon
- calling attention to oneself (when kept waiting at counters, etc.)
- as a guest, departing
- seeing off guests
- the bow and bowing

Morain suggests that such a list might be useful to students studying other languages and cultures as well.

There are a number of imaginative teaching and learning strategies by which students can work towards an understanding and appreciation of the culture of the linguistic groups they are studying. Jenks (1976) has suggested that students undertake cross-cultural research through interesting exercises of discovery and inquiry. In their study of Spanish, for example, they may undertake an inquiry into what distinguishes a Spanish "bocadillo" from a

Mexican "quesadilla" or, in the study of French, they may be asked what they would prefer to receive in exchange for one Canadian dollar—2 Swiss francs, 33 Belgian francs or 7 French francs? A pooling by groups of their findings in response to such sociocultural puzzles as these can lead to a discussion of larger cultural themes.

Besides being a vehicle for understanding another culture, second language studies can help to develop a consciousness of perspective. Knowledge of another language and its associated culture can lead to a recognition on the part of individual students that the way they view the world is not universally shared, and that others have perspectives that may be quite different from their own. Different cultural and linguistic perspectives may exist within a country that has two or more official languages, as do Belgium, Canada and Switzerland, for example.

Students may be able to develop a greater awareness of perspectives within bilingual or multilingual countries through simulating a forum on national issues in which the participants use the actual languages of the cultural groups they are representing. Similarly, a greater awareness of international perspectives can be developed through simulations of meetings such as those of the Organization of American States (English, Spanish and Portuguese) or the more linguistically complex European Parliament (English, French, German, Spanish, Italian and Greek). A knowledge of different perspectives is helpful in understanding perceptions in intranational and international conflicts and, indeed, for working towards a reconciliation of different points of view.

Rivers (1983) describes yet another way in which second language instruction can contribute to intercultural education: it can help students to understand the global interdependence of nations and can engender in them the feeling of belonging to a shrinking world. Many languages, she points out, have moved beyond their countries of origin as a result of colonization, emigration, and borrowing from one culture to another. English belongs as much to Jamaica, Alaska, the Philippines and India as it does to the British Isles. Spanish and Portuguese are spoken by more people in Central and South America than in their countries of origin. And French is spoken in such far flung places as Montreal, Haiti, Tahiti and Madagascar. Second-language teachers need to emphasize that languages such as these are important vehicles for widespread international communication.

In discussing essentially the same theme of globalizing foreign languages, Strasheim (1981) suggests that students examine the linguistic connections that they have to the world's peoples. This goal can be achieved in part by studying derivations from the second language found are in the first tongue, by examining more broadly the way English has borrowed from other languages and by considering the various families of languages in the world. Besides such academic exercises, an appreciation of our interconnectedness may be developed through a variety of practical activities. Rosenbusch (1992) suggests the study of global units such as "Housing and Population" or "Environmental Quality" as vehicles for second-language education. In such units, the students investigate local circumstances and problems together with case studies of other parts of the world. Critical studies of this kind, placed within the framework of developing a sustainable environment, can do much to help language students acquire global perspectives.

In retrospect, therefore, we can see that second-language teaching has a special role to play in developing intercultural understanding and global perspectives as dimensions of education for peace. It can help to develop an awareness of other cultures, particularly those that use the second language. It can help bring about a consciousness of other perspectives, thereby supporting similar goals in subjects such as history, geography and science. By developing a recognition of patterns of modern international communication, it has a distinct contribution to make in helping our young people understand our global interdependence.

Summary

In this chapter, we have examined the acquisition of communication skills and the development of cultural understanding through the study of second languages. The pursuit of these goals in relation to peace-building involved, first, an exploration of values for peace that are inherent in the subject matter in second languages as well as those that can be conveyed in the methodology of teaching. Second, it included a consideration of the way language teachers can contribute to the development of skills in the management of conflict at all levels—intrapersonal, interpersonal, inter-group and at other more complex levels. Third, we discussed the link between second-language education and multicultural education, focusing on the way language studies can develop sensitivity to other linguistic and cultural groups and help to form positive attitudes towards them. The final section examined second-language teaching in relation to intercultural understanding and to the development of broader international and global perspectives.

REFERENCES AND SOURCES

Ashworth, Mary (1991), "Internationalism and Our 'Strenuous Family'", *TESOL Quarterly,* 25 (2), Summer, 1991: 231–243.

Beattie, Nicholas (1986), "Use or Ornament? Values in the Teaching and Learning of Modern Languages," in Peter Tomlinson and Margret Quinton (eds.), *Values Across the Curriculum,* London: The Falmer Press: 109–133.

Beck, David J. and Catherine Simpson (1993), "Community Service and Experiential Language Learning", *TESL Canada Journal,* 11 (1): 112–121.

Cadd, Marc (1994), "An Attempt to Reduce Ethnocentrism in the Foreign Language Classroom", *Foreign Language Annals,* 27 (2): 143–152.

Curran, Charles (1983), "Counselling-Learning," in John W. Oller Jr. and Patricia A. Richard-Amato (eds.), *Methods That Work:* *A Smorgasbord of Ideas for Language Teachers,* Rowley, Massachusetts: Newbury House: 146–178.

De Berkeley-Wykes, Jonathan (1983), "Jigsaw Reading," in John W. Oller Jr. and Patricia A. Richard-Amato, *Methods That Work: A Smorgasbord of Ideas for Language Teachers,* Rowley, Massachusetts: Newbury House: 313–319.

Gibson, Robert E. (1978), "The Strip Story: A Catalyst for Communication," in Elizabeth Joiner and Patricia Westphal, (eds.), *Developing Communication Skills,* Rowley Massachusetts: Newberry House: 130–135.

Green, Kathleen, (1975), "Values Clarification Theory in ESL and Bilingual Education," *TESOL Quarterly,* 9 (2): 155–164.

Grittner, Frank M. (1970), "Pluralism in Foreign Language Education: A Reason For

Being," in Dale L. Lange, (ed.), *Britannica Review of Foreign Language Education,* 3: 9–58.

Hamil, Ralph E. (1981), "One World, One Language", *The Futurist,* 15 (3): 16–18.

Jenks, Frederick L. (1976), "Fifteen-Year Old Students Can Do Cross-Cultural Research: Basic Enquiry Strategies and Exercises for Teachers and Pupils," in Frank M. Grittner (ed.), *Careers, Communication and Culture in Foreign Language Teaching,* Skokie, Illinois: National Textbook Company: 65–71.

Kreidler, William J. (1990), *Elementary Perspectives 1: Teaching Concepts of Peace and Conflict,* Cambridge, Mass., Educators for Social Responsibility.

Kulick, Katherine M. and M. Clare Mather (1993), "Culture: Cooperative Learning in the Second-Year Foreign Language Curriculum," *The French Review,* 66 (May 6, 1993): 900–907.

Large, Andrew (1985). *The Artificial Language Movement,* New York: Basil Blackwell and London: Andre Deutsch.

Mantle-Bromley, Corinne (1992), "Preparing Students for Meaningful Culture Learning," *Foreign Language Annals,* 25 (2): 117–127.

Morain, Genelle, G. (1970), "Cultural Pluralism," in Dale L. Lange (ed.), *Britannica Review of Foreign Language Education,* 3: 59–95.

Ortuño, Marian Mikaylo (1991), "Cross-Cultural Awareness in the Foreign Language Class: The Kluckhohn Model," *The Modern Language Journal,* 75 (4): 449–459.

Omaggio, Alice C. (1978), "Real Communication: Speaking a Living Language," in Elizabeth Joiner and Patricia Westphal, (eds.), *Developing Communication Skills,* Rowley, Massachusetts: Newbury House: 125–129.

Preller, Arno G. (1976), "Building Better Bridges in a Kaleidoscopic Society," in Frank M. Grittner (ed.), *Careers, Communication and Culture in Foreign Language Teaching,* Skokie, Illinois: National Textbook Company: 72–83.

Rinvolucri, Mario F. G. (1980), "Action Mazes," *English Language Teaching,* 35 (1): 35–37.

Rivers, Wilga M. (1983), *Speaking in Many Tongues: Essays in Foreign Language Teaching,* Third Edition, Cambridge: Cambridge University Press.

Robinson, Gail L. Nemetz (1981), *Issues in Second Language and Cross-Cultural Education: The Forest Through the Trees,* Boston: Heinle and Heinle.

Rosenbusch, Marcia H. (1992), "Is Knowledge of Cultural Diversity Enough? Global Education in the Elementary School Foreign Language Program," *Foreign Language Annals,* 25 (2): 129–136.

Scarcella, Robin (1978), "Socio-Drama for Social Interaction," *TESOL Quarterly,* 12 (1): 41–46.

Scebold, C. Edward (1979), "Foreign Language and International Education in the Twenty-First Century," *Foreign Language Annals* 12: 27–28.

Stern, H. H. (1983), "Toward a Multidimensional Foreign Language Curriculum," in Robert G. Mead Jr. (ed.), *Foreign Languages: Key Links in the Chain of Learning,* Middlebury, Vermont: Northeast Conference on the Teaching of Foreign Languages: 120–146.

Strasheim, Lorraine A. (1979), "An Issue on the Horizon: The Role of Foreign Languages in Global Education," *Foreign Language Annals* 12: 29–34.

Strasheim, Lorraine A. (1981), "Broadening the Middle School Curriculum through Content: Globalizing Foreign Languages," in June K. Phillips (ed.), *Action for the '80s: A Political, Professional, and Public Program for Foreign Language Education,* Skokie, Illinois: National Textbook Company: 129–145.

Wallerstein, Nina (1983), *Language and Culture in Conflict: Problem Posing in the ESL Classroom,* Reading, Massachusetts: Addison-Wesley.

Zelson, Sidney N. J. (1978a), "Skill-Using, Self-Expression and Communication: Exercises in Three Dimensions," in Elizabeth Joiner and Patricia Westphal, *Developing Communication Skills,* Rowley, Massachusetts, Newbury House: 44–56.

Zelson, Sidney N. J. (1978b), "Skill-Using Activities in the Foreign Language Classroom," in Joiner and Westphal, (eds.), *Developing Communication Skills,* (quoted above): 161–165.

CHAPTER 6

History and Civics

EACH YEAR, *on the anniversary of the dropping of the atomic bomb on Hiroshima, the mayor of that city commemorates the event in a ceremony in the Peace Memorial Park, built upon the site marking ground zero of the blast. In 1991, the following message was delivered by Mayor Takashi Hiraoka, and distributed throughout the world[1]:*

The City of Hiroshima

PEACE DECLARATION

August 6 is a profoundly sad day for the people of Hiroshima. Yet it is also a day of renewing our dedication to peace and a day that we hope will live forever in the world's memory.

Forty-six years ago today, Hiroshima was devastated and countless lives were lost as a result of a single atomic bomb. This was the first wartime use of nuclear weapons in human history. Knowing from bitter experience how very easily the use of nuclear weapons could lead to

---

[1] The text has been slightly abbreviated.

the extinction of the human race, Hiroshima has sought untiringly to transcend hardship and hatred and to call unwaveringly for the abolition of all nuclear weapons and the attainment of lasting world peace....

Japan inflicted great suffering and despair on the peoples of Asia and the Pacific during its reign of colonial domination and war. There can be no excuse for these actions. This year marks the 50th anniversary of the start of the Pacific War. Remembering all too well the horror of this war, starting with the attack on Pearl Harbour and ending with the atomic bombings of Hiroshima and Nagasaki, we are determined anew to work for world peace.

Peace, of course, is more than the mere absence of war. Achieving peace also means eliminating starvation, poverty, violence, threats to human rights, refugee problems, global environmental pollution, and the many other threats to peace; and it means creating a climate in which people can live rich and rewarding lives.

The world today is groping its way towards a new world order successor to the Cold War. Major progress has been made toward nuclear disarmament. The heavy portals barring the way to peace are slowly being opened, and they can only be opened fully with the weight of our collective wisdom and concerted efforts.

Hiroshima thus renews its appeal:

> Let all nations everywhere put an immediate and complete end to nuclear testing and strive for the earliest possible abolition of nuclear arms.

> Let all peoples everywhere recognize the folly and futility of war, reaffirm the treasure of peace, and work together for human happiness.

> Hiroshima's appeal is a plaintive cry for the preservation of the human race, and we hope that the world's leaders will heed this plea.

> Today, in this Peace Memorial Ceremony to commemorate the 46th anniversary of the atomic bombing of Hiroshima, I would like to express my heartfelt condolences to all the victims of that bombing and to pledge myself to join the people of Hiroshima in working untiringly for peace.

❑

In this very moving declaration, the mayor speaks of the bombing of Hiroshima as an event that must live on in our collective memory of the past. What other key events of the Second World War should also be part of our collective memory? How can our larger collective memory, our history, serve to guide us individually and collectively in the conduct of our present affairs, especially in our determination to build peace? The mayor emphasizes that we must transcend hardship and hatred in history. How can the teaching of history, while dealing with past realities, contribute to healing relationships and reconciliation between peoples?

In this chapter we will explore the contribution that the teaching of history can make to the process of peace-making and peace-building. First, we will consider the teaching of values in history, with particular reference to values that make for the building, or weakening, of the peace-making process. Second, we will investigate the opportunities that a genuine study of history provides for developing multiple perspectives and larger understandings of the past. Third, the special opportunities for studying conflict and its resolution afforded by history will be reviewed. Finally, the concept of a global, or universal, history of humankind will be discussed.

Teaching Values in History

Because of the very broad scope of its subject matter, history offers a great opportunity for the study of values, and particularly for considering the values that make for the building, or weakening, of the peace-making process. In this section we shall consider, in turn, values that are largely implicit in the study and teaching methodologies of history; values as central to the culture of any historical society; the concept of changing values over time; and the teaching of values in contemporary history.

History has been used by nation states for the purpose of developing national unity and solidarity but, regrettably, sometimes at the expense of the development of good international relations. As shown in such classical studies as E.H. Dance's *History the Betrayer: A Study in Bias* (1964) and R. H. Billington's *The Historian's Contribution to Anglo-American Misunderstanding* (1966), the teaching of his-

tory has frequently suffered from the use of textbooks that are poorly researched, show biased treatment of historical topics, provide only one-sided accounts of history, or use language that creates bias in favour of one country while derogating the achievements and actions of others. At the base of such problems is often a disregard of the principles of scholarly research and writing and of the values that are implicit in them.

History places a value upon curiosity in framing questions and problems for critical inquiry. In the gathering of data, it requires comprehensiveness and the context of multiple perspectives, as opposed to a unidimensional investigation. In the analysis and interpretation of data, it values detachment, logic and rationality. History writing and teaching that takes these values lightly, or disregards them, can manipulate learners. Perceptions of other groups and other nations can become easily distorted, leading to unnecessary and unwarranted prejudices. Upholding scholarship in history and other attendant values such as balance and comprehensiveness is therefore, in itself, an important step in the building of inter-group and international relationships.

In the study of historical content, substantive values (rather than the procedural values just discussed) are central. The Greek communities of Sparta and Athens in the fifth century BC are often used to show similarities and differences in culture, particularly differences in values. The authoritarianism of Sparta is contrasted with the partial direct democracy of Athens; the value placed on physical fitness, might and aggression in one is placed against the value of "roundedness" (a cultivated mind in a healthy body) in the other; obedience to authority in Sparta is contrasted with self-control and self-regulation in Athens. Students could also be asked to analyze relative structural violence in the two societies. They might assess the peaceful or violent nature of these societies judging them by standards accepted at that time and also from the standpoint of contemporary values. Case studies like these, drawn from various cultures and continents, can provide students with a pool of experience about historical values, and they can serve as a basis for understanding the way in which values change.

To discover that values evolve is to find the essence of social and political change in history. Change often comes about as a result of social criticism of existing values, either by individuals or by groups. Such individuals give leadership in the identification of new values and to the process of reaching a new values consensus. Historical biographies can provide interesting accounts of the ways in which individuals help to advance new social values. The stories of Florence Nightingale and Henri Dunant show compassionate help to the

injured in time of war, when the norm was to leave the stricken on the battlefield to die. The biographies of Maria Montessori and Alfred Nobel reveal a philanthropic spirit and pursuit of peaceful international relations. The lives of Emily Pankhurst and Mahatma Gandhi model non-violence as a means of achieving political change. The lives of Martin Luther King and Mao Tse Tung provide insight into the struggle for economic and social justice. These individuals are exemplars of values-making for progress towards more peaceful societies.

Great movements in history involving the transformation of whole societies occur when one set of values is replaced by another. The rise of feudalism in Japan and in Europe sacrificed much of the personal freedom of individuals for the collective security of the manorial system. In colonial territories in Africa, Asia and America, the spread of imperialism meant the replacement of cultural and economic independence by dependence and cultural interpenetration. Industrialism in Europe and elsewhere replaced the value of relative self-sufficiency with interdependence, productivity and consumerism. Some of the value shifts may have been beneficial, while others led to social and economic injustice. It is valuable for students to investigate whether such value changes created more or less peaceful societies.

Although these kinds of changes in values may be controversial, those having to do with the recognition of human rights clearly reflect the evolution of more peaceful societies. The abolition of slavery in the United States and other countries represents a change from bondage to freedom; the abandonment of the policy of apartheid in South Africa is a move from racial separation and discrimination to racial and social integration; and removing differential treatment of men and women in law and political rights represents a change of values towards the equality of the sexes. These and other struggles for human rights help to diminish elements of structural violence in various societies and contribute significantly to the building of social justice and peace.

Another way of focusing on values in the teaching of history is to examine links between past, present and future. This may be done for virtually any thematic or problems approach to history and civics where the story of the past continues into the present and raises questions about future developments. Many writers believe that history and civics studies must necessarily be related to important questions concerning the future of humankind and of planet earth. Among them, for instance, Tooke (1988: 416) proposes that the idea of interdependence may be considered "as a new paradigm to propel the search for stability in the twenty-first century". By interdependence, Tooke refers to the connectedness that all human beings have one to another as well as the connectedness that all living organisms have with the planet's environment. She points out that all societies share the planet; they all are affected by one another's actions; and they all have an interest in, and concern for, each other's development. Ponting (1991) and LeSourd (1991) have already shown respectively how these relationships may be viewed from their historical and contemporary perspectives.

By acquiring a greater awareness of values and value shifts in history, students will be in a much better position to clarify and affirm what values they associate with the future development of a peaceful national and world society. They may, for example, consider the validity of such value transitions as the shift from ethnocentrism and intolerance to respect for diversity and tolerance; from personal and group self-interest to respect for human rights; from the institutionalization of inequities within and between societies to the application of the principle of equity for all; from exploitation of natural resources to stewardship of the earth; from national rigidities and aggression to flexibility and negotiation in the settlement of differences. The study of history can fully document the values of the past, whereas civics can help to teach the transformation of values that, it is hoped, will bring stability and security to the future.

Multiple Perspectives in History

In virtually all parts of the world, history has played an important part of the education of youth because it contributes to the development of group and national identity. In some countries, however, history is written and taught from a single point of view. The intention is to cultivate feelings of loyalty to the home country. Often, however—through default—it engenders prejudice against others. It also has the effect of reinforcing negative attitudes towards neighbouring groups or countries that may historically have been considered hostile to the home country. In effect, history teaching then becomes one of the barriers, rather than one of the vehicles, to the improvement of inter-group or international relations.

There are a number of approaches that can be used by history specialists to counter such unidimensional studies of the subject. One is to help students to understand better the ways in which bias creeps into the the learning of history. History teaching can be one-sided through *the bias of omission*: what is included in the history curriculum is perceived as important and what is left out tends to be seen as unimportant. If the curriculum in large part consists of national history, the history of the rest of the world will likely be perceived as irrelevant. Similarly, within national history, if the contributions of different ethnic groups, or those of women, are omitted, only the contributions of men in the dominant group are perceived to be important. When teachers and students together are aware of bias of omission, they are conscious of the limitations of the curriculum and are in a better position to correct it.

Another form of bias has been called *the bias of unconscious falsification*. This is the bias we acquire as a result of growing up in a particular culture, a bias of which we are hardly aware. It is acquired through the learning of stereotypes and through the folklore of culture and nationalism. We do not project this bias *intentionally* into the teaching and writing of history but, nonetheless, it results in history imbued with an aura of ethnocentrism and national superiority. In some British school textbooks, for example, Billington (1966) found references to the American colonies as "backward lands" and, in the discussion of the American Revolution, the assertion that Britain's "professional army...could be relied upon to beat the irregular levies of the rebels whenever they fought on anything like equal terms." Numerous other examples of bias have since been documented in a variety of studies (O'Neill, 1984; Dhand, 1988; Lowean, 1995).

History teaching can also be distorted through *the bias of monocultural perspectives*. In international affairs, this bias is conveyed when events are presented principally on the basis of documentary evidence of only one of the participating nations. In national history, it is apparent when the sources are largely those of a particular interest group such as an aristocracy, church, business, or military establishment.

Yet another type of slanting in the writing and teaching of history is *the bias of language*, which is well illustrated by Billington (1966). The choice of words used by the teacher or writer may stereotype people of other nations and be openly derogatory. For example, a reference to "Prussianism" strongly suggests that only German people are militaristic, or the term "colonials" may be used to suggest that settlers are inferior to the residents of the imperialist nation. Language may, however, be more nuanced, conveying bias through greater subtlety. There are differences between "non-believers" and "infidels", "rebels" and "patriots", between a "crowd" and a "mob", between an "uprising" and a "riot".

These and other mechanisms of bias such as the use of certain types of maps and illustrations serve to limit or circumscribe our field of vision. To wrest ourselves free of these limitations, it can be helpful to perceive two fundamental kinds of perspectives that operate in history teaching and that together form a matrix of possible complex perspectives. The first includes various cultural perspectives, such as those of ethnic and national groups or of "East" and "West" ideologies. The second includes the spatial perspectives of the local community, the province or region, the nation, the continent, the northern and southern hemispheres, and the globe. The nature of the matrix changes with time: a local community which at one point in history may have been culturally homogeneous may later on, through the migration of peoples within or between countries, have become culturally and racially diverse.

It is important that young people develop an appreciation of different perspectives in history, yet there is some difficulty in achieving this goal. Brown (1976) discusses the point that children acquire the ability to understand other perspectives only with intellectual maturity. From infancy to adolescence, they gradually mature from egocentric thinking to sociocentric thinking. It is usually only by the ages of 12 to 15 that they acquire multiple role-taking ability, where they can "put themselves into the shoes" of members of other cultures.

Other writers, such as Banks (1986), have theorized that there are various stages of development in acquiring perspectives. These include (1) ethnocentric encapsulation, where individuals practise ethnocentric separatism; (2) cultural identity clarification, where individuals accept themselves in relation to other cultural groups; (3) biculturalism, where individuals have the ability and skills to function in two cultural groups; (4) multiculturalism, where individuals have the ability to function in a range of cultural groups; and (4) globalism and global competency where individuals have the ability to function world-wide.

Applied to history teaching, such a scheme of development can include selective depth studies at certain points in the history curriculum. At the elementary or intermediate level, for instance, students can be introduced to the concept of "another culture" by reconstructing life in another era. As an example, the Stone Age could include the study of homes, technology, livelihoods and the beginnings of trade. Through making and using tools of the time (hand-formed ceramic bowls, fire bows, bone needles, picks made from deer antlers and shovels made from an ox shoulder-blade), they can identify more readily with the quality of life at that time and achieve a rudimentary understanding of the concept of culture.

After developing experience with different historic cultures, students can proceed to the concept of different perspectives within a given culture. For example, in feudal society in Medieval France or Britain, students could investigate the different points of view of the clergy, the nobility, the peasantry and the bourgeoisie towards the Pope's call in 1095 for a Crusade to effect a Christian occupation of the Holy Land. In such an exercise, students will learn the diversity of values and interests in a society.

In the sequence of more sophisticated approaches to the study of perspectives, students could then examine the different viewpoints between larger political entities. For instance, in carrying the previous example forward, they could examine the different viewpoints towards the Crusades of the West, Byzantium and the Seljuk Kingdom. This conflict between Christian and Islamic cultures has been described as the medieval equivalent of the modern conflict between "East" and "West". The Seljuk Turks, having conquered Palestine, were relatively new converts to Islam: they believed strongly in the spread of their faith and in its defence against Christian influence from Europe. The West believed that it should liberate the Holy Land from Islamic domination; some also believed that the Crusades would be an opportunity to establish trade links with the Byzantine Empire and the Seljuk Kingdom. Located between these two religious and cultural groups, the Christian Byzantine Empire viewed Western Christians as barbaric and predatory but nevertheless saw the Crusades as a means of containing the expansion of the Seljuk Kingdom into its territory.

The teaching of larger and larger perspectives helps students to acquire a greater degree of objectivity and scholarship in history. In effect, it is a procedure that allows them to step back to obtain a more holistic view and to achieve a wider vision. Young people skilled in perspective-taking are better equipped with skills to live in a multicultural community and in a world society.

Studying Conflict in History and Civics

While the subjects of literature and drama are especially helpful to us in understanding the nature of intrapersonal and interpersonal conflict, history and civics deal more directly with inter-group and international conflict. As Will and Ariel Durant (1968) pointed out, war is a constant throughout the ages and there have rarely been any times over the last three thousand years when there has been no war. Further, history, as our collective memory of the past, contains an enormous amount of knowledge concerning conflict as well as its control and mismanagement.

Case studies of different historical periods can help to reveal the kinds of social conditions that lead to civil wars and international conflict. In analyzing these conditions, Nesbitt et al. (1973) first point out that conflict often develops when there is rapid and profound change in a society. Industrialization in Europe, for example, created in the industrializing countries a new internal distribution of wealth. This caused internal conflicts within nations as well as the expansion of empires that brought nations into violent conflict with one another. Similarly, decolonization, involving relatively rapid changes in the shift of political power, resulted in civil wars in many countries including Afghanistan, India, Sri Lanka, Nigeria, and the Congo.

A second condition creating conflict is the kind of slow change that gradually produces significant economic discrepancies in a society. With time, if the rich get richer and the poor become poorer, and if those in power remain unwilling to change the status quo, internal stresses and strains build to the point where there is an explosion of violence, as in the Russian Revolution of 1917.

Economic conditions, by themselves, are usually not the sole cause of conflict in a society. There may also be an intellectual ferment in the form of new creeds, ideologies or belief systems that cause people to compare their existing state of affairs with a preferred state of affairs. The critical writings of Voltaire, Rousseau and others contributed significantly to events leading to the American and French Revolutions. In the same way, the works of Marx and Engels provided an ideological basis for the Russian and Chinese Revolutions of the twentieth century.

If we examine conflicts more closely, we will see that there is always, at the centre, a conflict of values. The values conflict may concern the material well-being of a population; it may be expressed in terms of egalitarianism and socialism in opposition to elitism and capitalism. Alternatively, the conflict may be based on the distribution of power, where the value of political elitism (as in an oligarchy) is pitted against the value of democracy and political participation. The conflict may have to do with status, where values of social inequality and discrimination conflict with a belief in equality and human dignity. The values conflict may, therefore, be interpreted generally as being concerned with economic, political or social justice.

In *The Gaia Peace Atlas: Survival into the Third Millenium*, (Barnaby, 1988: 38-39), Petra Kelly discusses the bases of conflict. In her scheme, the roots of war are human poverty, unsustainable ecology (a breakdown in a society's relationship with the environment), political elitism, government without consensus, and militarism. In each case, there is some form of structural violence that must be minimized if war is to be eliminated. It will be seen that the value conflicts implicit in this classification correspond closely with those advanced by Nesbitt.

Traditionally, the accounts of wars in history textbooks have been somewhat limited to their causes, events and results. They tend not to deal in any detail with the process by which conflicts escalate into the violence of war, an understanding of which is essential to a more complete comprehension of conflict. Nesbitt (1973) provides a helpful overview of the theoretical developments in the spiralling of international conflict. He says that they usually begin with an action that one nation considers both necessary and justifiable. Another nation then usually reacts with a more severe response. The reaction produces a counter-reaction by the first nation. While the parties perceive their own actions as defensive, they perceive those of the other side as aggressive.

As the action-reaction process develops, the participants increasingly justify their new actions by the previous actions of the adversary, rather than by the original issues in the conflict. At the same time, they develop feelings of suspicion, distrust and, eventually, hatred towards one another. Simultaneously there is a breakdown in communication: each side tends to perceive in the adversary's actions only what reinforces its image of the enemy. Information or perceptions that contradict those images tend to be ignored. Each side becomes willing to believe the very worst of the other, to believe that the enemy is less than human, and to justify the use of its most destructive weapons.

As the spiralling of conflict proceeds, each side becomes increasingly unwilling to explore alternatives for solving the initial issues. Each side loses objectivity, increasingly being unable to see the perspective of the other. As each side is committed to a solution by force, the probability of a negotiated settlement becomes increasingly unlikely. Case studies of the First or Second World Wars, as well as of the Gulf War of 1991, can do much to illuminate in detail this theoretical process of conflict escalation.[2]

School textbooks have not only failed to present an understanding of the process of conflict, they have also tended to accept the legitimacy of war as a way of resolving disputes. A survey of the treatment of war in American textbooks by Wigutoff and Herscovici (1983) found that none raised questions about the acceptability of war. While statistics were presented on the costs in lives and money, none showed the extent of human suffering. The costs for conducting wars were not weighed against the results. Moreover, none gave consideration to the possibility of alternative measures, and the choice of language used by the authors appeared to reveal an unconscious admiration of military power. What is true for the United States appears also to be true for other nations: students are not challenged to consider the legitimacy of war as an institution.

While students often study wars, they rarely examine examples of conflict control in history, even though such examples should help them understand the course of the past and deal with significant issues now. There have been many instances in the past where nations with serious differences have not gone to war, but have solved problems by other means. The long-standing North Atlantic Fisheries Dispute between Canada and the United States was referred to The International Court at The Hague in 1910 and was successfully resolved through international adjudication. Possible nuclear war between the US and the USSR was averted during the Cuban Missile

---

[2] An especially helpful study of communication and perception in the First World War is contained in Ole R. Hosti (1972).

Crisis in 1962, when the problems of Cuban and US security were resolved in a climate of exceptional stress through improved communications and a willingness on the part of the respective leaders to find a mutually agreeable solution to the problems. Students need to acquire a pool of experiences of this kind from which they may draw principles of both violent and non-violent conflict resolution.

The understandings and skills they develop through study of history then need to be brought to bear upon our contemporary world problems. Barnaby (1988: 224-225) believes that coercion, which is so amply illustrated in history books, is an unacceptable way of dealing with conflict, as it can lead to further violent action. Other ways of conflict control include avoidance (a withdrawal by one, or both, parties to avoid conflict), smoothing (emphasizing areas of agreement and ignoring those of disagreement) and compromise (bargaining). However, historical examples may also show that these measures are only temporary, short-term ones, at best. Since they present partial solutions and problems continue to smoulder beneath the surface, conflict is likely to recur. The only real solution is through problem-solving—cooperating to find ways that meet the needs of both sides without either one feeling that it has lost.

As noted earlier, in the discussion of values, human development rests on changing values. There is, in effect, a conflict between the old values (ethnocentrism, intolerance, self-interest, inequalities, etc.) and the new values (tolerance and respect for diversity, human rights, equity, etc.) The teaching of history has the potential to help young people not only to understand the contradictory values implicit in the major problems confronting humankind, but also to contribute to the resolution of these conflicts in non-violent ways that will help in the transformation of values.

Teaching World History

Many historians feel that their subject can make a major contribution to peace-building through the teaching of global history, or history in a world perspective. They argue that the bonding of the world's peoples is developed through the perception that humankind as a whole has a shared historical past, an increasingly shared present identity, and the desire for a prosperous and just future together on the planet. History therefore holds a key place in the development of citizenship at the global level.

What exactly is meant by "world" history? Bonnaud (1990) has explored the idea of identifying "world rhythms" as a basis for developing a new model of universal history. He provides an overview of the work accomplished by a number of historians who, over the last century and a half, have taken up the enormous challenge of writing a history of humankind. These writers include Oswald Spengler, H. G. Wells, Arnold Toynbee, Guiseppe Ferrari, Pierre de Coubertin and many others. Their work has been shaped by a variety of influences and written for varying purposes. For these reasons, the historiography of world history is of special interest to teachers. The purposes of writing world history have included examining the forces of change in different societies; comparing historical cultures, all of which are assumed to be of equal worth; portraying the identity of humankind; and providing a picture of the norms of human behaviour across the ages. In reviewing such histories to date, Bonnaud believes that there are still a number of obstacles to be overcome in seeking more authentic versions of universal history. They include overcoming the "backward state of Western historical studies on non-Western peoples", reconciling the concept of the universality of history with the unevenness of development of different societies at various stages of history, and developing an adequate theory for judging major turning points in universal history.

Within this framework, those who have given thought to the teaching of world history in the secondary school curriculum have recognized the need for the development of new purposes and new perspectives. Woyach and Remy (1988) noted that typical world history courses in North America have either centred too much upon the Western experience or they have been, in effect, unrelated parallel regional and national histories of various civilizations. In their view, such courses of study have not been based upon a conceptually integrated world history that would be relevant to young people whose working lives will be entirely in the twenty-first century. They advocate the development of world history and world studies courses that would strive for better integration.

Kniep (1989) has proposed that world history should be integrated around various themes including the evolution of human values and unique world views; the historical development of the systems that unite peoples in the modern world; and the historical antecedents of the major global issues of our time. These themes, Kniep recommends, should be taught through five central concepts in the social studies: interdependence (the interaction of world systems that form a functioning whole for the globe); change (shift and movement within different systems that constitute part of life and living); culture (social environments and social systems that meet basic human needs); scarcity (systems for the distribution of limited resources); and conflict (modes of resolving differences in values and goals between people and nations). Case (1993) has advanced a synthesis of the writings of Kniep and others, and underlined the importance of the perceptual values that learners bring to the study of world history. The knowledge, skills and values learned in world history become significant tools for analyzing and resolving contemporary global issues.

While not directed specifically at secondary schools, John Burton's *World Society* (1972) provides an analysis of political theory behind the development of modern world society. He does not deal with the history of earlier political units such as the city states, tribal groupings, dukedoms, feudal holdings, principalities, or kingdoms, but rather with the rise of the sovereign nation-state in modern times. The set of relationships between sovereign nations is termed the *billiard-ball model* of world society. In it, each nation is perceived as a sovereign independent unit. The internal affairs of nations are strictly domestic affairs and not the business of other nations. Relations between states are like those of differently-sized billiard balls in which the larger and faster ones push the smaller ones aside. Governments are the point of contact: international affairs are intergovernmental relations.

Burton states that, while this understanding of world society was realistic earlier in the twentieth century, a number of changes have taken place that make us search for alternative ways of understanding the world. These changes include a sharp increase in the number of nations, the growth of interdependence, constraints on the actions of various states, and the rapid development of education and communications. There have been great increases in the movement of people and ideas over the surface of the globe that do not directly involve members of the government. Tourists, professionals, technical advisers and business people all now create contacts. The expertise and transactions of the last groups form new international networks. Ideas are communicated through newspapers, telegrams, fax messages, telephone calls, electronic mail, the World-Wide Web, international radio and television transmission, and the like. Because we have developed systems that greatly transcend the contacts of governments, Burton describes these systems as *the cobweb model* of world society.

Concomitant with the development of international systems and the growth of global economic interdependence has been the rise of what Rosecrance (1986) refers to as the "trading state" as contrasted with the "territorial state". The traditional territorial state depended directly upon the control of its territory and upon its military strength for prosperity and security, and international peace was preserved through the balance of power. The trading state, typified by Japan and Germany, derives its strength from its successful participation in the interdependent global trading network, and world peace is based upon the mutual realization that the cost of prosperity and security through cooperation is much less than it is through aggression and territorial expansion.

While the cobweb model of world society is helpful to us in understanding the inter-relatedness of world affairs, it does not adequately portray the different levels of systems that operate in the world. Nations themselves are still the basis of important national systems, political, economic and social. In all cases, they are involved in complex regional relationships having to do with economic development, language and/or religious affinities, and sometimes with ideological or military relationships. Overlaying these regional systems are world-level social, economic and political systems, including international associations and organizations. Burton refers to this conceptualization as *the systems model* of a world society. It implies the development for world citizens of multi-levelled understandings and the tolerance of multiple loyalties.

It is our understanding of the kind of world we live in now and want to inhabit in the future that will determine our interpretation of world history and the purposes for which it is taught. It is important, however, that there be some common understandings of present global realities and of the values needed for humankind to build a common future of prosperity and justice. World histories that explain the ways in which we have been developing our political, economic and social institutions, together with civics, which will help us to resolve world problems now and adapt those institutions for the future of the human adventure, will need to find their place in the history curriculum.

Summary

In this chapter, we first considered the wide possibilities for studying values in history, including the values implicit in different historical cultures, significant shifts in social values over time, and the major changes in values that are now required for human development on a planetary scale. The second topic was the teaching of multiple perspectives in history, which includes developing an awareness of biases in history and of the possibilities of studying multiple perspectives in both national and world history. Third, we considered the study of conflict in history and civics, noting the conditions within and between societies that lead to conflict, the way in which history can illuminate conflict escalation and de-escalation as a process, and the need for skills in conflict resolution to be brought to bear upon contemporary human problems. The final section in the chapter examined the teaching of world history as a crucial compo-nent in the bonding of humankind. World history, when conceptually integrated and viewed as the evolution of the contemporary world community, can help to provide the story of humankind's common past.

REFERENCES AND SOURCES

Angell, Ann V. (1992), "Examining Global Issues in the Elementary School Classroom", *The Social Studies,* 83 (3) May/June 1992: 113–117.

Banks, J. A. (1986), "Multicultural Education: Development Paradigms and Goals", in J. A. Banks and J. Lynch (eds.), *Multicultural Education in Western Societies,* London: Holt Rinehart.

Barnaby, Frank (ed.) (1988), *The Gaia Peace Atlas: Survival into the Third Millenium,* New York: Doubleday.

Billington, R. A. (1966), *The Historian's Contribution to Anglo-American Misunderstanding: Report of a Committee on National Bias in Anglo-American History Textbooks,* London: Routledge and Kegan Paul.

Blow, Michael (1968), *The History of the Atomic Bomb,* New York: American Heritage.

Bonnaud, Robert (1990), "A New Model for Universal History: World Rhythms", *The UNESCO Courier,* April 1990: 40–42.

Brown, James A. (1976), "Intercultural Understanding", *McGill Journal of Education,* XI (2), Fall, 1976: 190–197.

Burton, John W. (1972), *World Society,* Cambridge: Cambridge University Press.

Case, Roland (1993), "Key Elements of a Global Perspective", *Social Education,* October, 1993: 318–325.

Chartock, Rosselle and Jack Spencer (1978), *The Holocaust Years: Society on Trial,* New York: Bantam.

Cogan, John J. (1989), "Citizenship for the 21st Century", *Social Education,* April/May 1989: 243–245.

Cortés Carlos E. and Dan B. Fleming (1986), "Social Studies Texts Need a Global Perspective", *Social Education,* September, 1986: 376–384.

Dance, E. H. (1964), *History the Betrayer: A Study in Bias,* London: Hutchinson.

Dhand, Harry (1988), "Bias in Social Studies Textbooks: New Research Findings", *History and Social Science Teacher,* Fall, 1988: 25–27.

Durant, Will and Ariel (1968), *The Lessons of History,* New York: Simon and Schuster.

Education Advisory Committee of the Parliamentary Group for World Government (1966), *Cyprus School History Textbooks: A Study in Education for Misunderstanding,* London: Education Advisory Committee of the Parliamentary Group for World Government.

Fleming, Daniel B. (1983), "Nuclear War in High School History Textbooks", *Phi Delta Kappan,* Vol 64, April, 1983: 550–551.

Heinrich, Dieter (1988), "Evolution of World Society: Process and Prospects", in Janis Alton, Eric Fawcett, and L. Terrell Gardner (eds.) *"The Name of the Chamber Was Peace",* Toronto and Fort Meyers: Science for Peace, Samuel Stevens and Company.

Hersey, John (1966), *Hiroshima,* Toronto: Bantam.

Hosti, Ole R. (1972), *Crisis, Escalation, War,* Montreal: McGill-Queens University Press.

Joyce, James Avery (1964), *The Story of International Cooperation,* New York: Franklin Watts.

Kirman, Joseph M. (1990), "Women's Rights in Canada: A Sample Unit Using Biographies and Autobiographies for Teaching History Chrono-logically", *Social Education,* January 1990: 39–42.

Klopfer, Gretchen (1987), "A Multicultural Approach to High School History Teaching", *The Social Studies,* November/December, 1987.

Kniep, Willard M. (1989), "Social Studies Within A Global Perspective", *Social Education,* October, 1989: 399–403.

Ladson-Billings, Gloria (1992), "The Multicultural Mission: Unity *and* Diversity", *Social Education,* September, 1992: 308–310.

LeSourd, Sandra (1991), "Integrating Pluralistic Values for Reconstructing Society", *Social Education,* January, 1991: 52–54.

LeSourd, Sandra (1992), "A Review of Methodologies for Cross-Cultural Education", *The Social Studies,* 83 (1), January/February 1992: 30–35.

Loewen, James W. (1995), *Lies My Teacher Told Me: Everything Your American History Textbook Got Wrong,* New York: Norton.

NCSS Task Force on Ethnic Studies Curriculum Guidelines (1992), "Curriculum Guidelines for Multicultural Education", *Social Education,* September, 1992: 274–294.

Nava, Julian (1988), "Cultural Pluralism and Global Interdependence: Teaching and Learning for the 21st Century", *Social Education,* March 1988: 215–216.

Nesbitt, William A. (1972), *Teaching About War and Its Control,* Albany: The University of the State of New York, The State Education Department and the Center for International Programs and Comparative Studies.

Nesbitt, William A., Norman Abramowitz and Charles Bloomstein, (1973), *Teaching Youth About Conflict and War,* Washington: National Council for the Social Studies.

O'Neill, G. Patrick (1984) "Prejudice Towards Indians in History Textbooks: A 1984 Profile", *History and Social Science Teacher,* Fall, 1984: 33–39.

Ponting, Clive (1991), *A Green History of the World,* London: Sinclair-Stevenson.

Rosecrance, Richard (1986), *The Rise of the Trading State: Commerce and Conquest in the Modern World,* New York: Basic Books.

Smith, Robert Irvine (1986), "Values in History and Social Studies" in Peter Tomlinson and Margret Quinton (eds.), *Values Across the Curriculum,* London: The Falmer Press.

Terray, Emmanuel (1990), "A Universal History—Possibility or Pipe Dream?" *The Unesco Courier,* April, 1990: 36–40.

Tooke, Moyra (1988), "A View from Canada", *Social Education,* October, 1988: 414–420.

Tucker, Jan L. (1988), "Social Studies for the 21st Century", *Social Education,* March 1988: 209–214.

Wigutoff Sharon and Sergiu Herscovici (1983), "The Treatment of Militarism in History Textbooks", *The Education Digest,* 48, March, 1983: 46–48.

Woyach Robert B. and Richard C. Remy (1988), "Strengthening World Studies: The Challenge of Conceptualization", *Social Education,* November/December, 1988: 484–488.

CHAPTER 7

Geography and Economics

The Riverbankers

"So-this-is-a-river!" (The Mole had never seen a river before.)

"*The* River," corrected the Rat.

"What lies over *there*?" asked the Mole....

"That? O, that's just the Wild Wood," said the Rat shortly. "We don't go there very much, we Riverbankers."

"Aren't they—aren't they very *nice* people in there?" said the Mole a trifle nervously.

"W-e-ll," replied the Rat, "let me see. The squirrels are all right. And the rabbits—some of 'em, but rabbits are a mixed lot. And there's Badger, of course.... Nobody interferes with *him*. They'd better not," he added significantly.

"Why, who *should* interfere with him?" asked the Mole.

"Well, of course—there—are others," explained the Rat in a hesitating sort of way. "Weasels—and stoats—and foxes—and so on. They're all right in a way—I'm very good friends with them— pass the time of day when we meet, and all that—but...well, you can't really trust them and that's the fact...."

"And beyond the Wild Wood again?" [the Mole] asked: "Where it's all blue and dim...?"

"Beyond the Wild Wood comes the Wide World," said the Rat, "and something that doesn't matter to you and me. I've never been there, and I'm never going, nor you either, if you've got any sense at all. Don't ever refer to it again, please. Now then! Here's our backwater at last where we're going to lunch." (Grahame, 1987)

❑

This brief extract from Wind in the Willows *provides an interesting analogy between the Mole, as a student of geography or economics, and our own young people as they are stimulated to look out across the world. At the beginning of the conversation, the Mole is genuinely curious about the surroundings. His interest is blunted by the Rat who actively discourages him from inquiring into the wide world beyond the woods. Furthermore, the Rat passes on to the Mole, in a very assertive and authoritative manner, his biases concerning the others who dwell along the riverbank, openly transmitting an attitude of mistrust towards some of the inhabitants. We might think of the Rat as representing the ethnocentric influences of socialization within society.*

Geography teachers, by contrast, are ideally much more positive agents of socialization. Besides teaching an understanding of the immediate environment, they encourage students to go up-river and down-river, to explore the woods on the other side, to understand the relationship between the inhabitants of the woods and the land upon which they live, as well as to inquire fully into "the wide world beyond". Geography, along with history and second languages, has long been considered one of the key subjects that can help to promote international understanding and peace. But more precisely, what contribution can it make to the peace-building process? In this chapter we will consider the teaching of values inherent in geographical studies and the way in which they may relate to values for a peaceful world; we will examine the special contribution that geography can make towards the teaching of cultural and other perspectives; and we will consider the teaching of world geography and the opportunity it presents for conveying the interconnectedness of human activity and the wholeness of planetary life. Reference to the teaching of economics is made where specific topics or approaches are relevant, and where topics are related to economic geography.

Teaching Values in Geography

Like many other subjects in the curriculum, especially those having a scientific component, geography has not traditionally been viewed as a subject that conveys values to young people. However, analytical and critical studies by geography educators show that geography is a value-laden subject both in its content and its methodology. Statements of aims in geography teaching are, in essence, value choices: they both select and emphasize what is valued and, by implication, the values to be taught. The questions that we wish to consider are, What values tend to be examined in geography? Which ones may be considered as peace-building values? How may geography students be encouraged to choose peace-building values in applying their knowledge to critical issues and problems?

The trend towards using an inquiry approach to the study of geography carries with it certain values. Observation, fieldwork and the evaluation of data for higher-level knowledge tends to value intellectual *curiosity* rather than *indifference*, *objectivity* rather than *bias*, *logic* rather than *irrationality*, and *sharing* (of knowledge) rather than *secretiveness*. In such procedures, both *abstractness* and *practicality* may be equally valued. These values implicit in geographical inquiry may be thought of as peace values, since the development of verifiable knowledge idealistically contributes to the pooling and sharing of knowledge for the benefit of all humankind.

Not only are values embedded in the methodology of the discipline; they are also implicit in the methods of teaching chosen by geographers (Wiegand, 1986). It is the teacher who makes value choices between a *participation* model and the *authoritarian* characteristics of the transmission-reception model of

teaching. Students can participate in planning—as, for instance, in the design of fieldwork in urban or rural studies—thereby exercising some responsibility for their own learning. Similarly, it is the teacher who makes value choices between *activeness* or *passiveness* in learning. Active, meaningful learning through inquiry, simulations, and project work and through the use and application of geographical knowledge reinforces student responsibility. It is the teacher, also, who makes value choices between *cooperation* and *discordance* in learning. Cooperative experiences in the study of weather, for instance, can be designed so that students help each other to learn and become interdependent: groups can be arranged to study local wind and weather, weather in the news, models of weather patterns, the function of weather stations, the role of the World Meteorological Organization and other topics, with a view to building together an understanding of global weather patterns. Methodologies that emphasize the values of responsible participation, active learning and cooperation contribute effectively to the classroom climate of peace.

Values are also conveyed more explicitly through the substantive content of the subject. More than most subjects in the curriculum, geographical studies contribute to an understanding of the state of the planet and, especially, some of the problems that create instability: climatic change; the decline of fishing resources; deforestation; soil depletion; water pollution; depletion of mineral resources; poverty in urban areas; and other similar geographical topics. Fien and Gerber (1986) and Cox (1986) suggest that students need actively to explore human values and the root causes of such problems from a geographical point of view, as well as the value alternatives for creating a better world. Some of the principal value alternatives would be as follows:

Desecration of
the earth ↔ Caring and stewardship
Wastefulness ↔ Conservation
Exhaustion ↔ Sustainability
Indulgence ↔ Constraint
Racial divisiveness ↔ Racial harmony
Social inequity ↔ Social justice
Indifference ↔ Participation
Powerlessness ↔ Conscientization

The contribution of geography to peace is, in good part, helping students to understand the value premises of what is being studied, to clarify their own value stances and, through critical reflection, to internalize peace-building values. The movement towards value goals such as these is conceptualized by Hicks (1988) as "positive peace".

Similar shifts in the teaching of values are proposed in the field of economics. Goodland and Daly (1990) state that economics has never been viewed within the context of a finite environment, and that government and business policies have operated on the now-outmoded assumptions of frontier economics when air was pure, water clean, and forests and other resources abundant. A whaler, for example, may be allowed to make a profit of 15 percent per year, by exterminating whales over a 10-year period. Having harvested the whales to extinction, the same individual could then invest the proceeds in the exploitation of another resource. There is no incentive to reduce profit to, say 10 percent per year, thereby allowing whales to be harvested on a sustainable basis. The authors believe that if we are to achieve a steady state, the economy must be seen as a subsystem of the global environment. The transition to a steady-state economy implies a shift in values to constraint, stewardship, conservation and sustainability.

Another approach to the teaching of peace values through geography and economics is to relate their subject matter to human rights education, since human rights are, in effect, statements of values to be pursued to achieve economic, social and political justice. Burnley and Pettman (1986) examine the theoretical basis for linking geography to human rights and suggest a variety of associated teaching activities. Some of the opportunities for linking values, human rights and geography are as follows:

(1) **The right to life:**
   (*survival* ↔ *mortality*)
   The global variability of life expectancy and infant mortality rates.

(2) **The right to health:**
   (*health* ↔ *disease*)
   The global variability of diet and nutrition, of access to safe water and medical services, and the geography of disease.

(3) **The right to an appropriate standard of living and life quality:**
   (*prosperity* ↔ *poverty*)
   Global variations of income distribution, educational provision, welfare provision and housing.

(4) **The right to freedom of information and expression:**
   (*communicativeness* ↔ *suppressiveness*)
   Global communications systems (newspaper, radio, television, telephone, mail, and computer network services) including restricted services.

(5) **The right to equality:**
   (*egalitarianism* ↔ *elitism*)
   The geography of discrimination on the basis of gender, ethnicity or racial background.

(6) **The right to participate in the political processes of one's own country:**
   (*enfranchisement* ↔ *subjugation*)
   The geography of political ideologies, or economic communities, and of prisoners of conscience.

(7) **The right to depart if one feels unsafe or oppressed**

   (mobility ↔ confinement)
   The geography of refugees.

(8) **The right to work**

   (livelihood ↔ privation)
   The geography of employment and unemployment, working conditions of migrant and foreign workers.

A values approach can help students understand that when negative values are be upheld and defended, human rights are abridged. Further, tensions associated with the denial of rights create psychological terrorism and structural violence. The peace process is one that involves transformation to the values implicit in the recognition of human rights.

Students can explore human rights in a variety of contexts and perspectives. First, case studies can be undertaken in the local community where students have the advantage of concreteness and availability of learning resources. Community studies can help to counter the belief that human rights are denied only in societies other than our own. Second, studies of human rights issues in other places and other countries are appropriate where teaching materials are available. In the 1990s, world attention was frequently focussed on the abridgement of human rights in such places as China, Indonesia, Myanmar, Rwanda and Burundi. Third, human rights may be presented in an international perspective as is achieved through the use of world maps showing the distribution of human rights abuses (Kidron and Segal, 1987; Barnaby, 1988).

As Huckle (1981) points out, some educators believe that the teaching of values, including those implicit in human rights, is not complete without there being some kind of action learning, in which students may experience a transformation of values and a deep sense of concern for the society they live in. The geography teacher can respond to this need by searching for local community projects and others that reach out to the world. Projects for improving the environment with a local conservation or ecological group would exemplify action learning. Through such activities, young people can contribute in a meaningful and responsible way to peaceful social reconstruction.

Teaching Multiple Perspectives in Geography and Economics

Just as one of the strengths of history is that it can provide multiple perspectives in a historical dimension, so geography and economics are excellent vehicles for developing perspective-taking skills in a spatial context. In the previous chapter, two important ideas were discussed: one was the ability of young people to see other points of view as they mature from egocentric to socio-centric thinking; the other was the need for them to acquire and understand different perspectives so that they are better equipped to function well as peaceful individuals in a multicultural community and in world society. In this section, we will examine ways in which the study of geography and economics can help to develop critical abilities in three areas: spatial perspectives, social and economic perspectives, and cultural and racial perspectives.

Young people are usually introduced to spatial perspectives with the study of mapping in elementary education. They learn more sophisticated skills in cartography at the secondary level. It is customary for young people to learn about the principal kinds of map projections— the Mercator, Mollweide, Peters, homolosine, conic and others—which helps them to understand the concept of distortion of space and the kind of bias that can be introduced into its representation. The concept of visual perspective may also be taught with a map or, preferably, with a globe. How does the world appear from such diverse places as Canberra, Lagos, Bogota, Reykjavik, Anchorage—or even from the moon? Some teachers have simulated the idea of visual perspective by drawing a huge map of the world on the classroom floor or playground and asking their students to "walk to different parts of the world" or to try to view it from afar.

Perspective, however, consists of more than what we can see from a particular place in space. It is a mental picture of the relative importance of things, a frame of reference that may include such factors as place, language, religion, social structure, economic organization and political ideology. With their many connections to other subject matter, geography teachers are in a good position to help students develop an awareness of perspectives in this larger sense.

Saunders (1985) has suggested that map postcards, or maps prepared by tourist information bureaus, can be studied by students to advance their understanding of the way in which maps are selective in the kinds of information presented. Map postcards, for example, usually omit many streets and have miniature pictures of places of interest to visitors. They are created from the perspective of the tourist industry and are designed to advance the cultural and economic interests of an urban centre or region.

A more comprehensive study of bias in mapping and propaganda cartography is presented by Burnett (1985), who has examined maps in relationship to the theme of war and peace. Drawing upon work by Bunge (1982) and others, Burnett shows how international organizations, governments and pressure groups use maps to express and emphasize particular points of view. Examples include a 1980s map from the USSR Ministry of Defence to illustrate the threat of nuclear attack from Western Europe and a corresponding map from the United Kingdom showing the menace of Soviet nuclear arsenals to Western Europe. These maps were prepared by the respective defence departments to argue for increased defence spending. A cartoon from the Cold War period used by Burnett shows vividly different spatial perspectives of the US and the USSR. The Russian bear perceives encirclement by American capitalism while a diminutive Uncle Sam perceives the global encroachment of Russian communism. Burnett finds that a number of techniques are used by cartographers to express perspective. They include selecting a favourable map projection; selecting some factual data while omitting others; using certain symbols and colours; and manipulating the size and distribution of symbols. Students need to be made aware of these techniques and the way in which they are used to create visual and spatial perspectives.

A second area in which students can gain a deeper understanding of the idea of perspectives lies in the social and economic spheres. In geography and economics, as in history, it is the selection and interpretation of facts that can convey a particular point of view. Fien and Gerber (1986: xiii–xiv) argue that through selection, much current geography teaching is biased away from "the teaching of geography for a better world". They cite the teaching of world trade that omits the arms trade and its consequences; the teaching of manufacturing without including the environmental consequences of the processes and products of manufacture; the teaching of agriculture that omits a study of the effects of herbicides, insecticides and fungicides on food and water run-off; the teaching of development that leaves out the role of women; and the teaching of nuclear power without including the problems of disposal of nuclear wastes and the place of nuclear weapons in the nuclear fuel chain. Geography teaching biased in these and other ways leads to limited perspectives and to the inability of students to associate major world problems with threats to global security and stability.

Much attention has been given by geographers to the study of development, particularly as it applies to the "developed" and "developing" countries or to the groupings sometimes referred to as the North and the South. In examining perspectives on development, it is important to understand in a critical way the perceptions of these groupings and some of the difficulties associated with teaching about the countries of the South. Mason (1989) believes that geography teachers may unwittingly contribute to the perpetuation of stereotyping of countries of the South by implying that the problems of poverty, malnutrition, hunger and disease are the fault of the people who live there. Similarly, they may convey a feeling of helplessness and despair about the future prospects of these countries. Mason reports on the use of geography materials that convey more positive images of the South as well as those that are critical of the student's own environment. Such materials help students explore their perceptions and examine the bases of their images and perspectives.

Part of the examination of bias can be a consideration of the terms "developed" and "developing", since all countries are, in fact, developing countries. The term "development" has been interpreted as economic development—industrialization; higher production, incomes and consumption; and increases in the GNP. It should be noted, however, that

the lifestyle of the "developed" world, based on such an interpretation, is largely unsustainable. It is having serious effects on the environment and resulting in planetary distress.

Liongson (1989), writing from the point of view of a "developing" country, advances an alternative conception. He defines development as liberation—liberation from poverty, malnutrition, hunger, disease, exploitation and oppression. "Unless we are liberated from dehumanizing and violent structures," he states, "we cannot claim to be truly developed." This conception of development implies the kind of transformation of values discussed in the previous section. It also requires perspectives that are larger than economic ones alone.

The third area in which students can gain deeper insight into perspectives is in the cultural and racial sphere. As geography deals with human culture and development in relationship to the environment, it contributes significantly to a study of the way in which different cultures view each other. Often, without intention, geography textbooks in one culture have portrayed the peoples in other cultures as inferior. They convey this impression through the selection of content, through oversimplification and stereotyping, and through textual illustrations (Slater, 1983; Bunge, 1984; Marsden, 1992). Special care needs to be taken in presenting a fair and realistic picture of other cultures. Various checklists have been developed to help make teachers and students aware of cultural and racial bias. Daws (1986) includes the following:

1. Illustrations (Does the material use stereotypes and tokenism?)

2. Values (Does it uphold the values of a dominant group or culture?)

3. Lifestyles (Is the explanation of lifestyles over-simplified or is it dealt with compre-

hensively by relating to the physical, economic, social and political environment?)

4. Political relationships (Does the material omit reference to political relationships, or does it clearly convey questions of leadership, control and power?)

5. Author's perspective (Does the author's cultural perspective produce a message in the material?)

6. Language (Is the language biased in reference to people of other cultures?)

Various means have been proposed for eliminating cultural and racial bias in geography textbooks. They include drawing more teaching materials from other countries; having teaching material vetted, or edited, by scholars of other cultures; bilateral and multilateral consultations on textbook revision; and encouraging producers to follow guidelines developed by professional organizations and by UNESCO (Boden, 1977). Such measures can help correct errors and identify prejudicial or misleading text.

No matter what steps are taken, developing an awareness of perspectives by students is a crucial part of their training in the social science disciplines. Students will learn what constitutes a perspective; they will understand the way in which the selection of information is what limits or shapes a perspective; they will discover the relationship between perspectives and purposes; and they will understand the advantages of seeking larger perspectives. The study of world perspectives in geography will be examined next.

Global Perspectives

Teaching global perspectives contributes to the peace-building process in at least two ways. First, geographic and economic theories need to be as comprehensive as possible in order to take into consideration the realities of the planet as a whole. In that sense, global scholarship becomes a common pooling of knowledge to which the earth's people can constantly add and from which they can draw for their common benefit. Second, understanding the earth as a whole system, and understanding the way in which the earth's inhabitants have become increasingly integrated and interdependent, adds to the process of human bonding and to the building of human solidarity. Students need to be acutely aware that we are all travelling together on Spaceship Earth.

Teaching for global perspectives can be carried out in a variety of interesting ways, each of which can complement and inform the other. Community studies and practical field work in the school environs can be placed effectively into a global context, as the following examples illustrate. As a means of developing cultural perspectives, Smith (1974) designed a study in which secondary students collected data on newsagents' publications, cinema programs, record and cassette shops, art galleries, radio and television programs, toy shops, post offices, hotels and airports. The students later analyzed their findings to determine domestic and overseas content, clientele and international networks, with a view to drawing conclusions about the extent of regional and international influences on the life of the community. In another project, Trudgill, Thomas and Coles (1990) organized a "hydrology day" in which students undertook comparative studies of water infiltration in nearby pasture, woodland and arable land. The conclusions of the fieldwork were linked to global problems of soil, water and forest conservation. In yet another study, Crooker (1990) designed a mapping exercise of world narcotics production and distribution which required that students develop hypotheses about the place of their own community in the distribution system. In this way, students could comprehend local problems of illegal drug distribution in relation to global drug routes and the illicit world drug trade.

Regional studies need also to be placed effectively into a global perspective. Writing on world geography and international understanding, Libbee (1988) advocates linking regional case studies and world themes, such as world population, world economic development, urbanization, world resources and global environment impact. Taking world population as an example, students could study global population data and the world pattern of population development. At the same time, specific students would be assigned separate case studies of families in different regions of the world. The case studies would examine such factors as family occupation and income, family size, infant mortality, levels of education, religious affiliation and social and health care policies. Throughout these family case studies, students would reflect upon what they regard as the most important population problems of their chosen societies, and they would engage in problem-solving exercises in a regional context. The next step would be to project what effects population changes would have upon the stability of the different societies and of the globe as a whole.

Another example of an activity that links global and regional studies is presented by John (1990). As an introduction to the study of development, the teacher assigns a country to each student. The countries are chosen for economic contrast and distribution across the world. The rectangular floor of the classroom is then used as a projection of the globe and students go to the approximate points of location of their countries. Those who represent developing countries are then told to sit on the floor. A discussion ensues on the meaning of "developed" and "developing" countries, the idea of "North" and "South" and the interrelationships between different regions. A number of variations of this activity can be used also to understand the relationship of global perspectives, such as those of the World Bank and UNICEF, to the regional realities of particular states.

Over the last decade, there have been efforts to build world perspectives in a great variety of materials as a means of better understanding global dynamics. Meyers' *GAIA: An Atlas of Planet Management* (1984) provides an excellent array of geographical and economics topics with accompanying world maps. Some examples of the groupings of topics are given below:

The Land Potential
Global Forests
Croplands
Grazing Lands
The Global Larder

The Land Crisis
Soil Erosion
Forest Depletion
Encroaching Deserts
Hunger and Glut

Managing the Land
World Cash Crops
Harvesting Forests
Green Revolution?

The Ocean Potential
The World's Ocean
Marine Pastures
Mangrove Wealth
The Global Shoal
Wealth and Investment
Polar Zones

The Ocean Crisis
Fish Stock Declines
Ocean Pollution
Habitat Destruction
Territorial/Resource
   Disputes

Managing The Ocean
Harvesting The Sea
Pollution Control
Managing Antarctica
Laws of the Sea
Marine Migratory Routes

Global perspectives like these focus essentially on earth systems that are syntheses, or inter-relationships, of the earth's subsystems. They are useful because they give meaning and context to local and regional studies and they provide insights into the complex nature of the global biosphere. Hicks (1992) has drawn attention to the need for geographical education to develop a futures orientation to global issues. Such concerns as climate change, biodiversity, aid to countries of the South, forest exploitation and sustainable development may all be integrated into the teaching of geography. The clash of values inherent in the study of such issues can be studied through alternative future scenarios for the planet.

As noted earlier, Goodland and Daly (1990) propose that the study and application of economics also need to be placed in the context of the global ecosystem. Economics, as a discipline, has historically developed without reference to the environmental limits to growth, and therefore needs to be modernized to take into account the goals of sustainable growth and environmental ethics. As shown in Figure 7–1, the world economic system is a part of the larger global ecosystem. In such a new economic view, the production and consumption of goods and services require raw materials and energy from the environment. This process, in turn, releases waste and pollution into the ecosphere. Since the environment is finite, economics must be viewed as a subsystem of the global ecosystem.

The same forces that have moved the study of geography from regional perspectives to global ones have been underpinning changes in emphasis in economics. Ankrim (1990) states that economic models that have treated regions as self-contained entities have been rendered obsolete. Using such indices as imports and

FIGURE 7–1 The steady-state economic vision

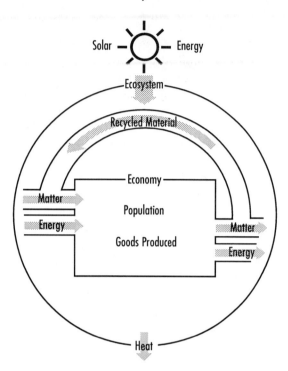

exports as percentages of the GNP, national percentages of world markets, foreign investment, international banking activity and international trade as a percentage of world production, he shows the increasing interdependence of the world economy over the past two decades. As a means of helping students understand these interrelationships, Ankrim suggests a series of teaching activities that show how economic decisions affect both domestic and foreign workers, markets and consumers. In the same vein, Lamy et al. (1981) have designed a series of games and simulations on such topics as multinational corporations, economic priorities and world trade specifically for the development of global awareness.

Summary

In this chapter, we examined the teaching of peace values in relation to inquiry in the disciplines of geography and economics, in relation to teaching methods, and in relation to substantive content. The discussion included reference to values implicit in human rights and ways of living out our values through action projects within our own communities. Next, we considered the importance of developing a critical awareness of perspectives in geography, including not only the biases encountered in mapping and other spatial representations, but also the way in which social, economic, cultural and racial perspectives are often prevalent the study of geography. Finally, we examined the teaching of global geography and economics, examining the way in which local, regional and global studies inform and complement each other and contribute to an understanding of planetary wholeness and unity.

REFERENCES AND SOURCES

Ankrim, Ernest M. (1990), "International Economics: A Path to Understanding the World", *Social Education,* February 1990: 90–92.

Barnaby, Frank (1988), *The Gaia Peace Atlas: Survival into the Third Millenium,* New York, Doubleday.

Boden, Philip K. (1977), *Promoting International Understanding through School Textbooks: The project for multilateral consultations on secondary school history, geography and social studies textbooks (1971–1974),* Berlin, Georg Eckert Institute for International Textbook Research.

Bunge, W. (1982), *The Nuclear War Atlas,* Victoriaville, Quebec, The Society for Human Exploration.

Bunge, W. (1984), "Racism in Geography", *Contemporary Issues in Geography and Education,* Vol. 1, No. 2: 10–11.

Burnett, Alan (1985), "Propaganda Cartography", in David Pepper and Alan Jenkins (Editors), *The Geography of Peace and War,* London, Basil Blackwell.

Burnley, Jenny and Ralph Pettman (1986), "Teaching About Human Rights in Geography", in John Fien and Rod Gerber, *Teaching Geography for a Better World,* Brisbane, Australian Geography Teachers Association with The Jacaranda Press.

Burton, John W. (1972), *World Society,* Cambridge, Cambridge University Press.

Butt, Graham and David Napper (1993), "A Global Warming Game for Key Stage 4", *Teaching Geography,* Vol. 18, No. 2, April, 1993: 70–73.

Cohen, Saul B. (1990), "The World Geopolitical System in Retrospect and Prospect", *Journal of Geography,* January-February, 1990: 2–12.

Cox, Bernard (1986), "Reflections on Geography Teaching for a Better World", in John Fien and Rod Gerber, *Teaching Geography for a Better World,* Brisbane, Australian Geography Teachers Association with the Jacaranda Press.

Crooker, Richard A. (1990), "Learning About Global Interdependence: An Area-Value Mapping Exercise", *Social Education,* September, 1990: 320–322.

Daws, Leonie (1986), "Geography and Minority Groups", in John Fien and Rod Gerber (Editors), *Teaching Geography for a Better World,* Brisbane, Australian Geography Teachers Association with The Jacaranda Press.

Demko, George J. (1987), "International Refugees: A Geographical Perspective", *Journal of Geography,* September-October, 1987: 225–228.

Fien, John and Rod Gerber (1986), *Teaching Geography for a Better World,* Brisbane, Australian Geography Teachers Association with the Jacaranda Press.

Goodland, Robert and Herman Daly (1990), "The Missing Tools", in Constance Mungall et al, *Planet Under Stress,* Toronto, Oxford University Press.

Grahame, Kenneth (1983), *The Wind in the Willows,* New York: Adama Books. (Originally published 1908)

Grant, James P. (1990), *The State of the World's Children 1990,* Published for UNICEF by Oxford University Press.

Harper, Robert A. (1990), "Geography's Role in General Education", *Journal of Geography,* September-October, 1990: 214–218.

Hicks, David (1986), "The Geography of War and Peace" in John Fien and Rod Gerber, *Teaching Geography for a Better World,* Brisbane, Australian Geography Teachers Association and The Jacaranda Press.

Hicks, David (1988), *Education for Peace: Issues, Principles and Practice in the Classroom,* London, Routledge.

Hicks, David (1992), "Mapping the Future: A Geographical Contribution", *Teaching Geography,* Vol. 18, No. 4, October, 1993: 146–149.

Huckle, John (1981), "Geography and values education" in Rex Walford (Editor), *Signposts for Geography Teaching,* London, Longman.

Jenkins, Alan (1985), "Peace Education and the Geography Curriculum", in David Pepper and Alan Jenkins (Editors) *The Geography of Peace and War,* London, Basil Blackwell.

John, Andrew (1990), "An Active Approach to Global Location", *Teaching Geography,* June, 1990: 124–125.

Kenney, Marianne (1992), "Geography and Mutual Understanding: `Harvest of Hope'", *Journal of Geography,* Vol 91, No. 4, July/August 1992: 177–185.

Kidron, M. and R. Segal (1987), *The New State of the World Atlas,* London, Pan Books.

Lamy, Steven L., Roger B. Myers, Debbie Von Vihl and Katherine Weeks (1981), *Teaching Global Awareness with Simulation Games,* Denver, University of Denver, Center for Teaching International Relations.

Libbee, Michael (1988), "World Geography and International Understanding", *Journal of Geography,* January-February 1988: 5–12.

Liongson, Raymond (1989), "Education for Development and Peace", *Social Education,* April/May 1989: 246–249.

Lyons, Robin R. (1992), "The Community Service-Minded Geographer: Geography and the Boy Scouts of America Merit Badge Program", *Journal of Geography,* Vol. 91, No. 1, January/February 1992: 24–27.

Marsden, W. E. (1992), "Cartoon Geography: The New Stereotyping?" *Teaching Geography,* Vol. 17, No. 3, July, 1992: 128–130.

Mason, Peter (1989), "Geography and Development Education: Recent Teaching and Future Strategies", *Teaching Geography,* January, 1989: 2–5.

Myers, Norman (1984), *Gaia: An Atlas of Planet Management,* New York, Doubleday.

Pepper, David and Alan Jenkins (1985), *The Geography of War and Peace,* London, Basil Blackwell.

Saunders, Mark N. K., (1985), "Teaching about Bias in Maps: a consideration of map postcards", *Teaching Geography,* October, 1985: 15–17.

Serf, Jeff and Vivienne Hoyte (1988), "South Africa: Geography and Human Rights", *Teaching Geography,* January, 1988: 10–13.

Slater, Frances (1983), "Sexism and Racism", *Contemporary Issues in Geography and Education,* Vol. 1, No. 1: 271–273.

Smith, David C. (1974), "Teaching International Relations Using Community Resources", *Horizon/Exploration,* Vol. 14, No. 2, September, 1974: 12–16.

Trudgill, Stephen, Tony Thomas and Nigel Coles (1990), "The Global Context: Developing a Local Fieldwork Day", *Teaching Geography,* June, 1990: 106–110.

Wiegand, Patrick (1986), "Values in Geographic Education" in Peter Tomlinson and Margret Quinton (Editors), *Values Across the Curriculum,* London, The Falmer Press.

CHAPTER 8

Mathematics

SHAKUNTALA DEVI, *whose home is in India, makes her living by travelling around the world giving demonstrations of her amazing ability to do complex mathematical calculations to students, teachers and other interested people.*

While on a tour of Canada in 1989, she gave a remarkable display of her powers. Someone asked her to give the cube root of 82,312,875, a number chosen at random, and quickly she gave the correct answer: 435.

Asked to name the day of the week for the date August 15, 1980, the date of a reporter's wedding, she correctly identified it as a Friday. Devi can provide the day of the week for any date within 2,000 years.

She is particularly adept at other kinds of mental arithmetic, such as multiplying numbers of many digits by other large numbers and lengthy addition, subtraction and division. In fact, she holds the world record for multiplying two 13-digit numbers in her head: the Guinness Book of World Records *has honoured her with the record in which she multiplied 7,686,369,774,870 by 2,465,099,745,779 to obtain the correct answer of 18,947,668,177,995,426,462,773,730 in a mere 28 seconds.*

Devi was born in Bangalore, India, and gave at only the age of three the first public demonstration of her prowess with numbers at Mysore University. She has become known as the Human Calculator, and has been travelling the world giving performances of her mathematical genius.

Asked how she manages to do such difficult calculations, Devi replied that her ability is a manifestation of divine power. Her Hindu acquaintances believe that she is a reincarnation of Srinivasa Ramanujam, a brilliant Indian mathematician who undertook research at Cambridge University, but who died at the early age of 32 in 1920.

Devi has written a book on mathematical calculations, entitled, Figuring: The Joy of Numbers *(1990). Asked about her fascination with the subject of mathematics, she said that mathematics for her is a labour of love. She sees in the purity of numbers the essence of truth and other universal values. "Numbers," she says, "have life—they signify something beautiful. They help bring all humanity together, a universal bond for humankind."*

Can mathematics indeed bring humankind together and help to form, as Devi asserts, a universal bond? Does the subject of mathematics have a role to play in the development of peace? In this chapter, we will explore ways in which this subject may convey values, help in the understanding of other cultures, contribute towards thinking in a global perspective and enhance our creative abilities.

Teaching Values in Mathematics

Of all the subjects in the school curriculum, mathematics is the one that is most often thought of as being "value-free". Even in the sense that the subject of mathematics is a coherent body of abstract knowledge, however, that assertion is only partly true. The very study of "pure mathematics" in some cultures links it to religious or cultural values. In some Islamic countries, for example, abstract mathematics is viewed as a manifestation of symbols or signs of God (Wilson, 1986: 101).

106

In the general study of mathematics as a school subject, certain values may be inherent both in the content used and in the methodology employed. One of the obvious values implicit in mathematics is the value of truthfulness as opposed to falsehood. In mathematical tasks involving fundamental operations or the solution of equations, for example, the only right answer is the one that is correct, and it is usually highly valued by instructors. Wrong answers are generally devalued: only occasionally do we find them genuinely valued by teachers for remedial purposes.

Another value implicit in mathematics lies in the stability, consistency and reliability of the subject matter. In a world where much of our knowledge quickly becomes obsolete, the durability of mathematics knowledge is highly valued and overlaps in this respect with its perceived value of truthfulness.

Implicit in mathematics instruction is the value of abstraction, as in the case of principles and theorems that are key parts of the structure of the subject. However, in school mathematics, the application of abstractions to practical problems also makes concreteness an important value. Since mathematics would have little value for most students if it were limited to only one of either abstraction or concreteness, these two values are usually held in creative tension with each other.

It is in the concrete applications of mathematics, particularly in the problems posed to students, that values are either explicit or implicit. The values espoused usually reflect those for which there is a consensus in our society, but are they necessarily those that make for a peaceful community or world society? A few examples of problems adapted from North American textbooks currently in use may help us to consider this question carefully.

Two bicyclists decide to have a 100 km race. A rides at 15 km per hour and B rides at 20 km per hour. Since B is faster, B agrees to give A a 10 km advanced start. Which cyclist wins the race?

Many examples can be found of mathematics problems that emphasize the value of competition. When they deal with examples of friendly rivalry, as in the example above, they may be approving the sublimation of aggressive tendencies into harmless activity. On the other hand, the omission of examples dealing with cooperation may carry the message that competition is preferred over cooperation.

A girl regularly saves $10 per month from her allowance, placing it into a daily interest savings account. If she makes her first deposit on May 31, and interest is added at the end of each month, how much will she have in her account by November 30, assuming that the rate of interest is 8%?

An underlying value in this problem is that of thriftiness and delayed gratification as opposed to extravagance and immediate consumption. Some similar problems dealing with savings, however, have more complex value underpinnings, as in the following example.

When his daughter was born, a father set up a fund for her university education. He invested $1,000 at 9% compounded annually. If no withdrawals are made from the fund, how much will have accumulated on her 18th birthday?

In addition to the value of thriftiness, the values for education, sharing and farsighted planning are also evident. Seldom in our society, preoccupied with immediate consumption, do we see examples of concern for the welfare of people so many years in advance. It may also be noted that both of these problems, posed in a society where many families experience financial hardship through declining income or unemployment, tend to reflect middle class values rather than the shared values of the population as a whole.

Mathematics textbooks and computing programs usually have multiple problems dealing with the income of sales representatives who work on a basic salary plus commission, and with various types of problems such as those involving furniture and appliances that can be bought at a discount. Consider the following problems:

A sales representative is paid $50 per week basic salary plus $20 for each vacuum cleaner he sells. Write the formula that shows the relationship between his weekly income, I, and the number, n, of vacuum cleaners he sells. Draw the equation of this relationship on a graph.

A washing machine normally listed at $560 is put on sale at a discount of 25% and then is further reduced by 10% of the discount price. What is the sale price of this item?

Such individual problems are relatively innocuous in themselves, but grouped together *to the exclusion of other kinds of problems*, they can represent the values of consumerism, acquisitiveness and materialism. On the other hand, seldom-found problems that involve the repair of appliances, the reupholstering of furniture, the mending of shoes, the rebinding of books and the like would convey the values of conserving and durability, rather than those of a consuming and wasteful society.

Other examples of problems containing important values are those requiring a comparative study of the nutritional content indicated on food labels (emphasizing the value of healthfulness); those pertaining to municipal budgets (conveying a sense of social integration and community); and those that require income tax calculations taking into consideration deductions such as charitable donations (underpinning the values of honesty in making a return and sharing personal income with the less fortunate).

It is important that students and teachers should not be unknowingly manipulated by the implicit or explicit values contained in the teaching materials prepared for young people. Shan and Bailey (1990, 1991 a, b, c), in writing on educating for equality and justice through mathematics, propose that teachers develop sensitivity to the messages of race, class and gender conveyed by mathematics textbooks. They should be taught to recognize and critique the social values context of the mathematical problems and visual illustrations used in teaching. Teachers have a responsibility to prepare materials which contain values that promote community building on the broadest possible scale.

Mathematics and Intercultural Understanding

Just as school mathematics in our society tends to reflect our social values, so the mathematics studied in other countries reflects different histories, ideologies and cultures. In his book *Socialist Mathematics Education*, Frank Swetz (1978) presents some stark examples of such differences. Two examples are given below.

During the Cultural Revolution in China from 1966 to 1976, comparisons of modern economic conditions in the country were often made with the conditions for peasant farmers that existed before the revolution. Consider the following problem from a mathematics textbook used widely at the time:

When worker Tung was six years old, his family was poverty-stricken and starving. They were compelled to borrow five dou [215 pounds/100 kilograms] of maize from a landlord. The wolfish landlord used this chance to demand the usurious compound interest of 50 percent for three years. Please calculate how much grain the landlord demanded from the Tung family at the end of the third year. (Swetz, 1978: 171)

This example could well lead to questions such as: What were the relations between landlords and peasants in pre-revolutionary China? What other evidence might we find that could help us to understand the nature of Chinese society at that time? What transformations took place between pre-revolutionary and post-revolutionary China? What purpose might have been served in using such examples during the Cultural Revolution?

This example shows how mathematics can be used to whet the appetite for knowing more about the people of another country. A case study approach, in which students understand something of the way in which a mathematics system is a function of a culture, can be an effective way of promoting inter-cultural understanding.

In her book *Africa Counts,* Claudia Zaslavsky (1973) includes a number of such studies, one of which is that of the Yoruba people of Nigeria. Nigeria has a long and rich history with evidence of human settlement going back nearly 40,000 years. Different cultures and empires have flourished over various historical periods. The Yoruba people themselves are believed to have come from the east and to have been well established in West Africa by the year 1300 AD. Their custom was to build walled cities, such as the ancient city of Ibadan, and to surround them with a large band of farms. However, they were traders,

and they also carried on commerce in cloth, food and hardware outside the city, particularly with people of the north.

While some trade took place by means of barter, the Yoruba developed their own currency system long before any contact with Europeans. The system began with the cowrie, a shell found in Nigeria, and excavated in quantity at the ancient city of Ife. The cowrie served as the basic unit of currency and was traded for goods. A sixteenth-century European observer noted that 100 cowrie shells were required to pay for 2 gallons of honey and a honey comb. In addition to being used in trade, the cowries would also be used for calculations and record keeping.

In a typical trading session, a bag of 20,000 shells, which had previously been counted, would be emptied on the floor. A cowrie-counter, who would be seated beside the pile, would rapidly make 4 piles of 5, which would be moved together to form 20. When 5 piles of 20 had been formed, they would be collected together to form 100. And 2 piles of 100 would be swept together to form the important number 200. Such a procedure would continue to the point where the required number of shells had been counted out. In some parts of the country, the shells of 2 piles of 20 would be pierced and threaded together for convenience on a string, and groups of 200, 2,000 and 20,000 would also be kept separately as special numbers.

It is believed that, because the shells were used for trade, the Yoruba developed an interesting number system that is both additive and subtractive. The numbers 1 to 10 have different terms, as do the numbers 20, 30, 200 and 400. The rest are formed by multiplying, then either adding or subtracting the basic numbers, as can be seen from a study of Table 8–1.

TABLE 8–1   The Yoruba Number System

1. okan	31. (30 + 1)
2. eji	32. (30 + 2)
3. eta	33. (30 + 3)
4. erin	34. (30 + 4)
5. arun	35. (20 x 2) – 5
6. efa	36. (20 x 2) – 4
7. eje	37. (20 x 2) – 3
8. ejo	38. (20 x 2) – 2
9. esan	39. (20 x 2) – 1
10. ewa	40. (20 x 2)
11. ten plus one (10 + 1)	41. (20 x 2) + 1
12. ten plus two (10 + 2)	42. (20 x 2) + 2
13. ten plus three (10 + 3)	43. (20 x 2) + 3
14. ten plus four (10 + 4)	44. (20 x 2) + 4
15. twenty less five (20 – 5)	45. [(20 x 3) – 10] – 5
16. twenty less four (20 – 4)	46. [(20 x 3) – 10] – 4
17. twenty less three (20 – 3)	47. [(20 x 3) – 10] – 3
18. twenty less two (20 – 2)	48. [(20 x 3) – 10] – 2
19. twenty less one (20 – 1)	49. [(20 x 3) – 10] – 1
20. twenty (ogun)	50. [(20 x 3) – 10]
21. twenty plus one (20 + 1)	51. [(20 x 3) – 10] + 1
22. twenty plus two (20 + 2)	52. [(20 x 3) – 10] + 2
23. twenty plus three (20 + 3)	53. [(20 x 3) – 10] + 3
24. twenty plus four (20 + 4)	54. [(20 x 3) – 10] + 4
25. thirty less five (30 – 5)	55. [(20 x 3) – 5]
26. thirty less four (30 – 4)	56. [(20 x 3) – 4]
27. thirty less three (30 – 3)	57. [(20 x 3) – 3]
28. thirty less two (30 – 2)	58. [(20 x 3) – 2]
29. thirty less one (30 – 1)	59. [(20 x 3) – 1]
30. thirty (ogbon)	60. (20 x 3)

The number 35 would be expressed as "five less than two twenties"; 45 as "five from ten from three twenties"; 53 as "three more than ten less than three twenties"; 60 as "twenty in three ways"; 105 as "five from ten less than six twenties", etc. We can see how such a system grew out of the counting of cowries by fives, and by the traditional groupings of the cowries into piles of 20 to make larger and larger numbers.

In traditional Yoruba society certain numbers have special significance, especially the number 4. There are 4 days in the week and this rhythm determines the frequency of market days. The names of each of 4 major deities (Shango, Obatala, Orunmila and Oduduwa) are given to the days in the week. In each town, there are 4 gates in the walls, and the 4 major deities are respectively linked to each of the points east, north, west and south.

In the nineteenth and twentieth centuries, a number of changes occurred that have discouraged the used of the cowrie number system. The introduction of the larger Zanzibar cowrie, which was in abundant supply, meant added weight and created problems of transportation. When coinage was introduced to replace the shells, problems of differences in the rate of exchange for the cowrie in different parts of the country made it difficult to continue with it as an internal unit of currency. Today, the shells are used for decoration on clothing, drums, headdresses, ritual masks and furniture. They are also used as special-purpose currency particularly for ceremonial occasions, including bride-price payments, funerals and initiation into secret societies. The cowrie as a currency and its mathematical system were replaced earlier in this century by the Nigerian pound, which was made up of 20 shillings. In 1972, this system was, in turn, replaced by a new system of decimal currency of which the unit is the naira, made up 100 kobo.

It might be noted that besides the system developed in Nigeria, there were hundreds of other numeration systems developed in Africa, south of the Sahara. Some of them, described by Mozambiquan mathematicians Gerdes and Cherinda (1993), show that they were somewhat unique to their geographical and cultural settings.

In summary, it may be said that mathematics may play a unique role in promoting intercultural understanding by helping us to consider and appreciate the mathematical systems of other cultures. As in the case of the numeration system of the Yoruba peoples, it may help us to understand the relationship between mathematics and culture and the cultural integrity of a society. Yet this case study illustrates as well that there are tensions in every society between one sub-culture and another and that new and peaceful accommodations, including those in the realm of mathematics, may need to be made in the process of development of national and international communities.

Mathematics and Global Perspectives

We have seen that the teaching of mathematics can contribute to the building of peace through a greater awareness of values in problem-solving and through developing a more critical consciousness of the relationship between mathematics and culture. Mathematics may also contribute to peace by playing a role in the development of global perspectives.

Many of the applications of mathematics have traditionally been taken from very local or national sources on the grounds that the problems students deal with should relate to matters within their own experience. While this practice may be appropriate to some degree for elementary school children, the global events that young people are now exposed to, particularly when they reach the secondary level of education, make it both parochial and ethnocentric.

Increasingly, mathematics teachers need to draw applications from subjects that are not only of local importance but, because of the interdependence of nations, are also of worldwide significance. A number of authors have pointed the way by developing examples of problems that deal with local issues in global perspective: population growth patterns and infant mortality, pollution, energy consumption, food consumption, distribution of wealth, language, the arms race and nuclear peril. Such problems can be used to develop mathematics skills in interpreting charts and graphs; in calculating fractions, ratios, proportions, and percentages; and in the solving of word problems. A few examples will be reviewed here.

World Population Characteristics

The human family depends upon the earth's resources and environment for survival. Weeden (1985: 22) has developed mathematical exercises in which students construct geometrical representations of the world population by regions and compare them to the corresponding representations of the world's land area. These exercises provide an excellent beginning to the study of population distribution and density and to the varied circumstances of the relationship between population and space in different regions of the world. Swetz (1985: 6-7) has prepared tables showing world population projections for different constant rates of growth over the next 700 years. Using these projections, students can tackle the following questions:

Estimates of the world's agricultural resources (soil, water, sunlight, etc.) indicate that the planet can support 217 billion people at a bare subsistence level. If our present population of 6 billion continues to grow at its present rate of 1.7%, in about how many years will subsistence existence be reached? If the population grew at a higher rate of 2.5%, how long would it take? If the rate were 1%, in how many years would we reach the theoretical subsistence level?

The mathematics of population distribution and population growth can lead into the study of some other characteristics of the earth's peoples. Weeden (1985: 16, 19-20) has devised a number of ratio and percentage problems around the theme, "If there were 100 people in the world...". Students are given a sheet of paper with 100 figures of people on it and are then asked to use coloured pencils to indicate their estimates of answers to such questions as:

- How many people would be American, Indian, Chinese...?
- How many would speak English, Chinese, Russian...?
- How many would be suffering from malnutrition?
- How many would be in the "North" and how many in the "South"?

Following the exercise, students may compare their guesses with the correct answers supplied by the teacher, or calculate the correct answers from given statistical information. They may reflect upon the differences between their guesses and reality or test the general knowledge of other people. Such an exercise could also be effectively incorporated into studies of sets and their operations. Weeden recommends the same technique for studying the global distribution of wealth by having students determine the answers to "If there were 100 banknotes in the world...". Similarly, global patterns of food consumption can be better comprehended through a corresponding exercise, "If there were 100 Smarties in the world...". With younger students, this exercise can be made more concrete by using the same total number of recipients as the number of pupils in the class. In this way the class may be divided into world regions, and the pupils themselves can become a microcosmic world population.

Pollution

Other world problems are also amenable to mathematical treatment at the secondary level. Schwartz (1981) presents a number of problems, including those related to pollution and the arms race. To give pupils practice in reading and interpreting graphs, he provides a graph indicating the lead content in the Greenland ice cap. From their studies of the graph, pupils are then asked:

1. What was the approximate lead content in the Greenland ice cap in
   a) 1900?
   b) 1950?

2. In about what year was the lead content (micrograms of lead per ton of snow) equal to
   a) 100?
   b) 200?

3. What might explain the sharp rise in lead content between 1930 and 1970? (Schwartz, 1981: 7)

Students will recognize that the Greenland ice cap is an accumulated record of pollution built up from precipitation over many years. They can become aware that lead pollution is a global problem because it has come about as a result of the increased use of gasoline in the industrialized nations, which are thousands of kilometres away from Greenland.

Military Expenditures and Social and Economic Development

Schwartz (1981:5) recommends that students explore the relationship between the arms race and aspects of national development through the creation, or solution, of appropriate mathematical problems. The example below, an application of Schwartz's idea, is designed to help students understand the way in which different nations allocate their resources, and

to begin to assess the social consequences of different kinds of national policy. Using the figures in the table, students can be asked questions such as the ones that follow.

CENTRAL GOVERNMENT EXPENDITURES[1]

COUNTRY	PERCENT OF TOTAL EXPENDITURES					
	Defence		Education		Health	
	1980	1992	1980	1992	1980	1992
Low income economies						
Pakistan	30.6	27.9	2.7	1.6	1.5	1.0
Malawi	12.8	4.8	9.0	10.4	5.5	7.8
Middle income economies						
El Salvador	8.8	16.0	19.8	12.8	9.0	7.3
Morocco	17.9	12.8	17.3	18.2	3.4	3.0
High income economies						
Netherlands	5.6	4.6	13.1	10.8	11.7	13.9
New Zealand	5.1	3.9	14.7	13.9	15.2	12.1

[1] Figures extracted from World Bank (1994: 180-181)

1. Calculate the rate of increase, or decrease, in military expenditures over the period 1980 to 1992 for each of the six countries listed above.

2. Find the average rate of increase, or decrease, in military expenditures for each of the above three categories (insofar as the countries listed represent those categories).

3. On the basis of the countries listed above, do you think that any relationship exists between level of economic development and the pattern of expenditures for defence and social development?

4. Note that these statistics represent central government expenditures and do not take into account expenditures of political units within each country. Why might such tables have to be interpreted cautiously?

These problems provide mathematics practice in the use of ratios, calculation of rates of change, calculation of averages, extraction of meaning from statistics and interpretation of statistics. At the same time, they may help students begin to consider both the internal insecurities and the perceived external threats of certain nations as well as the economic and social benefits of achieving stable and peaceful relationships with planetary neighbours.

Statistics can also be used to create problems related to specific military expenditures; for example, the cost of purchasing aircraft carriers, military aircraft and other weaponry in trade-off for improving food and water supplies and raising the standards of health in developing areas. By considering such problems, students can become aware of questions of equity and social justice on a world scale.

Mathematics, Creativity and Conflict Resolution

Mathematics, like any other subject that involves problem-solving, requires both divergent and convergent thinking. When mathematics cultivates such thinking, it contributes to the development of creativity and to attitudes that favour flexibility and reflectivity in our thought processes.

In his book *Lateral Thinking*, Edward de Bono (1979) writes that problems involving conflict may be solved either through confrontation between opposing ideas or through changing ideas from within ourselves as a result of information. We often have difficulty changing our ideas because thought patterns tend to become firmly established in our minds and we routinely call upon them to resolve the problems that confront us. While initially useful, these patterns tend with time to become idea-clichés, and may restrict our ability to find new and fresh solutions to emerging problems. The reason for our difficulty with fixed thinking patterns is partly that our education has emphasized logical, or vertical, thinking to the exclusion of lateral thinking—thinking that generates new ideas and helps us to break away from the restrictions of

fixed ideational patterns. The development of lateral thinking can make an important contribution to solving problems of many kinds.

De Bono and other writers on creativity draw heavily upon mathematics to illustrate the principles of creative thinking and to develop exercises that help our minds to play with ideas, to form new relationships between ideas, and to develop our imaginations. It is interesting to examine some ways in which mathematics can therefore be used to encourage creativity.

Generating Alternatives

Very often, because of our tendency to rely upon previous thought patterns, we are inclined to look at something (an object, a concept or an idea) in a limited number of ways. But in lateral thinking (de Bono: 58), we learn that any particular way of looking at something is only one of many possible ways. How can we develop mental habits of exploring more possibilities? One way to improve our creative thinking is to practise generating alternatives. For example, students could be presented with Figure 8–1, and asked to give as many interpretations of it as possible.

FIGURE 8–1

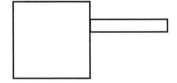

Some responses we might get from students include:

1. A large rectangle from which two smaller rectangles have been removed
2. A small rectangle added to a square
3. A small "slice" taken from the top of a rectangle and placed at the side

4. A saucepan

5. A butcher's cleaver

6. A turret gun

7. A caricature of a person with a long nose

8. A bird's eye-view of a building with a long entrance hallway, or possibly with a connecting hallway

9. A picture of a building with a tall chimney (when viewed from the left)

10. A rectangular sign affixed to a wooden stake (when viewed from the right)

Note that some alternatives are generated by consciously thinking of the particular point from which you view the figure. A series of exercises of this type can help to develop the habit of lateral thinking. No matter how absurd some responses may be, judgment should be suspended on the acceptability of any one suggestion (as an interpretation, idea or solution) until the class has run out of ideas. Only when freewheeling thinking is exhausted, should some evaluation be made of the best way to proceed.

The kind of divergent thinking stimulated by this sort of activity is akin to the need to understand that a given conflict can be perceived in different ways and to the brainstorming required to generate imaginative, alternative solutions to conflict situations.

Challenging Assumptions

De Bono (82-92) also used a number of mathematical examples to illustrate ways in which lateral thinking can help us to challenge assumptions. We usually believe that our assumptions are correct, and we build our thinking upon sound assumptions. Basic ideas, however, may need to be tested. In this case, lateral thinking can help us achieve a

FIGURE 8–2

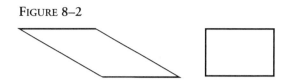

restructuring of basic ideas. Consider Figure 8–2. It shows two shapes, a parallelogram and a rectangle. Suppose we want to arrange the figures in such a way that they form a square. We would normally assume that we must try to place one side of the rectangle adjacent to one side of the parallelogram to see whether we could come up with a square. In this case, using that assumption, it is impossible. Suppose now that the parallelogram is bisected along its shorter diagonal, we have two small triangles that can be fitted together to form a rectangle, and then placed upon the first rectangle to make a square. As de Bono points out, such a manoeuvre may be regarded as "cheating", which really indicates that there have been assumed limits or constraints in the thinking process.

Experience with lateral thinking in mathematics can be transferred to thinking about real-life problems. For example, boundaries between nations have often been matters of dispute, and wars have been, and are still being, fought over them. One assumption we often have is that boundaries are fixed and permanent and can only be changed by force. Another is that only one nation can have jurisdiction over territory adjacent to a boundary. Lateral thinking could help us to restructure our concept of boundaries. We could consider that they might have varying degrees of permeability; that there might be joint jurisdiction of disputed boundary zones; that there could be multi-national government of disputed zones; that under certain conditions boundary changes could become normative practice, perhaps under the supervision of a third party such as the International Court of Justice; or that a boundary could be entirely removed.

Analyzing and Synthesizing

In their book, *Creativity Training,* Kirst and Diekmeyer (1973) also use a variety of mathematical examples (statistics, graphs, sets, geometric figures, algebraic formulas and the like) as a means of developing and improving creative abilities. Sets may be created to help students develop such skills as analysis and synthesis. Suppose, for example, students are asked to consider buying the ideal bicycle. They would need to analyze the component features of a bicycle and then to assemble and draw the final product. In doing so, they might first create a number of feature sets as follows:

Frame	**Handle Bars**
Men's	Drop
Women's	Standard
Wheel Size	Straight
40 cm	**Gears**
60 cm	1-speed
66 cm	3-speed
Tire Size	12-speed
Thin	**Lights**
Regular	Reflectors
Mountain	Battery
Colour	Dynamo
Gold	**Wheel Guards**
Silver	With
Black	Without
White	**Brakes**
Red	Caliper
Green	Disk

Creating such a list stimulates the imagination by requiring an analysis of features and characteristics of bicycles. The features can be broken down into as many different sets as one can find. An interesting mathematical problem can be devised by asking, "How many different bikes could be built based upon the above features?" ($2 \times 3 \times 3 \times 6 \times 3 \times 3 \times 3 \times 2 \times 2 = 11,664$).

Choosing the particular features of a bicycle when trying to customize a personal design requires a reflection upon values and choices represented by each set, and it embraces the idea of the intersection of sets. The choice may involve considering such values as fitness, competitiveness (speed), status, prestige, durability (toughness), safety, sociability (riding with friends and family), etc. This stage of the exercise of selecting features and assembling an idea of the whole requires construction and synthesis of information, another step in creativity.

How might these same thinking skills be applicable to conflict resolution? Let us suppose that bad feelings have developed between two young friends, Gill and Kim, because Kim borrowed Gill's bicycle without asking permission. Not knowing that her friend had borrowed her bike, Gill subsequently reported it as missing to the police. The police found the bike in Kim's possession and took her to the police station for questioning.

An analysis of the problem could involve (1) the steps leading up to the conflict; (2) the perceptions that each one has of the problem; (3) the alternatives that might be pursued to resolve the difficulty; (4) the values implicit in each alternative action; and (5) the likely consequences that would follow from each alternative action.

When the two friends see each other, Gill learns that Kim had borrowed the bike to go quickly to the drug store to fetch a medication for her mother who has a heart ailment. Kim thought that Gill would not mind if she took the bike in an emergency, because Kim is her friend. Kim had felt extremely humiliated to be apprehended by the police. Gill had not known Kim's circumstances and had felt that Kim had abused their friendship. The two could keep their grudges against each other with the consequence that their friendship would be diminished. However, if reconciliation were to occur, Kim could apologize for her somewhat precipitant action. Gill could forgive Kim, understanding that Kim's motive was not to hurt her, but to help her mother. Gill could apologize to Kim, explaining that it was not her intention to humiliate her. They could both say how much they valued each other's friendship. Putting the pieces together, and deciding what values have overriding importance, the two could apologize and forgive each other, with the consequence that their relationship would be healed and their friendship immeasurably strengthened. The actual decision made with regard to the conflict depends upon the creativity that Gill and Kim bring to bear upon generating alternatives, and the values they hold (sympathy–indifference; friendship–egotism; reconciliation–vengefulness) which they bring to bear upon effecting a synthesis of their information.

Carrying Through

Another example of using mathematics to develop creativity is what Kirst and Diekmeyer (1973:121) call "carry-through" activities that require purposeful and systematic use of our creative resources to yield solutions. One such exercise is that of linked words. While this exercise appears to be a word game, it has important mathematical implications. Students are asked to think of two four-letter words, such as "flip" and "tree", that do not have any letters in common. Then, by changing only one letter at a time, they are chal-lenged to build a bridge between the words; in this case: flip/flop/flow/flew/flee/free/tree. The examples can be made more imaginative. For example, students could be asked to suppose that there are two points of view, black and white, and that they are challenged to reconcile their differences by building a symmetrical bridge to peace. A solution is offered below:

```
                    peace
               place     pease
            plane           phase
          plank               chase
        clank                   chose
       clonk                     whose
      clock                       whole
     block                         while
    black                           white
```

Mathematical thinking may help in the search for a solution to such a problem. What is the minimum number of steps that could be taken on each side to achieve a solution? Notice the order in which the letters are changed. Are there alternative orders for changing the letters? In a trial and error procedure, how can systematic efforts be used to try the five different vowels? How could the twenty-one different consonants be tried systematically? In developing a strategy for finding solutions, is it fruitful to try a branching technique with different trial words? Is it fruitful to work systematically from both ends? How many different words containing at least one vowel could theoretically be made from four letters? How many could be made from five letters? In the above example, the gradual reconciliation between black and white may be regarded as a good illustration of incremental change towards compromise and a successful symmetrical resolution of conflict.

In review, we can see that mathematics can play an important role in developing lateral thinking and in cultivating habits of creative thinking generally. If such skills and attitudes can be brought to bear upon the great range of problems confronting humankind, we may be more inventive in finding solutions that are agreeable to various parties and that lead to reconciliation.

Summary

In this chapter, we first explored the way in which mathematics can be an effective vehicle for teaching values that enhance community-building and peace-making activities. Second, we considered the ways in which school mathematics, while building fundamental skills and concepts, can help to promote inter-cultural understanding. We then considered the need for refurbishing mathematics programs so that the content reflects a better balance between local, national and world perspectives, since all are now important in the lives of our young people. Finally, the ways in which mathematics can make a contribution to the development of creativity and conflict resolution were explored. Fertile thinking combined with appropriate knowledge, values and attitudes, can help each individual to become a more productive global problem-solver.

REFERENCES AND SOURCES

Allard, André (1993), "Hindu-Arabic Roots of Medieval Europe: a numeration system transmitted to the West from India via the Arab world", *The UNESCO Courier*, November, 1993: 34–36.

Burton, John W. (1972), *World Society*, Cambridge: Cambridge University Press.

Clanson, Tandy (1991), "Mathematics Therapy", *Mathematics Teaching*, September, 1991: 21–23.

Cotton, Anthony (1990), "Anti-Racist Mathematics Teaching," *Mathematics Teaching*, September, 1990: 22–25.

de Bono, Edward (1979), *Lateral Thinking*, Harmondsworth, Middlesex: Penguin Books.

Devi, Shakuntala (1990), *Figuring: The Joy of Numbers*, London: Viking Penguin.

Dodd, Phil (1992), "Maths from Around the World", *Mathematics Teaching*, December, 1992: 23 (Insert).

Filliozat, Pierre Sylvain, (1993), "Making Something Out of Nothing: Inventing the zero in India", *The UNESCO Courier*, November, 1993: 30–33.

Foster, Leslie (1986), *Rand McNally Mathematics Encyclopaedia: Maths Puzzles, Graphs, Weights and Measures*, New York: Rand McNally and Company.

Gerdes, Paulus and Marcos Cherinda (1993), "Words, Gestures and Symbols: traditional counting methods in Africa", *The UNESCO Courier*, November, 1993: 37–39.

Gill, Dawn, (1986), "Politics of Per Cent", *Mathematics Teaching*, Nos. 114–121: 12–14.

Howson, H. G. (1980), "Socialist Mathematics Education: Does It Exist?" *Educational Studies in Mathematics*, 11: 285–289.

Hudson, Brian (1985a), "Peace Education and Mathematics", *World Studies Journal*, 5 (4): 10–12.

Hudson, Brian (1985b), "Social Division or Adding Up to Equality? militarist, sexist and ethnocentric bias in mathematics textbooks and computer software", *World Studies Journal*, 5 (4): 24–29.

Ifrah, George (1982), "Knots as Numbers", *The UNESCO Courier,* February, 1982: 24–25.

Johnson, Peter (1990), "Creative Conflict", *Mathematics Teaching,* March, 1990: 23.

Kirst, Werner and Ulrich Diekmeyer (1973), *Creativity Training: Become Creative in 30 Minutes a Day,* (English Translation by Thomas Semon), New York: Peter H. Wyden Inc.

Lévy, Thomas (1993), "The Origin of Numbers: The story of a great intellectual adventure", *The UNESCO Courier,* November, 1993: 9–13.

Menninger, Karl (1969), *Number Words and Number Symbols: A Cultural History of Numbers* (Translated by Paul Broneer from the revised German edition), Cambridge, Massachusetts and London: M.I.T. Press.

Pool, Peter (1990a), "Other People's Mathematics", *Mathematics Teaching,* March, 1990: 32–33.

Pool, Peter (1990b), "Blinded by Culture", *Mathematics Teaching,* December, 1990: 12–14.

Ritter, James (1993), "Sumerian Sums: the origins of a positional system of numbering in ancient Mesopotamia", *The UNESCO Courier,* November, 1993: 14–17.

Schwartz, Richard (1981), "Teaching Global Issues Through Mathematics", New York, UNICEF, Educational Resources Information Center, (ERIC) ED 212411.

Selby, David (1985), "Global Perspectives in Mathematics and Science Education: A bibliography", *World Studies Journal,* 5 (4): 57–58.

Shan, Sharan Jeet and Peter Bailey (1990), "Education for Equality and Justice I: Whose Mathematics? What Mathematics?", *Mathematics Teaching,* December 1990: 42–43.

Shan, Sharan Jeet and Peter Bailey (1991 a), "Education for Equality and Justice II: Appropriate learning context for raising issues of culture, equality and justice", *Mathematics Teaching,* March, 1991: 58–59.

Shan, Sharan Jeet and Peter Bailey (1991 b), "Education for Equality and Justice III", *Mathematics Teaching,* June, 1991: 40–41.

Shan, S.J. and P. Bailey (1991 c), *Multiple Factors: Classroom Mathematics for Equality and Justice,* London: Trentham Books.

Shi-ran, Du (1993), "The Mathematics of Early China: an original system of counting using counting rods", *The UNESCO Courier,* November, 1993: 18–21.

Swetz, Frank (1978), *Socialist Mathematics Education,* Southampton, USA: Burgundy Press.

Swetz, Frank (1985), "Mathematics: a vehicle for better global understanding", *World Studies Journal,* 5 (4): 5–9.

UNESCO (1993), "The Story of Numbers", *The UNESCO Courier,* November, 1993.

United Nations Development Programme (1993), *Human Development Report 1993,* New York: Oxford University Press.

Weeden, Paul (1985), "Numbers in an Unequal World", *World Studies Journal,* 5 (4): 15–23.

Wilson, Bryan (1986), "Values in Mathematics Education", in Peter Tomlinson and Margret Quinton, *Values Across the Curriculum,* London: The Falmer Press: 94–108.

Woodrow, Derek (1984), "Cultural Impacts Upon Children Learning Mathematics", *Mathematics in School,* Vols. 13–14, 1984–85: 5–7.

World Bank (1994), *World Development Report 1994: Infrastructure for Development,* New York: Oxford University Press.

Zaslavsky, Claudia (1973), *Africa Counts: Number and Pattern in African Culture,* Boston: Prindle, Weber and Schmidt, Inc.

CHAPTER 9

Science and Technology

IN THE EARLY *morning hours of March 13, 1989,
Quebec experienced a massive province-wide power failure, resulting
in a total black-out for several hours. At the same time, hydro-electric transmission was also disrupted, but less severely so, in Ontario
and British Columbia. When the power failed in Quebec, traffic
lights were inoperative, causing rush-hour tie-ups for commuters;
schools and businesses closed; and airports were temporarily para-
lyzed. Hydro officials blamed the power failure on unusual flares of
activity on the surface of the sun. But how could events over 1.34
billion kilometres away affect us here on earth?*

*Solar physicists have observed that there is a cycle of exceptional
activity at the surface of the sun every 11 years. They theorize that
such activity is initially caused by an unevenness in the speed of the
sun as it rotates upon its axis, and that this unevenness periodically
results in solar flares——huge eruptions of energy from the sun's fiery
surface. Scientists know that such explosions cause bubbles of magnetic field to poke through the regular magnetic field lines of the sun and
to be hurled far into space. Emissions of charged particles, mainly*

protons, are thus sent spiralling away in a solar wind, travelling at speeds of hundreds of kilometres per second.

It takes several days for these particles to reach the outer atmosphere of the earth. As they funnel into the earth's magnetic field, they cause the regular field pattern to wiggle and to be disturbed: compass needles are deflected by those changes. At the same time, the particles ionize gases in the upper atmosphere, causing them to glow and produce bright displays of the aurora borealis. The wiggling of the earth's magnetic field lines also causes an induction of electricity in power transmission cables. Under these circumstances, circuit breakers are automatically activated, shutting down the provincial power grid.

Four days before the massive power failure, scientists had observed the movement of a flare 36 times the size of the earth on the sun's northeast quadrant. This flare resulted in the strongest pulse recorded on the earth's magnetic field in a decade. As we reflect upon the sensitivity of the earth to forces at great distances from it, we cannot help but consider the use of electricity in our homes, streets and work places in different perspectives. Normally we might think of electricity as energy that comes into our homes by way of a wire attached to our house or apartment. We can also think of it further afield in terms of our connection to a regional grid and the effect upon it of a lightning storm hundreds of kilometres distant; we can also understand how our electrical system can be be dramatically affected by a solar storm millions of kilometres away.

Expanding on these ideas, we might also ask, In what ways can science help enlarge our perspectives as human beings on the planet earth? Can the methods of science and the knowledge they generate help to bring together the people who inhabit the earth? Is there a special contribution that the study of science and technology can make to the kind of human experience needed to help build a peaceful world?

In this chapter we will investigate the values inherent in scientific study and the way in which they may relate to values for a peaceful world. We shall also consider key issues relating to science, technology and society. Finally, we will look at some of the ways in which the study of science and technology may be able to contribute to thinking about the welfare of the planet and its people.

Teaching Values in Science and Technology

The teaching of science in schools—based on scientific principles, experimentation and theory—has for a long time tended to assume that the subject is value-free, and that the culture of the knower is not relevant to scientific knowledge. However, recent writers in science education including Thelen (1983), Miller (1984), Layton (1986), and Stanley and Brickhouse (1994) point out that certain values arising from the nature of the subject have traditionally been highly prized among the scientific community. They include the values of curiosity and questioning that give rise to investigation and experimentation, as opposed to values of complacency and smugness; the values of humility and cautiousness, in the sense that our thoroughly tested forms of knowledge are still incomplete and that science itself is subject to errors of measurement; the values of objectivity and detachment, since scientific knowledge is verifiable by investigators in different social and cultural contexts; the values of precision, exactness and logic, which are prized in standard scientific procedure; and the value of courage, as against despair, since knowledge is pursued in spite of the fact that we know the universe is forever beyond our total understanding.

The traditional values in science, sometimes taught implicitly as part of the hidden curriculum, are important to peace education in at least two respects. The first is that, although science may be perceived somewhat differently in various cultures, there is a sense that many of these values are shared and that scientific knowledge, too, because of the value of openness, is shared. The world has, then, a common pool of knowledge to which it gradually adds. It also has a set of common value dispositions by which the knowledge can be used for the benefit of all humankind. In this sense, the earth's people theoretically share a common scientific culture and can experience a sense of unity within that culture. The second way in which these values are important to the building of peace is in the influence they may bring to bear upon that part of our knowledge that is less scientific and exact in nature. As Miller (1984) states, the scientific values of humility, cautiousness and tentativeness can be applied to such ideologies as free enterprise or collectivism, thus helping us to appreciate the relativity of alternative political and economic systems and to build tolerance of differences.

In the application of science to human endeavours, tremendous advances have been made in such areas as information technology, computing, chemical technology, agricultural technology and biotechnology. Advances in these areas are creating new possibilities for increasing production, improving standards of health and meeting more satisfactorily the material and cultural needs of humankind. Yet, as Klein (1988) has pointed out, these developments have in some cases been accompanied by large-scale unemployment, new forms of poverty, major damage to the environment and other problems. To build better links between science, technology and society, James and Kurtz (1985) discuss the importance of integrating new values into science education. They include the values of resourcefulness, which involves drawing intelligently upon varied sources of knowledge in the physical and social sciences in the solution of persistent problems; creativity, in terms of throwing knowledge areas into fresh combinations or viewing problems from new and different perspectives; and social cohesiveness in the face of new technologies to counter the alienating effect that they have upon human beings. To that list, Layton (1986) would add the value of stewardship, especially the stewardship of the earth as the home of humankind. Everything we possess is not owned absolutely; we hold it in trust for all, including future generations.

Just as there is sharing of scientific knowledge, there needs to be a sharing of technology: hence the phenomenon of technology transfer where it is appropriate. Under conditions of war, technology is not shared, as countries hostile to each other always seek advantages in military technology over their enemies. By contrast, the building of a peaceful world requires the sharing of technology for mutual benefit and especially for the establishment of social justice on a global scale.

So far, our discussion has dealt with the values that are explicit or implicit in the content of science and technology education. As in the case of other subjects in the curriculum, however, values are also conveyed by the methods used in teaching. Layton (1986) points out that the methodology of teaching science, especially in Europe, has emphasized individualism. This value has been taught through individual laboratory experimentation, individual science projects and other forms of learning that have tended to emphasize learning in isolation. Such heuristic forms of learning are aimed at individual development without much reference to the social context of learning. Linked to such methods are the values of secretiveness and competition, which encourage students to work for, and by, themselves. As science teaching moves more towards consideration of the cultural contexts of learning, and begins to include a different mix of pure science and technology, such values may become incompatible with curriculum objectives. New forms of cooperative learning that provide not only for individual reflection but also for group accomplishments, and that promote openness in sharing information and experimental findings, would reinforce the constitutive values of science discussed above.

In summary, there has been a trend away from the disengagement of science from values towards a conscious re-engagement of values in science, technology and society, a process described by Layton as "a revaluing of science education". Incorporating into the teaching of science such values as questioning, accuracy, perception, openness, resourcefulness, creativity, courage, cooperation and stewardship serves as a basis by which students can grapple with difficult science-related issues, and favours the kind of personal and social development needed for peace-building in the community and in the world at large.

Some Critical Issues in Science and Peace

This section will present some of the most urgent science-related problems that affect good order either within, or between, nations around the globe and have, as a result, direct implications for international security and peace. In each case, major concepts and scientific principles are discussed in relation to the problems, and the new values and new technologies proposed to alleviate the problems are also described. While the problems themselves are described separately, it is recognized that they are intricately related to each other. Overall solutions require scientists and technologists to recognize the inter-relationships, and to deal with problems in a more unified way than they have in the past.

World Population and Food

The population of our globe is increasing at the rate of an additional 90 million per year. It is expected to reach 6 billion by the year 2000 and 10 billion by the year 2050. Population growth in the "rich" countries is level, or in some cases it is declining; however, population in the "poor" areas is growing rapidly, with the continent of Africa having the highest rate of growth in the world.

In 1995, world food production stood at 4 billion tonnes per year, and was increasing gradually. Theoretically, there is enough food for all the world's population, but cultural food preferences and food distribution problems result in surpluses in some areas and severe shortages in others. Although food production is increasing, it cannot keep pace with the needs of a rapidly-growing population.

The gap between population growth and food supplies is, therefore, widening, with catastrophic results. Food shortages are leading to widespread poverty, famine, malnutrition, disease and, in areas of severe famine, high rates of mortality. At the same time, these enormous stresses lead to a frantic scramble for food, causing prices to rise in the global economy, making food all the more costly in low-income countries. Such trends have a destabilizing effect upon governments in these countries, which are unable to cope with the crisis. Lester Brown (1991) points out that the concept of national and international security needs to be redefined to recognize that the principal threat to our future comes not from the relationships between nations, but from the relationship between ourselves and the natural systems and resources upon which we depend.

Population control is a complex question since it involves social customs, religious beliefs, education, government policy and a variety of other factors. High rates of population growth result in urban sprawl, which diminishes agricultural land and increases pressure on agricultural productivity. Through the increased production of urban and industrial waste, urbanization results in general environmental degradation. Such countries as India and China have well-established policies of population control, but the policies and their application are highly controversial from a moral standpoint. One important known trend is that when levels of education are raised in a society, the rate of population increase declines.

There are a number of biological forces at work that make increases in agricultural production in various parts of world more difficult. The first is desertification, the spread and expansion of desert land. Desertification occurs in semi-arid regions and is caused, in some instances, by the cultivation or overgrazing of lands and, in other instances, by successive below-average rainfalls. The deserts of Ethiopia and Sudan have been spreading for decades, but the threat of desertification exists on all of the continents of the world. Approximately one third of the surface area of the earth is affected by desertification and about 6 million hectares of land are turned into desert each year, while another 21 million hectares are degraded to the extent that they can no longer be used as economically viable farmland.

Another reason for the decline of farmland is deforestation. Forests, particularly tropical forests, are vital to the planet's climate system, soaking up rainfall like a sponge and releasing water slowly over time. The razing of forests for the purpose of expanding farmland often results in a temporary increase in agricultural production, but the erosion of topsoil into waterways and oceans and the depletion of already nutrient-poor soils soon leads to a decline in the production of crops or livestock. In 1995, it was calculated that 11.3 million hectares of forest were being lost every year, principally in Latin America, Africa and Asia.

Declining agricultural production also results in the long term from the practice of chemical farming. When the soil is under continuous cultivation with the use artificial fertilizers, herbicides and pesticides, yields from the land are excellent for a number of years. Over the long term, however, such practices eventually result in a reduction of the organic content of the soil, lessening both its tilth and its ability to retain moisture, and turning it into "hard pan". Under these conditions, depleted soils are less productive and are at greater risk of erosion from wind and water.

In the face of these difficulties, much attention has been given to the development of science and technology to increase food production both on a short- and long-term basis. Research on desertification has focused upon sand-dune stability and desert revegetation. Work has been done, for example, on hydro-mulching techniques to develop stable cover-crops (Guinon and Allen, 1990), the development of vegetation and the improvement of soils through nitrogen-fixing plants (Ross, 1990) and the planting of food-producing bushes adapted to arid land (Meyers, 1984). Developments of this kind, combined with other programs such as new water-saving methods of irrigation, make it possible to halt and reverse the process of desertification and to increase the yield of food in arid lands.

Scientists are also concerned with finding effective ways of forest regeneration in areas that have been destroyed through logging, cutting and burning. Protection of the tropical rainforests, which are believed to play a major role in regulating world climate, has become a priority. New highly efficient wood-burning stoves have been developed that, if used in low-income countries, could cut in half the consumption of wood for fuel, and would significantly reduce the rate of deforestation (Maini, 1990). In addition, the development of better logging and forest management practices, based upon the ecological principles of sustainability, could play an important part in restoring the earth's forests (Horowitz, 1990).

New approaches to farming are being developed to avoid the harmful effects of chemical agriculture and improve food production on a sustainable basis. They include preserving genetic diversity, since the practice of genetic uniformity in crops makes them more vulnerable to infestation and disease (Meyers, 1984); biological methods of pest control that cause sterility in pests or impede their maturation; recycling organic materials to replenish the soil; using "green manure" crops to increase soil fertility; and planting shrubs and trees to slow the velocity of the wind and prevent soil erosion (Johnson, 1990).

These developments may not be enough in themselves. What is needed is a new sense of values—sharing resources more widely, accepting stewardship of that part of the earth for which we are responsible, and conserving and living with the natural environment. As Meyers points out, there needs to be less emphasis on industrialization, urbanization and the export of cash crops and more on rural self-sufficiency. Ultimately, new lifestyles that will support a sustainable future will need to be developed in all countries.

World Energy Resources

The major sources of the world's energy at present are petroleum, coal, natural gas and wood. The first three are non-renewable resources, and are sometimes referred to as fossil fuels. Hydro-electric power and nuclear power are also important sources of energy but make smaller contributions to energy supply. These energy sources are used principally for the operation of industry and transportation, and for homes, farms and commerce.

Throughout the latter half of the twentieth century, the consumption of energy worldwide has increased enormously, producing a growing energy crisis that poses a great threat to international peace and security. The crisis is associated with three factors. The first is that traditional energy resources are distributed unevenly over the surface of the globe; there are some nations that have rich endowments of energy resources and others that do not. The German occupation of the territory of Lorraine in the Second World War, and the occupation by Iraq of Kuwait in the Gulf War were, in part, brought about by the coveting of neighbouring energy supplies.

The second factor associated with the crisis is the uneven consumption of energy among the world's nations. Current estimates (1998) indicate, for example, that North America, with just 5 percent of world population, consumes about 30 percent of all energy produced, whereas Asia, with over 60 percent of the population, uses only 30 percent of the energy. Although the poorer nations aspire to develop their economies, they will never be able to use energy at the same level of per capita consumption as the developed nations since there are simply insufficient world supplies to make that possible. The inequitable consumption of energy resources therefore creates a condition of economic injustice and consequent tension between members of the world community.

The third factor, which is bringing the energy crisis to a head, is that non-renewable energy resources are finite and, with the exception of coal, fast being depleted. The developed world has been heavily dependent upon petroleum for domestic, industrial and commercial purposes and will experience a critical shortage within 30 years unless alternative sources of energy are used. Apart from the energy crisis in the countries of the North, a second crisis exists in the South. There, by far the greatest amount of energy is derived from wood, or wood products such as charcoal. This continuing use of wood is contributing in some areas to deforestation and desertification.

Science has an important role to play in helping us to know the different effects of energy production and use. Knowledge of energy is also central to the creative development of alternative energy technologies that will help to slow, halt, or reverse trends that lead to energy-related conflicts.

Most of the fuels currently used throughout the world are carbon compounds. When they burn, they combine with oxygen to produce carbon dioxide as shown by the following chemical equations:

For anthracite coal
$$C + O_2 \rightarrow CO_2 + Heat$$

For wood or cellulose
$$C_6H_{10}O_5 + 6O_2 \rightarrow 6CO_2 + 5H_2O + Heat$$

For methane in natural gas
$$CH_4 + 2O_2 \rightarrow CO_2 + 2H_2O + Heat$$

For heptane in gasoline
$$C_7H_{16} + 11O_2 \rightarrow 7CO_2 + 8H_2O + Heat$$

Carbon dioxide, along with nitrous oxide (N_2O, which comes from vehicle exhaust, coal combustion and the decomposition of chemical fertilizers), and methane (CH_4, the product of rotting garbage in landfill sites and the combustion of wood) all enter the atmosphere. They are the primary causes of the rise in the surface temperatures of the earth due to the greenhouse effect. Global warming, in turn, is a cause of massive dislocation of people and consequently of conflict, as noted later in this chapter.

Hydro-electric power is produced by water falling through turbines that, in turn, drive electrical generators. People tend to think of hydro-electric power as a clean and renewable source of energy. However, there is a growing understanding of the various costs of this form of energy, particularly when it is obtained through very large hydro projects. The construction of huge dams in river valleys floods the habitat of plants and animals and, as in the case of the James Bay Project in Quebec, displaces large numbers of people from their lands. Fish life in the waterways is often permanently affected. Regional, perhaps even continental, weather and climate are altered. And thousands of hectares of forest and farmland are necessarily affected by the construction of power transmission lines. Increasingly, the environmental costs, in addition to the capital construction costs of such projects, are being placed under close scrutiny in cost/benefit analysis.

The other principal form of energy, nuclear power, was originally seen as a cheap, clean and abundant supply of energy that would make up for the anticipated decline in oil supplies. In nuclear reactors, neutrons bombard uranium or plutonium atoms, causing them to release other neutrons that bombard more atoms in a controlled chain reaction called breeding. The immense amount of heat released in this reaction is carried by a coolant to a heat exchanger, which heats water to steam that, in turn, is used to drive turbines and electric generators. The prediction that nuclear power would provide 50 percent of the world's energy needs by the year 2000 now appears to be excessively optimistic. The construction of nuclear power plants has slowed considerably throughout the world due to escalating costs and huge cost-overruns that have made nuclear energy less competitive. The construction of such plants has also slowed because of the unsolved problem of the disposal of highly radioactive wastes. Public opinion, too, has disfavoured nuclear power, after the events of Chernobyl in the former Soviet Union, Five Mile Island in the United States, and scores of other accidents in nuclear power plants.

A variety of proposals have been presented to resolve the problems of environmental degradation, inequitable consumption and diminishing supplies of traditional resources caused by current energy consumption patterns.

As a first step, the high consumption of energy in the countries of the North needs to be reduced through fuel efficiencies, fuel economies and changing lifestyles. It is possible to make cars much more fuel efficient; to reduce dependence upon cars through greater use of bicycles and public transportation; to make use of less energy for lighting, heating and cooling homes, offices and factories. Flaven and Lenssen (1991) estimate that it is possible for developed countries to reduce their per capita energy consumption by at least 50 percent without detrimentally affecting their economies, while, in the developing countries, improvement in energy efficiency could result in substantial growth to their economies.

A second major step forward would be the development of new technologies for renewable energy resources that do not harm the environment. Chief among them would be solar energy, which has been described as the cornerstone of a world energy system. Solar energy can be used directly through solar collectors to heat water for homes and industries, and is already used extensively in some countries for that purpose. Future possibilities include the collection of solar energy using parabolic dishes in arid and semi-arid lands, and transmitting the energy to accessible urban areas. The photovoltaic cell, which converts light energy directly into electrical energy and is already used extensively in millions of pocket calculators, has enormous potential for expanded use. One possibility is electrolysis of water to produce hydrogen as a clean-burning fuel.

Wind power, caused by the uneven heating of the surface of the earth, is another renewable source of energy. Certain areas of the globe are subject to relatively constant winds, and have great potential for wind power. They include northern Europe, northern Africa, the southerly part of South America, the western plains in North America, and the trade wind belt in tropical areas. It is estimated that wind could provide up to 20 percent of the energy needs of some countries. It can be harnessed by relatively small windmills for pumping water for irrigation and for watering animals. New technology windmills are also efficient in generating electricity. Some modern experiments have also been carried out to use wind as a supplementary source of power for ocean-going ships.

Wave energy, which is derived from wind power over large bodies of water, is also being explored. Meyers (1984:78) reports that various means are being developed to extract wave energy and convert it to electrical energy. Other efforts are being made to harness the energy of tides, caused not by winds but by the gravitational pull of the moon. In some areas of the world the difference in water level between high tide and low tide may be as much as 12 metres. Where significant differences of this order occur, tidal basins can be constructed in such a way that both rising and falling tides can be harnessed by turbines to produce electricity.

Another potential source of power is geo-thermal energy, the energy in the latent heat of the earth's core. Flavin and Lenssen (1991) state that countries around the Mediterranean, around the Pacific Rim and along East Africa's Great Rift Valley can tap geo-thermal energy. Currently, El Salvador obtains 40 percent of its electricity from geo-thermal sources; however, Iceland, Indonesia and Japan are among the countries that have the greatest potential. According to Meyers (1984), ocean thermal energy conversion, which exploits the difference in temperature between the surface and depths of the oceans, has massive potential. These sources of energy could be used in certain areas when there is no sun or wind.

It is important that our students build confidence in the way in which they personally can contribute towards the resolution of energy problems in their own lives. Reference works such as those by Johnson (1990) and Naar (1990) contain practical suggestions for improving energy efficiency and contributing to the development of renewable energy resources. Our energy-consuming lifestyles, however, need always to be seen within larger contexts: modest advances in energy technology combined with energy efficiency measures, and the willingness to share and acquire new knowledge and technology *can* produce sustainable energy systems. The solutions will require that different countries use a variety of combinations of renewable energy resources that draw upon their geography and location.

Rich nations will have the capital necessary to convert to new systems; developing nations, which in most cases have abundant renewable energy resources, will not be burdened with extensive conversion costs. Moving ahead swiftly with conversions will avoid international energy crises over limited supplies of fossil fuels and help to avert energy-based conflicts.

World Climate

The problem of world climate is closely related to energy supply and consumption patterns, but it is posing a different set of threats to economic and political stability around the globe. As noted earlier, there has been a significant rise in the amount of carbon dioxide in the atmosphere, especially in recent decades. Its concentration increased from 280 parts per million in 1850 to 350 parts per million in 1995. If unchecked it is expected to reach 600 parts per million by the year 2050. Increasing emissions of methane, nitrous oxide and chloro-fluorocarbons are adding to the change in the composition of the atmosphere.

While the mantle of the earth has a great capacity for absorbing carbon dioxide, the actual absorption has been reduced by deforestation, agricultural development and urban sprawl. The result is that the net amount of carbon dioxide remaining in the atmosphere has increased dramatically. Carbon dioxide and the other gases that exist in minute quantities do not appreciably affect incoming solar energy, but together these "greenhouse" gases have an insulating effect upon the planet. They absorb energy, trapping heat near the surface of the earth, and resulting in a warming effect. This effect is most notable in urban areas where temperatures on windless days may be as much as 10°C higher than those in surrounding rural areas.

Global warming has already measurably occurred: the global mean temperature has increased 0.5°C within the last 100 years and the 1980s included the 5 warmest years on record. It is estimated that there will be a rise in the average temperature of 3°C over the next 50 years. Such an increase will not be evenly distributed over the globe, as there will be little change at the equator but as much as 7°C increase in the polar regions. The temperature increase will melt much of the ice and snow in the mountainous and polar regions of the world, causing ocean levels to rise in this period by as much as 5 to 7 metres. In addition, snow and ice surfaces normally reflect some solar energy back into space. Their loss for the greater part of the year will result in the absorption of even more energy, adding to the warmth of the earth. At the same time, the greater amount of moisture in the atmosphere may produce more clouds, cutting off sunlight and possibly moderating temperatures.

There appear to be at least three ways in which climate changes will have an effect upon international peace and security. As reported by Meyers (1984:117), rainfall patterns will change so that some areas will become drier and others wetter. It is foreseeable that some of the grain belt in North America could suffer permanent drought and become much less productive, while higher temperatures in Siberia could enable new and fertile land to come under cultivation. Climate change would therefore result in significant shifts of economic power, in which some nations would profit and others would lose. These changes in agricultural resources would certainly cause great stresses and strains in the international community, posing a threat to peace.

A second way in which global warming and climate shifts would create economic and political instability would be in those areas that would become drier as a result of diminished rainfalls. Land that once supported viable farming would dry up, resulting in the loss of livelihood for large numbers of people who would become, in effect, environmental refugees. The plight of more than one million refugees in Ethiopia in the 1980s (see Chapter 10) was caused by successive droughts and desertification in areas that once were agriculturally productive. The displacement of large populations and the problems of their resettlement will pose enormous challenges to the international community, especially when refugees cross international boundaries.

The third effect of climate change will be in rising sea levels caused by melting glaciers and ice caps in the polar regions. If sea levels were to rise between 5 and 7 metres, the low-lying areas most vulnerable to flooding would be the Netherlands, the delta of Bangladesh and the state of Florida in the United States. Since 40 percent of the world's population lives in coastal regions that could potentially be affected by rising waters, there would be major disruptions to human life for future generations. The problem of dislocation caused by flooding would produce another kind of environmental refugee. Mass migrations of populations could further compound problems of environmental sustainability and world stability.

The chemicals in the atmosphere that are causing global warming have been put there largely by the industrialized countries. As many of the countries of the South now feel that they have a right to use fossil fuels to industrialize and establish standards of living comparable to those in the North, they do not necessarily feel bound to reduce their emissions of greenhouse gases. The South, therefore, needs investment and technology from the North to help it convert to renewable energy resources. The countries of the North carry much responsibility for financially supporting the management of the planet on a sustainable basis.

Both adults and children, in looking at the predicted future climate of the planet, might easily feel overwhelmed by the immensity of the problem; yet there is a solution, which lies both in collective and individual action. There is much that can be done, as previously suggested in the discussion of energy, to reduce the consumption of fossil fuels that produce greenhouse gases and to encourage the development of renewable energy resources that do not so radically affect the planet's climate.

The process of forest regeneration can also play an important part in regulating the climate of the planet. Trees utilize carbon dioxide in the process of photosynthesis and store carbon as cellulose in the fibre of the tree, thus reducing the amount of carbon dioxide in the atmosphere. Although wood decays and eventually releases carbon dioxide into the atmosphere, it fixes and stores carbon for long periods of time. Wood used for construction, or furniture, or as recycled paper, locks in the carbon for even longer periods of time. Besides using carbon dioxide, trees have a cooling effect upon climate, since they use and store solar energy, reflecting less than other components of the environment. The United Nations Environmental Program estimates that it would be feasible to plant 500 million hectares of new forest over the next two to five decades as the most economical way of countering global warming.

Finally, the classroom, and the school itself, can be a model for contributing positively in the resolution of these problems through school and school board policies and actions—where appropriate, encouraging children to walk or cycle to school; using alternative energy sources for school heating and lighting; conserving heat energy through insulation; using environmentally friendly utensils and energy in the cafeteria; using environmentally friendly products for cleaning the school and caring for school gardens and lawns; and planting trees on school property.

World Military Technology

In the mid-1990s, the world was spending about $800 billion dollars per year for arms and military activities—more than 6 percent of the global GNP. About 70 percent of the investments in the arms industry were made by countries of the North, and the remaining 30 percent from countries of the South (there are more than 50 military governments in the South). It is notable that military expenditures in developing countries have been growing at a faster rate than those of the developed world. Expenditures for arms by the developed world are about 30 times larger than their aid budgets to developing countries.

A great deal of the world's scientific and technological development resources are being used for military purposes. Meyers (1984, 247) reports that of the 2.25 million research scientists world wide, 500,000 work on military-related research and development projects and, further, that 50 percent of the physicists and engineers in this group work exclusively on the development of weapons. Both the investment in military hardware and the intellectual resources of scientists and technologists draw significantly from national resource bases and increase the staggering debt of some Third World countries.

As evidenced in the Gulf War of 1991, conventional warheads can be delivered with deadly accuracy and even non-nuclear explosives have enormously devastating power. Although chemical and biological weapons are officially banned by the Geneva Convention, their secret manufacture and use have major environmental implications. Nuclear weapons that were stockpiled by the superpowers and other members of the nuclear club have the capability of destroying the earth many times over. Currently the weapons in possession of countries with nuclear capability have the destructive power of one million Hiroshimas.

The military policy followed by the major powers until the mid-1970s was centred on the principle of mutually assured destruction in the event of war. The "peace" was kept by nuclear deterrence—the fear of self-destruction in a nuclear war. Since then, the pin-point accuracy with which nuclear weapons can be targeted has raised the spectre that a nuclear power could use a preemptive strike at the nuclear silos and other military targets of an antagonist, giving way to the idea that it would be possible for there to be a "winner" in a nuclear war.

Current developments in world military technology pose a threat to peace in at least two fundamental ways. The first is that more and more countries are acquiring nuclear weapons capability. This increases the probability of the accidental start of a nuclear war; or of the use of such weapons by less rational leaders; or by a country, cornered in an international dispute, using them as a "last resort".

The second threat lies in the huge sums of money expended by countries of both the North and the South for their military arsenals. A substantial portion of those funds could be used to find solutions to the real problems that give rise to serious conflicts within and between nation states. Meyers (1984) points out the irony that some developing nations spend inordinate sums of money in acquiring military hardware while ignoring forestry and agricultural practices that erode millions of tonnes of precious top soil from their lands, permanently diminishing the natural resources upon which the future of their country depends. Hence, militarization, in effect, exacerbates food and energy shortages and other problems that can give rise to international conflict.

There have been a number of constructive proposals for addressing the predicament of modern warfare by science educators who believe that stronger connections should be made between science and society. Saperstein (1983), Wellington (1983) (1985), and Johns (1987) advocate teaching about nuclear arms, nuclear radiation and the effects of nuclear war as part of the science curriculum. The proposals specifically include an examination of the history of nuclear weapons with some reference to nuclear physics. They include, as well, developing a greater awareness of the destructive power of nuclear weapons as compared to conventional weapons. In his book *The Fate of the Earth,* Jonathan Schell (1982) perhaps more vividly than any other writer, has described the collective and catastrophic effects of a nuclear holocaust upon human life, social organization and the natural environment. Other scientists have, through modelling techniques, estimated the effect of a nuclear winter upon the globe, which would virtually extinguish any life of a higher order that would be left in the aftermath of a nuclear war.

Rapoport (1988) believes that the dilemma can be approached by universities, and possibly other institutions, from another direction. It is apparent, he states, that the power and prestige of the military establishment, or the war institution (which includes the armed forces, military academies, departments of national defence and industrial and scientific complexes), rest upon the superstition that

military establishments protect the societies upon which they feed. Disciplinary and interdisciplinary studies of the institution of war and the superstition upon which it rests could lead to a greater awareness of the risks it poses and to the eventual atrophy of its legitimacy.

Yet another approach is suggested by Meyers (1984), who proposes that world militarism needs to be seen in relation to the dynamics of planet management, including population and hunger, energy depletion and environmental abuse. The earth must make a transition in values from exploitation to restraint, from aggressiveness and destruction to the protection and sustaining of life, from short-term goals to long-term vision. These larger teaching perspectives will be considered next.

Teaching Science with a Global Perspective

In what ways can science teachers develop global perspectives in their teaching? Photographs taken of the earth from space show it to be a beautiful, live sphere. Satellite pictures provide us with new eyes to see ourselves and our earth. They help us to understand the oneness of the earth, the interplay and intricate connectedness of its various systems, bringing us to a greater awareness of our world as a single biosphere or ecosystem (Mayer and Armstrong, 1990). Through helping young people to understand the wholeness of the planet, science teaching reveals the values that support global ecology and advance global security.

There are a number of ways in which world perspectives can be developed in the sciences. The beginnings of larger perspectives can be taught through an approach developed by Williams (1982), who may have built upon earlier concepts of appropriate technology developed by Schumacher (1975). Through contact with voluntary workers overseas, Williams has compiled a series of units in multicultural science and technology, and more specifically in "Third World science", primarily for secondary students in the North. The units teach the application of scientific principles in different cultures, dealing with topics such as charcoal, distillation, fermentation, energy conversion, iron smelting, methane digestors, dyes, plants and medicines, salt and soap. Through these studies, students in developed countries can understand better the inventiveness of people everywhere, the application of science to practical problems in different cultural settings, and the frequent inappropriateness of attempts to transfer technology directly from the North to the South.

Another example that would establish links between culture and technology can be found in agricultural practice in China. The development of small, low-cost three-wheeled tractors for work on land plots and hillside terraced farms—tractors that require few spare parts and can be easily repaired on the land—is a good example of intermediate technology being used to suit the local topography and agricultural economy. Chinese agriculture also makes use of methane digesters, fish ponds and small-scale ecology generally. Science and technology studies of this type of topic can make an important contribution to understanding the uniqueness, value and integrity of cultures different from one's own.

A second approach, which develops perspectives further, is that advanced by Hazlewood (1984, 1985) and Hodson (1993) in which examples of scientific study are drawn from a variety of cultures and countries. Hazlewood gives a specific example of the way

in which the chemistry curriculum can be clothed with a world context. In the study of metals, such as tin, it is suggested that a class begin by considering the importance of the metal and its alloys, such as bronze, pewter and solder; the chemical reactions that tin has with other substances; and other aspects of the chemistry of tin. Further studies then widen horizons; for example, students consider the world-wide sources of tin, its extraction from the earth and its purification. The human dimensions of the tin industry are then explored by viewing a video of a case study of tin mining in Bolivia. Pupils learn about the squalid conditions of living for tin miners, the hardships for their families, and the uncertainties of the tin industry created by Bolivian politics and fluctuating world markets. Through the contextual studies of the theme, students are encouraged to relate science to questions of values—in this case to social and economic justice—and to consider ways in which they, too, may share responsibility for the plight of workers in other parts of the planet.

A third way in which science teachers can help their students to develop world perspectives is to make explicit the relationships between the various systems of the earth so that students can understand the wholeness of the earth as a biosphere. The Gaia Theory, developed by James Lovelock, and expanded by authors such as Meyers (1984) and Devereux (1989) is helpful in this respect. It holds that the earth is a living organism that regulates itself very much like the human body and other living things. Harman (1988) provides some good examples of the self-regulatory mechanism. The amount of oxygen at the earth's surface of the atmosphere, for instance, tends to remain constant at 21 percent by volume, a level that is required by most organisms for their survival. If the proportion drops below that level, much animal life would die; however, the surviving plant life would flourish, bringing the oxygen content of the air up to the original level again. On the other hand, if there were a level of oxygen higher than 21 percent, fires (such as forest fires) would burn out of control, destroying plant life and therefore bringing the oxygen content down to the normal level.

Similarly, the surface temperature of the earth tends to remain steadily between 10°C and 20°C as a result of the regulatory effect of plant life. If the temperature rises, there is more plant growth. Initially, the plants reflect some energy back into space, but they then have a cooling effect upon the atmosphere near the earth's surface. When there is a decline in temperature, plants grow less, absorbing and reflecting less energy; therefore, temperatures rise once more. Self-regulatory, or homeostatic mechanisms, are characteristic of all living beings.

Important, too, in the Gaia theory are the many intricate global interrelationships such as those between atmospheric gases and plant life, between soil acidity and plant species, between ocean chemistry and marine life. Major human interventions on the planet, as we have seen in the burning of stored fossil fuels, the manufacture and release of toxins, or the deforestation of tropical and other areas, affects the planet as a whole. Human decisions and actions can fundamentally affect the fragile planetary balance. In proposing a system of planetary management that will help our human population to continue in harmony and not in combat with the planet, Meyers emphasizes the importance of Gaia values: self-regulation and ecological constraint as against rapaciousness and greed for resources; sharing and cooperation as against assertiveness and aggressiveness; efficiency and recycling as against wastefulness; and sustainable development as against runaway growth. All humankind has a common responsibility for the health of the planet.

Summary

This chapter has considered the importance of linking science, technology and society in contemporary science teaching. It has reviewed some of the explicit and implicit values in content and methodology that can underpin the teaching of science and technology for peace. Four key issues—world food and population, energy, climate and military technology—have been identified as posing a threat to the current and future stability of the planet, with a view to proposing ways in which science teaching can contribution to their gradual resolution. Finally, the teaching of science and technology in a global perspective has been discussed to underline the shared responsibility that all humankind has towards the future of the earth as our home.

REFERENCES AND SOURCES

Aird, Forbes (1991), "Faucet Fuel: Tapping the water-bound energy of hydrogen", *Harrowsmith*, No. 99, September-October, 1991: 67–71.

Alton, Janis, Eric Fawcett and L. Terrell Gardner (eds.), (1988), "*The Name of the Chamber Was Peace*", Toronto and Fort Meyers: Science for Peace, Samuel Stevens and Company.

Atwater, Mary M. and Joseph P. Riley (1993), "Multicultural Science Education: Perspectives, Definitions and Research Agenda", *Science Education*, 77 (6), November, 1993: 661–668.

Berger, John J. (ed.), (1990), *Environmental Restoration: Science and Strategies for Restoring the Earth,* Washington: Island Press.

Blosser, Patricia E. (1985), "Science Education for the Year 2000 and Beyond", in Robert K. James and V. Ray Kurtz (eds.), *Science and Mathematics Education for the Year 2000 and Beyond,* Bowling Green, Ohio: School Science and Mathematics Association.

Brown, Lester et al., (1991), *State of the World 1991, A Worldwatch Institute Report on Progress Toward a Sustainable Society,* New York: W. W. Norton.

Burdett, Pat (1985), "What Have Science, Education in a Multicultural Society and All-White Schools To Do with Each Other?", *World Studies Journal,* 5 (4): 50–56.

Devereux, Paul, John Steele, and David Kubrin (1989), *Earthmind,* New York: Harper and Row.

Ellington, Henry, Eric Addinall and Fred Percival (1981), *Games and Simulations in Science Education,* London: Kogan Page.

Flavin, Christopher and Nicholas Lenssen (1991), "Designing a Sustainable Energy System", in Lester R. Brown, *State of the World 1991,* New York: Norton.

Fyfe, William S. (1990), "Our Planet Observed: The Assault by *Homo Sapiens*" and "Dynamics of Planet Earth" in Constance Mungall and Digby J. McLaren (eds.), *Planet Under Stress,* Toronto: Oxford University Press.

Guinon, Marylee and David Allen (1990), "Restoration of Dune Habitat at Spanish Bay", in John J. Berger (ed.), *Restoring the Earth,* Washington: Island Press.

Harman, Willis (1988), *Global Mind Change,* New York: Warner.

Hazlewood, Patrick (1984), "Teaching Chemistry with a World Studies Perspective", *World Studies Journal,* 4 (3), 28–30.

Hazlewood, Patrick (1985), "Developments in Teaching Chemistry with a World Studies Perspective", *World Studies Journal,* 5 (4): 44–49.

Hodson, Derek (1993), "In Search of a Rationale for Multicultural Science Education", *Science Education,* 77 (6), November, 1993: 685–711.

Horowitz, Howard (1990), "Restoration Reforestation", in John J. Berger (ed.), *Environmental Restoration,* Washington: Island Press.

James, Robert K. and V. Ray Kurtz (1985), *Science and Mathematics Education in the Year 2000 and Beyond,* Bowling Green, Ohio: School Science and Mathematics Association.

Johns, Frank (1987), "Nuclear Radiation: A Focus for Science/Math Educators", *Peace Education News,* 2, Summer/Fall: 27.

Johnson, Lorraine, (1990), *Green Future: How to Make a World of Difference,* Markham: Penguin Books.

Klein, Helmut (1988), "Education Today for Tomorrow's World", in Terrance Carson (ed.), *Toward a Renaissance of Humanity: Rethinking and Reorienting Curriculum and Instruction,* Edmonton: World Council for Curriculum and Instruction.

Layton, David (1986), "Revaluing Science Education", in Peter Tomlinson and Margaret Quinton (eds.), *Values Across the Curriculum,* London: Falmer Press.

Lindsay, Liz (1985), "Racism, Science Education and the Politics of Food", *World Studies Journal,* 5 (4): 32–37.

Maini, J. S. (1990), "Forests: Barometers of Environment and Economy", in Constance Mungall and Digby J. McLaren (eds.), *Planet Under Stress,* Toronto: Oxford University Press.

Mayer, Victor J. and Ronald E. Armstrong (1990), "What Every 17-Year Old Should Know About Planet Earth: The Report of a Conference of Educators and Geoscientists", *Science Education,* 74 (2), April, 1990: 155–165.

Meyers, Norman (ed.), (1984), *GAIA: An Atlas of Planet Management,* New York: Doubleday.

Miller, Ralph M. (1984) "Science Teaching for the Citizen of the Future", *Science Education,* 48 (4): 403–410.

Mungall, Constance and Digby J. McLaren (eds.), (1990), *Planet Under Stress: The Challenge of Global Change,* Toronto: Oxford University Press.

Naar, John (1990), *Design for a Livable Planet: How You Can Help Clean Up the Planet,* New York: Harper and Row.

Rapoport, Anatol (1988), "The Possible Role of Universities in the Preservation of Peace", in Janis Alton et al., *The Name of the Chamber Was Peace,* Toronto and Fort Myers: Science for Peace, Samuel Stevens and Company: 1–18.

Ross, Virginia A. (1990), "Desert Restoration: The Role of Woody Legumes", in John J. Berger (ed.), *Environmental Restoration,* Washington: Island Press.

Saperstein, Alvin M. (1983), "In My Opinion...Physicists Should Teach About War", *The Physics Teacher,* 21: 470–471.

Schell, Jonathan (1982), *The Fate of the Earth,* New York: Avon.

Schumacher, E. F. (1975), *Small is Beautiful: Economics as if people mattered,* New York: Harper and Row, 1975.

Selby, David (1985), "Global Perspectives in Mathematics and Science Education: A Bibliography", *World Studies Journal,* 5 (4): 57–58.

Souchon, Christian (1985), "Some Thoughts on New Approaches to Science Education", *Prospects,* 15 (4), 1985: 535–540.

Stanley, William B. and Nancy W. Brickhouse (1994), "Multiculturalism, Universalism and Science Education", *Science Education,* Vol 78 (4), July, 1994: 387–398.

Sund, Robert B. and Leslie W. Trowbridge (1973), *Teaching Science by Inquiry in the Secondary School,* Second Edition, Columbus, Ohio: Charles E. Merrill.

Thelen, Leverne J. (1983), "Values and Valuing in Science", *Science Education,* 67 (2): 185–192.

Thelen, Leverne J. (1987), "Values Clarification: Science or Nonscience", *Science Education,* 71 (2): 201–192.

Wellington, J. J. (1983), "Science and Peace Education—big bang or damp squid?" *Physics Education,* 18: 122–3.

Wellington, Jerry (1985), "Issues in Nuclear Education", *World Studies Journal,* 5 (4): 38–43.

Williams, I. W. (1982), *Third World Science: Resource Materials for Science Teachers,* Bangor, Gwynedd: Centre for World Development Education, University College of North Wales.

CHAPTER 10

Music

TOWARDS THE END OF 1984, *the world suddenly became aware that several million people in Ethiopia and the Sudan were tragically on the verge of starvation. Because there had been no rain in a large region of Africa, farmlands and pastures were parched dry, devastating crops, killing cattle, and causing a famine of unprecedented proportions.*

The television news in countries around the world carried pictures of people shrunken from starvation, their arms and legs as thin as sticks, their eyes staring vacantly into space. Many victims suffered disease and sickness as a result of prolonged malnutrition. Thousands trudged slowly into towns and hastily assembled feeding centres in the hope of finding emergency food from their governments and from international agencies, but there were frequently only pitifully small supplies to go around, and hundreds were dying daily.

People the world over were deeply moved by the television images that so forcibly expressed the plight of their planetary neighbours, and wondered how a disaster could have developed to such a scale before the media had brought it to their attention. They responded immediately with donations through many channels, including the International Red Cross, UNICEF, World Vision and Oxfam. Among those who who felt a compulsion to help personally, as well as to rally public support for famine relief, was the pop singer Bob Geldof.

Geldof first thought of producing a record by himself and sending the proceeds for famine relief, but on testing the idea with other well-known recording artists in Britain, he quickly gathered their support for making a combined record called Band Aid. *Initially he had expected to raise $150,000, but the idea so caught the imagination of the public and the media, that over $12 million was raised in Britain. Spurred on by collective achievement, Geldof inspired the production of records in both Canada* (Northern Lights) *and in the United States* (U.S.A. for Africa), *which were corresponding successes.*

Slowly, out of these experiences, emerged the idea of a global event—"Live Aid". There would be five-hours of concert from London, and five hours from Philadelphia, with another five hours of alternation of acts from the two cities as a transition from one concert to the other. The two concerts would be linked by satellites and would be televised live to the whole world. At the same time, appeals for funds would be broadcast and telephone numbers given to allow viewers to pledge donations. It was indeed to be a global telethon.

Geldof, with teams of volunteers from various countries, led the organization that arranged the use of stadiums in the two cities, the vast and complex communications network, and the mammoth program of individual artists and pop groups. The concerts included Bob Dylan, Phil Collins, Stevie Wonder, Paul McCartney, Mick Jagger, David Bowie, Madonna, Kenny Rogers, Sting, Status Quo, Queen, U2, Wham!, Duran Duran and The Who—in all, more than 50 performers.

The first global concert and telethon in history, seen by an estimated two billion people, ran to schedule on July 13, 1985. Among the performers and the audience, there was a tremendous sense of excitement and warmth. The audience knew that this was a world concert and that it was a massive and concentrated effort to help the hapless victims of famine in Africa. Some of the songs that day, such as Feed the World, *were an eloquent and direct statement of the human predicament. Others, such as* All You Need Is Love *and* Every Breath You Take, *took on new and significant meanings in the context of famine. The final performance by Lionel Ritchie, who sang* We Are the World, *capped the essence of fellow-feeling and world consciousness. As a result of the concert, $100 million was raised worldwide to help Africa.*

The Live Aid concert showed us that music can be used to make us conscious of an acute international problem, as well as to develop an awareness of global togetherness in helping to respond to that problem. Since music is the art that perhaps touches the lives of people throughout the world more closely than any of the other arts, it has enormous potential as a vehicle for giving us pride in our individual cultures and also for helping us build a more unified world. Yet music has been used not only as a means of creating unity, but also as a means of engendering cultural and social conflict.

In this chapter, we will discuss music and song as a means of social criticism in our society. We will consider ways in which music can convey social values and ways in which it may help us to understand other cultures and develop world perspectives. Finally, we will discuss some therapeutic aspects of music and its contribution towards conflict resolution.

Songs of Social Criticism

Folk and popular music, more than classical music, tends to mirror the society in which it is created (Hamm, 1995). An examination of popular song in relation to political and social concerns over the past forty years shows a story directly reflecting political developments and expressing social criticism. "Some of these songs," writes B. Lee Cooper (1991: 172) "are highly philosophical, stressing universal concern over war, freedom, equality, brotherhood, love and justice." The intent of the artists is often to develop an awareness of the issues and to shape public attitudes. These goals may be achieved both through the words of the songs and through the feelings conveyed by the music.

During the period of the war in Vietnam, Bob Dylan wrote *Blowin' In The Wind,* which has become a classic song emphasizing our imperviousness to the lessons of war. In it, he evokes a number of images, including those of the cannonball and the dove, and he asks a series of questions that encourage the listener to reflect upon the catastrophe and futility of war. The version by Peter, Paul and Mary has alternating solo and choral singing with simple guitar accompaniment, and conveys a sombre and melancholic tone. At about the same time, Pete Seeger wrote a song having a very similar theme, *Where Have All The Flowers Gone?,* made popular by The Kingston Trio. The lyrics of this song speak of the vicious cycle of war, and the melody, through a series of descending phrases and haunting tones, engenders a feeling of sadness at our inability to learn from the past.

The theme of war continued as performers sought to address world tensions through the 1980s and early 1990s. An outspoken social critic, reggae musician Bob Marley wrote *So Much Trouble In The World.* This song makes a number of references to the weapons of war and to the tensions that exist between ordinary people and those who control the weapons. In this case, a positive message that solutions are possible through openness and negotiation is carried along by hopeful and inspiring music. In the song *Us And Them,* Pink Floyd expresses the view that young men are frequently coerced into war and are controlled at the front by senior officers who make their decisions safely from behind the lines. At the very beginning of the record, the sound of an organ comes in waves, prompting the listener to think of successive lines of soldiers moving forward in battle. Special effects of background talking and echoing add to the active narrative of the song, and the variable volume of the music conveys force and meaning of the anti-war message. The song *Russians,* by the British singer Sting, is one that speaks out specifically against nuclear warfare. Although the probability of nuclear catastrophe is not now felt to be as great since this song and others in the same mould were written, the recordings still carry valid messages. Sting's song emphasizes that the Russians and those in the West have far more in common with each other than they realize: "[T]he Russians love their children, too". The song is sung to the accompaniment of the strong, driving, deep notes of an organ. And at the end of it, there is the sound of a clock ticking, intimating that there is little time left to live, unless we renounce nuclear war.

The theme of war is addressed by U2, and invariably includes the message of hope for humankind. Their song *Sunday Bloody Sunday* conveys images of death and destruction in the aftermath of war. The music has the marching rhythm and drum beat of a military band, and cymbals are used like rapid-firing machine guns. While the song throughout is disjointed in its sound to convey the sense of defeat for all in war, it concludes with the message that the real battle is a spiritual one for the hearts and minds of men and women. Another of the group's songs, entitled *Seconds,* expresses the fragility of the world's peace, which can be shattered simply by the press of a button. There may be only seconds in which to say goodbye to loved-ones and friends. Drums and bass provide a relatively slow beat, and a minor key is used to emphasize the sadness and introspectiveness of the message.

In some songs, war is considered with its causal factors or with associated social problems. For example, *Children's Crusade,* by Sting, laments the betrayal of children and young people first in a system that sends men in the flower of their youth to die in the battlefields of war, and second in a system where youth become enslaved to drug addiction. Initial discordant notes in this song suggest death, and the many discords present throughout the song reinforce the message of betrayal. The song *War,* composed by Allan Cole and Carlton Barrett and sung by Bob Marley, links war and racism. Its essential message in free verse form is that, until racist beliefs and practices are eliminated, there will be no peace. Our dreams of a permanent peace, of the ability of all human beings to enjoy world citizenship, of rule based on an international morality will not be realized. The words in this song are enunciated slowly, and sung reflectively, backed by a strong bass beat and reggae rhythm.

There are songs that deal with yet other matters that undermine world peace. The satirical song *Money,* by Pink Floyd, runs through many of the luxuries that a rich person can afford, and describes the ideology of self-interest. It implies that there is an acquisitiveness and smugness in Western culture and further that its dominant philosophy of materialism and consumerism perpetuates the gap between the rich nations and the poor, a major tension in world affairs. Special effects of a cash register and the sound of coins enhance its message and the effective use of the saxophone and electric guitar suggest that our society is living life in the fast lane. The song *Crazy Baldhead,* by Bob Marley, is a protest against the colonialization of indigenous peoples. The words express a determination towards decolonization, and the music, which consists of a strong bass rhythm and a mixture of different percussion instruments, conveys momentum. The use of the kazoo, especially, suggests a rapidity of movement.

More recent music reflecting social discontent has focused on other areas. The Australian group Midnight Oil, in its album *Blue Sky Mining,* has produced songs critical of the destruction of the earth's forests, of the pollution caused by huge industrial and urban centres, and of environmental degradation generally. Environmental problems are linked to the continuing increase in the supply of material goods and to the values of the consumer society. It may well be that the popularity in the mid-1990s of Gregorian chant music such as that of the Gregorian Chorale of Eglise Querin reflects disenchantment with the materialism of the lifestyle of the consumer society. The songs of other artist-critics have tended to focus upon a variety of social tensions. For example, the Haitian group the Fugees (short for refugees), in their album *The Beast,* are critical of police brutality. British singer Sting decries the lack of gun control. Irish singer Christy Moore sings of injustice and civil rights. American artist Ani DeFranco sings about such social issues as abortion, capital punishment and sexual identity.

As these examples illustrate, songs of protest and criticism may be drawn from the larger arena of world affairs, or they may reflect national or local issues, in which case they help to bring the criticism of our society even closer to home. Examples of social criticism in music can serve as an excellent springboard for research and discussion and can be linked effectively to other subjects such as the social studies and moral and religious education.

Teaching the Appreciation of Values in Music and Song

Every piece of music upholds a value or a cluster of values. Music which embodies the things that are important to us is usually the music that has more lasting popularity. Students enjoy identifying and articulating values in songs and are able to reflect seriously on values that promote peace-making and peace-building. In this section, we will examine some examples of songs that convey explicit values both through their lyrics and through the special quality of their music.

Let us consider initially examples of the values of sorrow and joy. In Karen Carpenter's version of Lennon and McCartney's *Ticket to Ride*, sorrow is expressed as a result of the severing of a relationship between two people who had loved each other. The tone of the singer's voice and the dirge-like accompaniment—which includes, at one point, the tolling of a bell—both support the sorrow of the song. By contrast, A. Podell's *Everybody Loves Saturday Night*, as sung by the New Christy Minstrels, is a song of unfettered joy. Its theme of fun on Saturday night is given first in English, then in Spanish, German, Italian and Hawaiian versions. Each verse is sung as a solo to the accompaniment of rhythmic instruments, including the banjo and tambourine, and is followed by a choral affirmation of joy. Reflection upon contrasting songs like these might well lead listeners to investigate how we might respond to emotions such as sorrow in others.

A second pair of values that relate closely to peace are those of belligerence and friendliness. Aggression and violence are reflected in the Sex Pistols' song, *Anarchy in the U.K.* The words reveal that the singer is an anarchist, bent on destruction. The punk rock music is noisy and monotonous and contains high-pitched chords that tend to heighten nervousness in the listener. At a different level, John Williams' *Imperial Attack,* from the motion picture *Star Wars,* includes a trumpet call to military action, a quickening tempo of music

that suggests the assembly of forces, followed by heavy drums simulating a military march, and finally staccato and dissonant music to accompany a battle in space. At the other pole of values are numerous songs that advocate friendship, kindness and caring. Three such examples are *Lean on Me* (B. Withers), *Stand by Me* (B. King and E. Glick) and *With a Little Help From My Friends* (J. Lennon and P. McCartney). All three emphasize being able to depend upon a valued and faithful friend to help in times of trouble. In each case, the music that interprets the words is appropriately constant, rhythmic and predictable.

A third pair of values that can be considered in relation to peace-building are those of indifference and compassion. The manifestation of these values has much to do with our ability to identify with others, particularly those who have some physical, psychological or spiritual need. The Sex Pistols' *No Feelings* expresses self-centredness; the singer declares repeatedly that he has no emotions for others. The musical accompaniment is a combination of guitar, drums and bass, which thump along together in a dominantly monotone melody. That song throws into stark contrast Nicholas Ashford and Valerie Simpson's *Reach Out and Touch Somebody's Hand.* The lyrics here offer a series of imperatives to give encouragement to those who are lonely or lost. In the rendition by Dana, on the album *Everything Is Beautiful,* bass and drums are used to provide a lively rhythm to the melody, and the chorale back-up reinforces the message of the solo singer.

Finally, let us consider the values of despair and hope, which are important in that they provide a broad mental set, or framework, for other kinds of decisions and actions. Despair is illustrated well in *I Just Don't Know What to Do with Myself,* composed by B. Bacharach and H. David and sung by Dionne Warwick.

This song tells of a break-down of a loving human relationship and the words express feelings of total dejection. The variable beat of the music and the vocal interpretation emphasize deep emotional loss and discouragement. Songs that express hope and renewal, however, are more numerous. In George Harrison's *Here Comes the Sun,* a series of images presents the transition from winter to spring and summer to express optimism and rebirth. The quick tempo of the music provided by guitar, bass and drums conveys reassurance and bright prospects. The theme of hope is the basis, too, of Cat Stevens' recording of *Morning has Broken.* This song speaks of seeing our surroundings with a freshness that recalls the first morning of creation in the Garden of Eden. The music is simple, involving a guitar with piano embellishments, and there is a choral backing for the last verse. Throughout the melody, phrases rise expectantly and hopefully, giving additional meaning to the words.

The examples given above constitute a small sample of the possibilities for considering values within music. Teachers and students will want to build their own repertories from songs and music familiar to them. However, as LeCroy (1992) has pointed out, quite apart from the lyrics and content of music, the methods employed by music teachers, especially those in group activities, have the potential to build a range of other values including self-esteem, tolerance and integrity.

Music and Intercultural Education

Studying the music of other cultures can make an exceptionally significant contribution to education for peace. Recorded music from other countries is becoming widely available and educational literature on music and cross-cultural understanding is growing rapidly. It is increasingly feasible for music specialists to integrate world music into their courses of study and to design programs that have special appeal to the cultural backgrounds and contexts of their students.

The music of other cultures may be studied at several different levels. At the first level, we may listen to it simply because we like it. Some patterns such as calypso from the Caribbean, rumba from Latin America, or gypsy music from Europe may already be partly familiar to some young people. But our students may also enjoy popular, or more traditional music, from Africa, the Middle East, Asia and other parts of the world, and gradually recognize that people everywhere create music, albeit in many varied forms and with instruments that are peculiarly their own.

At a second level, we may listen to the music of other people not for enjoyment alone, but as a serious effort to understand those people and their culture. In this respect, like the visual arts, music is a key to understanding the heart and the soul of a human society. In our multicultural cities, it may help us to appreciate one another's ethnic backgrounds better and, by contributing to a climate of mutual valuing, help in the bonding of larger communities. From there, it is only a small step to appreciate cultures in distant parts of the globe and the parallel building of global human society.

How, specifically, can music help us to understand better other societies that appear to differ from ours in so many ways? To answer that question, we need to have some systematic knowledge about the kind of people who live in the other country, their social and political organization, their language, their geographical environment, their natural resources, their occupations, the nature and development of their technology and other components of their culture. When we know something of these elements, we can ask, how is the music an expression of cultural lifestyles? How is it a manifestation of social values? How may it reveal some of the important social and political issues of that society? The music and songs may, in turn, lead to a deeper identification with that human community on the part of the learner. As an example of a way in which we can use music for inter-cultural education, let us consider the traditional music of the country of South Africa.

The Republic of South Africa occupies the southern tip of the African continent. Most of the land consists of broad, flat plateaus which are separated by mountains from a narrow coastal strip. The eastern plateaus are high and fertile and include much of the cultivated farmland. The central northern area is less fertile and is covered by vast grasslands used for cattle grazing. The western plateaus are dry and include, in the northwest, the Kalahari Desert. Apart from four major ports in the coastal area, the major urban areas are in the central and northeastern part of the country.

About four-fifths of the population of 30 million is made up of indigenous peoples, including groups of Zulus, Basutos, Xhosas and Pondos. There are some South Africans of Asian descent, but most of the remainder of the population is made up of white people. Many of this group have descended from Europeans who began colonizing South Africa from the seventeenth century onwards. Although the white population was a minority, it controlled government until 1994, promoting a policy of apartheid, or separate development of the races. About one third of all indigenous peoples lived on tracts of relatively poor rural land set aside for them by the government; about another third worked on farms owned by whites; and the remainder,

who worked in factories and mines or in other occupations, lived in designated parts of cities and towns reserved for them.

Many of the songs still sung today recall the history of the people of South Africa. *Zenizenabo* (Jonas Gwangwa and E. John Miller) and *Swazi Warriors* (Adolf Wood and Stanley Glasser) are war chants recalling old tribal feuds; *Ayababona Abelcingu* (Delisa Sibaya) is a song of the Anglo-Zulu wars; *A Piece of Ground* (J. Taylor) is a ballad that tells the story of South Africa as a struggle for the land and its resources and the domination of indigenous peoples by white settlers. Many of the traditional songs reflect ways of living that indigenous peoples had known before colonization and urbanization.

Traditional musical instruments are made from materials in the environment. Trumpets are made from the horns of such animals as the gazelle. The umqunge, or bow, is constructed from wood and string: one end may be held in the mouth as a resonator while the other end is flexed to alter the tautness of the string to allow for different vibrations. Drums are fashioned from wooden cylinders and the stretched skins of animals pulled tight by leather thongs. The materials and methods of building instruments have changed with time, but have always directly reflected the resources and technology of the culture.

The music of the majority people of South Africa has been woven around their occupations and lifestyles. Since many people are engaged in herding and pasturing animals, some of the music is associated with the tending of cattle, and with life in the grasslands. The book *Songs of Southern Africa* (Wood and Glasser, 1968) includes *Herd Boy*, which tells simply of the work of a young man who tends his father's cattle, and *Rain*, which describes the joy of seeing rain fall upon dry pastures.

The strategy of hunting a young impala is the theme of the song *Leopard.*

Tribal life in South Africa traditionally centred on the kraal, a cluster of mud huts that look like baskets that have been turned upside-down. Certain songs reflect the quality of life in and around such communities. In her book *World of African Song,* Miriam Makeba (1971: 74, 41, 98) includes such numbers as *Qhude,* which is about a daughter-in-law wakened by the shrill crowing of a cock at dawn and called to fetch water for the household; *Ngoma Kurila,* the lament of a mother who tries to comfort her hungry baby, perhaps in a time of famine; *Olili,* the song of a mother who lulls her child to sleep; and *Qongqothwane,* a nonsense ditty for children about an earth-beetle often seen by youngsters playing in the fields.

Some of the traditional folk songs deal with the theme of flirtation and love among young men and women. In *Listen, You Men!* (Wood and Glasser, 1968: 87), eligible girls, who liken themselves to young wild berries that may soon grow old, call out to prospective boy-friends to notice them. A converse situation exists in the song *Pumpkin,* in which a boy, seeing a girl cooking pumpkin, asks if he can have some when it's ready, but then actually confesses that he would rather have a kiss than eat the pumpkin (Wood and Glasser: 93). In another song, entitled *Nomthini* (Makeba, 1971: 56), a young man yearns to see a beautiful young woman who lives beyond the mountain, and only wishes that he had wings to fly him there. The themes of these and other love songs in South Africa may well be universal.

As South Africa is a major producer of gold, diamonds, uranium, nickel, copper and other minerals, large numbers of men work deep underground in the mines. *The Gold Is Waiting* (Wood and Glasser: 42) describes the drilling, fusing, shovelling and other work done by Zulu, Shangaan and Basuto miners. In another song, entitled *Gold Miner* (Wood and Glasser: 44), a man refers to the iron cage that takes him underground. The cage seems to be a symbol of the confining nature of his toil, but he feels that all the dust and backbreaking work is worthwhile if his loved-one back home is still waiting for him.

By far the largest number of indigenous peoples who live in or near towns or cities are employed in various types of commerce and industry. A great variety of music has developed about urban life dealing with themes such as work, shopping, leisure and recreation, celebrations and the disparity between the rich and the poor. The human dimension of urban living is found in such songs as *Stones Are Very Hard to Break* (Wood and Glasser: 41) in which a quarry worker reminisces about the tranquillity of the countryside. It is also found in *Woza* (Makeba: 68), a Zulu lament about an urban couple, who, in spite of trials and difficulties, are determined to be hopeful and optimistic.

Besides the songs that convey the quality of everyday life, there are those that criticize the political relationship that existed between the whites and the non-whites in South Africa. One such song, *Ntyilo-Ntyilo,* (Makeba: 36), played softly and delicately, tells of a bird singing from a bush, but as the listener draws nearer, he hears the real message of the bird: "There is trouble in the land." *Mayibuye* (Makeba: 91) is a more direct criticism of apartheid. Recollecting the words of a former king, who warned of the dangers of colonialism, and the anguish of generations who lived under apartheid, this song was a call to united action for freedom. It draws the listener to reflect upon the relationship between justice and peace.

Another anti-apartheid activist and singer, Vusi Mahlasela, wrote songs and poems reflecting the pain and suffering of oppressed South Africans.

With the transition from apartheid to democratic rule in 1995, popular music in South Africa has expressed a great sense of rejoicing and celebration as well as hopes and dreams for future development. Themes of some recent albums include "Let's Develop Peace" (Ladysmith Black Mambazo), "Eyes on Tomorrow" (Miriam Makeba), "Jump and Live" (The Soul Brothers) and "Wisdom of Forgiveness" (Vusi Mahlasela). The songs in albums such as these emphasize exuberance and joy; the oneness, rather than the separateness, of the people of South Africa; calmness and controlled purposefulness in effecting change, hope and peace.

These examples of music in South Africa are intended to show how music reflects the culture of another society and the way in which it can be a very meaningful point of entry into other cultures, helping us to understand their history and society. More importantly, it can help us to understand our common humanity with people who at first appear to be different, but who have the same fears, loves, anxieties and hopes as ourselves.

Music and World Perspectives

Some songs promote love and the building of trust between people as the means for developing a more united world. *One Love/People Get Ready* by Bob Marley and the Wailers cleverly interweaves solo and chorale singing to emphasize the need for one love, one heart and togetherness among the earth's peoples. A similar theme is contained in the song, *Citizens of the World* (by J. Morali, H. Belolo and V.

Willis) which is sung by the Village People. With the aid of electronic drums and background trumpets, they declare the message that by learning to love and trust, people will indeed become world citizens.

A second factor associated with human unity is tolerance of differences. Ray Stevens' *Everything Is Beautiful,* sung by Dana, tells us that external differences of skin colour and length of hair are really of little consequence, but that all people are beautiful in their own way. The music, with heavy rhythmic drums and bass, plus trumpet embellishments and choral back-up, gradually builds throughout the song and reinforces the idea that it is our internalized values and attitudes that are really important.

Recognizing the value of contributions to humankind from every part of the world is a third factor adding to a sense of global unity. *It's a Small World,* written by Richard and Robert Sherman and sung by Bob McGrath, uses primarily drums, piano and xylophone to accompany the words of the song. When references are made to particular parts of the world, musical instruments from those parts are used, including the Irish flute and several Chinese instruments. When the chorus assumes the melody towards the end of the song, all the instruments participate, thus reinforcing the verbal message of the song.

A fourth factor promoting human unity is the building of harmony by blending various unique contributions. In Bob McGrath's version of *I'd Like to Teach the World to Sing* (B. Backer, B. Davis, R. Cook and R. Greenaway), a number of poetic symbols are used to convey the idea that the whole world could be unified. A sense of global participation is achieved simultaneously by the gradual addition of musical accompaniment—drums, banjo, triangle, bass, piano, harmonica and tambourine—and by an increasingly complex harmony of an ecstatic children's chorus.

Finally, some songs advocate having a vision of the future in which we are all consciously aware that we are members of a unified human family. The song *Aquarius* (Ronald Dyson and Company), from the musical *Hair*, is a rock hymn in which the singers mystically call forth their vision of a planet guided by peace. John Lennon's *Imagine* is a reverie, in fittingly slow musical tempo, of a world in which there is neither greed nor hunger, one in which people share what they have, and live as one.

In recent years, there has been a trend towards what is invariably described as "world music". The trend reflects the increasing popularity of musicians who travel and perform across international boundaries, and also the international collaboration of musicians from different musical traditions (Gardinier, 1991).

In the streets and subways of many North American cities, small crowds gather around groups of native South American musicians. Performers such as Kassav (from the Caribbean), Ofra Haza (Israel), the Sabri Brothers (Pakistan), Johnny Clegg (South Africa) and The Gipsy Kings (France) have achieved international success performing music from their own traditions, and in some cases, from other traditions beyond their own cultural frontiers.

Artists such as Paul Simon and Peter Gabriel have played together with African, Indian and Latin American musicians, creating a new blending of sounds and a new dynamic in music. Paul Simon's album, *Graceland*, resulting from collaboration with South African musicians, helped a number of artists from other countries develop exposure to international audiences.

World music has developed because artists everywhere have found a need to widen their horizons and to experiment with new musical textures. Both the musicians and their followers have shown a real desire to learn the music of other cultures. This kind of blending of music across cultural boundaries — the interpenetration of musical traditions — is creating a new set of perspectives in music, bringing together people who before were strangers, rivals or antagonists.

Music, Therapy and Conflict Resolution

Music can contribute to education for peace both through its therapeutic qualities and, like the other arts, as a medium of creativity. As children grow up, especially through the critical period of adolescence, they experience rapid changes in their personal and social relations and are often faced with difficult social and emotional problems. At this stage, as well as throughout later life, music can provide a means of emotional release.

Murdock (1987: 120–126) provides some exercises in guided imagery which, in part, use music to remove stress and help children relax. In one such exercise, the students are asked to close their eyes and relax through deep breathing. They are then asked to imagine walking through a forest, and eventually to come across a house, which they enter. The house contains a room of mirrors and the students begin to dance to music, watching the movements of their own mirrored reflections. It is suggested that the teacher might play "Spring" from Vivaldi's *The Four Seasons* to assist students in mentally visualizing their dance. Such exercises, combining physical relaxation with visual imagery and music, can help to cultivate an inner peace.

There are, as well, a variety of commercial recordings that use music to help relieve stress. Such productions as Bloomfield and Vessette's *Relieve Tension and Anxiety* (1986) or Jim Oliver's *Healing Harmonies* (1993) use a combination of music, deep breathing and mental imagery to relieve stress. The music may use soothing chimes, soft flute and piano to enhance the exercises, which are designed to bring the listener into a state of calmness and serenity.

The effective fusion of intellect and emotions through music is illustrated in the work of Enigma II, each of their selections being an inward journey towards reconciliation. In their song *Return to Innocence* they take a number of apparently contradictory concepts, such as weakness and strength or sadness and laughter, and stimulate the listeners to turn towards their inner selves to discover that the concepts are not opposites, but different facets of each other.

Although we are not considering here the practice of professional music therapists, it is widely recognized that music also has value in helping to mitigate certain personal problems. Young people often find themselves in may different kinds of predicaments: loneliness, ridicule, embarrassment, discouragement, homesickness, shyness and the like. The songs of contemporary popular musicians often deal with such problems. Discouragement is the theme in Peter Gabriel's *Don't Give Up;* rejection in Tiffany's *Could've Been;* and personal abuse in Pat Benatar's *Hell Is for Children.* Although songs such as these will not solve problems, they may help individuals to recognize and release feelings by letting them know that others, too, have been in similar situations.

While it is generally accepted that music has therapeutic value at the individual level, less attention has been paid to the relationship between peace and creativity. Menuhin (1969: 167–70) asserts that the denial of the spontaneous creative impulse is regrettably a part of the ethos of our civilization. Such denial is exploited by the commercial world which tries to substitute new fashions in clothes, changing hairstyles, new models of cars, "in" books, "top of the pops" music, and other institutional modes of creativity for the exercise of our individual, naturally creative powers. "It is almost," he writes, "as if we were deliberately making life intolerably frustrating only to further the sale of appeasers and narcotics to forget and to escape, at a price." Optimizing individual creativity through many different channels, including music, helps to reduce frustrations and allows us more fully to exercise our capabilities. It can be argued that creative individuals make a creative society, one that is better able to solve its problems at all levels.

While music can provide young people with a means of resolving conflict within themselves, it may also be a channel for exploring the resolution of social tensions. Traditional ballads from many lands unfold stories of inter-personal and inter-group conflict. *Barbara Allen,* the most popular traditional ballad of the western world, is the story of a man who has slighted the beautiful Barbara Allen, but seeks her love as he is lying on his death bed. He sends a servant to the town to fetch Barbara Allen to his bedside. When she arrives, she cannot find it within herself to forgive him. The man dies. Barbara Allen, recognizing her hard-heartedness, then dies of her grief for him. The two are symbolically reconciled after death as a rose grows from his grave and a briar from hers, the two climbing an old wall and weaving themselves into a lover's knot. It can be interesting for students to extract their own meanings from traditional and contemporary ballads as a way of heightening their sensitivity to conflict and its resolution.

A more participatory mode of understanding conflict through music is through the composition of lyrics and music by the students themselves. A number of authors (Bland, 1993; Ames, 1993; and Speake, 1993) advocate having students create an opera as a highly collaborative artistic form. The exercise involves finding a meaningful story concept— perhaps one current in the newspaper—and developing an event sequence, involving the setting of the story, rising action and conflict, climax and its resolution; and then setting music and scenery to the dialogue. In contrast to a great deal of music teaching that is controlled by the music educator, the building of an opera is a team effort among students, each contributing in a specialized way to the whole production. The learning system itself, as well as the content of the opera, may help the student reflect upon and internalize significant values.

Summary

Music can become an important vehicle for peace because of its pervasiveness in our society. It can be studied as a channel of social criticism and as a window upon other cultures. By focusing on blends of different national musics, it can provide insights into international and world perspectives. At the personal level, music can be a means of reducing stress as well as mitigating problems that are often experienced by young people. Further, musical improvisation and composition can help individuals develop their creative potential and recognize the value of a society where creativity, rather than escapism or destruction, is the dominant value.

REFERENCES AND SOURCES

Ames, Roger (1993), "Collaborating to Build an Opera Ensemble", *Music Educators Journal,* February, 1993: 31–34.

Anderson, William and Patricia Shehan (eds.), (1989), *Multicultural Perspectives in Music Education.*

Bessom Malcolm E., Alphonse M. Tatarunis and Samuel L. Fortucci (1980), *Teaching Music in Today's Secondary Schools: A Creative Approach to Contemporary Music Education,* Montreal: Holt, Rinehart and Winston.

Bland, Anita (1993), "Original Opera in Middle School", *Music Educators Journal,* February, 1993: 27–30.

Blaukopf, Charles (1983), "National Identity and Universalism in Music," *The International Journal of Music Education,* 1 (1): 38–40.

Boyer-White, René (1988), "Reflecting Cultural Diversity in the Music Classroom", *Music Educators Journal,* December, 1988: 50–54.

Breskin, David with Cheryl McCall and Robert Hilburn (1985), *We Are The World,* New York: Putnam and Toronto: General Publishing.

Cooper, B. Lee (1991), *Popular Music Perspectives: Ideas, Themes and Patterns in Contemporary Lyrics,* Bowling Green, Ohio: Bowling Green State University Popular Press.

Cruickshank, John (1981), *Values Through Song,* Toronto: Berandol Music.

Dennislow, Candida (1994), "Southern Cycles: Rhythms and Melody of Indian Music", *Music Teacher,* January, 1994: 12–13.

Delaunay, Charles (1983), "Jazz and World Culture," *The International Journal of Music Education,* 1 (1): 41–48.

Dobbs, Jack P. B (1992), "Music as Multicultural Education", in Patricia A. Richard-Amato and Marguerite Ann Snow, *The Multicultural Classroom: Readings for Content Areas,* New York: Longman.

Fara, Frank, (1992), "The Saga of Diamondfield Jack", in *Songs of the Trail,* Fullerton, California: Centerstream Publishing.

Gardinier, Alain (1991), "'World Music' or sounds of the times", *The UNESCO Courier,* March 1991: 37–39.

Geldof, Bob (1987), *Is That It?* Harmondsworth, Middlesex, Penguin Books.

Gonzo, Carroll (1993), "Multicultural Issues in Music Education", *Music Educators Journal,* February, 1993: 49–52.

Griffin, John (1988), "Sting: Rock 'n' human rights," *The Gazette,* Montreal, February 12, 1988, p. C1.

Griffin, John (1988), "Rock 'n rollers give peace a chance," *The Gazette* Montreal, June 4, 1988: D1.

Hamm, Charles (1995), *Putting Popular Music in Its Place,* Cambridge: Cambridge University Press.

Kabalevsky, Dmitri (1987), *A Composer Writes about Music Education,* Paris: UNESCO.

Kaptainis, Arthur (1988), "Hands Across the Water: The World Philharmonic Orchestra," *The Gazette,* December 10, 1988: E–1.

Lai, T. C. and Robert Mok (1985), *Jade Flute: The Story of Chinese Music,* New York: Schocken Books.

LeCroy, Hoyt F. (1992), "Imparting Values: A Challenge for Educators", *Music Educators Journal,* September, 1992: 33–36.

Lingerman, Hal A. (1983), *The Healing Energies of Music,* London: The Theosophical Publishing House.

Makeba, Miriam (1971), *The World of African Song,* Chicago: Quadrangle Books.

McAllester, David P. (1983), "Music as Ecumenical Force," *The International Journal of Music Education,* 1 (1): 19–23.

Menuhin, Yehudi (1969), "Music and the nature of its contribution to humanity," in *The Arts and Man,* Paris: UNESCO and Englewood Cliffs: Prentice Hall: 153–170.

Moore, Gillian (1992), "Gaining Access: The Value of World Music in the Classroom", *Music Teacher,* June, 1992: 34–35.

Murdock, Maureen (1987), *Spinning Inwards: Using Guided Imagery with Children for Learning Creativity and Relaxation,* Boston: Shambhala.

Peggie, Andrew (1994), "Music: *Halal* or Haram" ("The difficulties of teaching music in a multiracial school"), *Music Teacher,* June, 1994: 10–11.

Peterson, J. W. (1983), *Great Hymns of the Faith* , Grand Rapids, Michigan: Singspiration Music of the Zondervan Corporation.

Reck, David (1977), *Music of the Whole Earth,* New York: Charles Scribner's Sons.

Sarath, Edward (1993), "Improvisation for Global Musicianship", *Music Educators Journal,* September, 1993: 23–26.

Shehan, Patricia K. (1988), "World Musics: Windows to Cross-cultural Understanding," *Music Educators Journal,* November, 1988: 23–26.

Sheftel, Paul (1986), *Folk Songs from Around the World,* Sherman Oaks, California: Alfred Publishing.

Speake, Constance J. (1993), "Create an Opera with Elementary Students", *Music Educators Journal,* February, 1993: 22–26.

Standifer, James (1986), "Everyday Music in a Chinese Province," *Music Educators Journal,* 73, November 3, 1986: 32–39.

Wood, Adolf and Stanley Glasser (1968), *Songs of Southern Africa,* London: Essex Music Limited.

Yudkin, Jacqueline (1993), "Choosing Pluralism or Particularism", *Music Educators Journal,* April, 1993: 46–48.

References to Records (R) , Cassettes (C) and Compact Disks (CD)

Artists Collection, *Serene and Uplifting Instrumental Music,* The Relaxation Company, (C) 3215.

Ashford, Nicholas and Valerie Simpson, "Reach Out And Touch Somebody's Hand", *Dana: Everything Is Beautiful,* Warwick Records, (C) WW4 5099.

Bacharach B. and H. David, "I Just Don't Know What To Do With Myself", *Dionne Warwick: Here Where There Is Love,* Scepter Records, (R) SPS 555.

Backer, B., B. Davis, R. Cook and R. Greenaway, "I'd Like To Teach The World To Sing", *Bob McGrath Sings for All the Boys and Girls,* Disneyland Records (R) 1357.

Barry, John, *Dances with Wolves,* Epic Associated, (CD) ZK 46982.

Blaisch, L. "Could've Been", *The Video Hits Album 2,* CBS Direct, (C) DMBT 116.

Bloomfield, Harold and Sarah Vitesse, *Relieve Tension and Anxiety,* Fullerton, California, Tape Data Media, Inc. 1986 (C).

Clegg, Johnny and Savuka, *In My African Dreams,* EMI Records, (CD) E2 7243 8 30073 25.

Clegg, Johnny and Savuka, *Cruel, Crazy, Beautiful World,* Capitol, (CD) CDP 7 93446 2.

Cole, Allan and Carlton Barrett, "War", *Rastaman Vibration,* Island Records, (R) ISM 9383.

Dylan, Bob, "Blowin' in the Wind" *The Best of Peter, Paul and Mary,* Warner Bros Records (R) 2552.

Dyson, Ronald and Company, "Aquarius", *Hair: The American Tribal Love-Rock Musical,* RCA Victor (R) LSO 1150.

Enigma, *Enigma I,* Virgin Records, (CD) V2 0777 7 86224 2 0.

Enigma, *Enigma II,* Virgin Records, (CD) V2 7243 8 392 36 25.

Gabriel, Peter, "Don't Give Up", *So,* Geffen Records, (CD) CD 24088.

Gabriel, Peter, *Shaking the Tree,* Geffen Records, (CD) GEFSD 24326.

Goldsmith, Jerry, *Schwarzenegger: Total Recall,* Varese Sarabande, Inc., (CD) VSD 5267.

Grammer, Red, *Teaching Peace,* The Children's Group Inc. (C) SAN 1015.

Gregorian Chorale of Eglise Querin, *The Inspiration of Gregorian Chant,* Medacy Music Group Inc., (CD) MSB-2-8705-2.

Harrison, George, "Here Comes The Sun", *The Beatles 1967–1970,* Capitol Records, (R) SKBO 3404.

Hill, Richard, "He's Got The Whole World In His Hands", *Dana: Everything is Beautiful,* Warwick Records (C) WW4 5099.

Kaleefah, *Listen to the World,* KC Records, (CD) KCD 1001.

Kamen, Michael, *Robin Hood: Prince of Thieves,* Polydor, (CD) 511050-2.

King, B. and E. Glick, "Stand By Me", *The California Raisins,* A & M Records (R) SP 9505.

Ladysmith Black Mambazo, *Let's Develop Peace,* Shanachie (CD) 64064.

Lennon, John, "Imagine", *Imagine,* Capital Records (CD) CDP 7 908032.

Lennon, John and Paul McCartney, "Ticket to Ride", on *Carpenters: The Singles 1969–1973,* A & M Records (C) CS 3601.

Lennon, John and Paul McCartney, "With A Little Help From My Friends", *Sgt. Pepper's Lonely Hearts Club Band,* EMI Records, (R) CDP 7 4644 2.

Mahlasela, Vusi, *When You Came Back,* Indigo, (CD) LBL 2505.

Mahlasela, Vusi, *Wisdom of Forgiveness,* Indigo, (CD) LBL 2518.

Makeba, Miriam, "Qonggothwane (The Click Song)", *Country Girl,* Sono Disc, (CD) CD 6518.

Makeba, Miriam, *Pata Pata,* Sono Disc, (CD) CD 6508.

Makeba, Miriam, *Eyes on Tomorrow,* Polydor, (CD) 849 313-2.

Marley, Bob, "So Much Trouble In The World", *Survival,* Island Records (R) ISM 9542.

Marley, Bob, "Crazy Baldhead", *Rastaman Vibration,* Island Records, (R) ISM 9383.

Midnight Oil, *Blue Sky Mining,* Columbia (CD) CK 45398.

Midnight Oil, *Earth and Sun and Moon,* Columbia (CD) CK 53793.

Morali, J., H. Belolo and V. Willis, "Citizens Of The World" *Village People Go West,* Can't Stop Productions, (R) NBLP 7144.

Oliver, Jim, *Music for Relaxation: Sound Therapy,* Vital Body Marketing, (C) 9582.

Oliver, Jim, *Healing Harmonies: Music Composed to Balance and Soothe,* The Relaxation Company, (C) 3205.

Pink Floyd, "Us And Them", *The Dark Side of the Moon,* (R) SMAS 11163.

Pink Floyd, "Money", *The Dark Side of the Moon,* (R) SMAS 11163.

Podell, A, "Everybody Loves Saturday Night", *Greatest Hits of the New Christy Minstrels,* (R) CS 9279.

Schwartz, E. "Hell Is for Children", *Pat Benatar: Courses of Passion,* Chrysalis Records, (R) CHE 1275.

Seeger, Pete, "Where Have All The Flowers Gone?" *The Best of the Kingston Trio,* Capitol Records, (R) ST 8-1705.

Sex Pistols, "Anarchy in the U.K.", *Never Mind the Bollocks,* Warner Bros. Records, (R) KBS 3147.

Sex Pistols, "No Feelings", *Never Mind the Bollocks,* Warner Bros. Records, (R) KBS 3147.

Sherman, Richard and Robert Sherman, "It's a Small World", *Bob McGrath Sings for All the Boys and Girls,* Disneyland Records, (R) 1357.

Sibaya, Delisa, "Ayababona Abelcingu", *Zulu Songs from South Africa,* Lyrichord Stereo (R) LLST 7401.

Simon, Paul, *Graceland,* Warner Bros, (CD) CD 2544/.

Songwriters and Artists For the Earth, *Put On Your Green Shoes,* Sony Kids' Music, (C) LT 53832.

Soul Brothers, *Jump and Live,* Earthworks, (CD) STEW33CD.

Springsteen, Bruce, *Chimes of Freedom,* Columbia Records, (CD) CEPK 44445.

Stevens, Cat, "Morning has Broken", *Cat Stevens Greatest Hits,* A & M Records, (CD) DIDX -63, CD 4519.

Stevens, Ray, "Everything Is Beautiful", *Dana: Everything Is Beautiful,* Warwick Records (C) WW4 5099.

Sting, "Russians", *The Dream of the Blue Turtles,* A & M Records, (C) CS 3750, and (CD) CD 3750.

Sting, "Children's Crusade", *The Dream of the Blue Turtles,* A & M Records, (C) CS 3750, and (CD) CD 3750.

Sting, *Nothing Like the Sun,* A & M Records, (CD) CD 6402/DX 2163.

Taylor, J, "A Piece Of Ground", *Miriam Makeba: Pata Pata,* Reprise (R) 6274.

U2, "Sunday, Bloody Sunday " *War,* Island Records (R) ISL 67.

U2, "Seconds", *War,* Island Records (R) ISL 67.

Various Artists, *The Best of Both Worlds,* Rykodisc, (CD) RCD 30298.

Various Artists, *Best of the World,* Declic Communications, (CD) 171001.

Various Artists, *Drums of the World,* Playasound, (CD) PS 6001.

Various Artists, *Global Celebration Gatherings: Authentic Music from Joyous Festivals Around the World,* Ellipsis Arts, (CD) CD 3234.

Various Artists, *Global Celebration Passages: Authentic Music from Around the World Celebrating Life's Turning Points,* Ellipsis Arts, (CD) CD 3233.

Various Artists, *National Anthems of the World,* Madacy Records, Inc. (C) LXC 6919, P.O. Box 550, Town of Mount Royal, Quebec, H3P 3C7.

Various Artists, *Planet Africa,* Charly Records, (CD) CD INS 5057.

Various Artists, *Plus From Us,* Real World, (CD) V2 0777 7 58 28.

Williams, John, "Imperial Attack", *Star Wars,* Musicor Records, (R) MUS 8801.

Williams, John, *The Star Wars Trilogy: Return of the Jedi, The Empire Strikes Back, Star Wars,* The Utah Symphony Orchestra, Varese Sarabande Records, Inc. (CD) VCD 47201.

Withers, B., "Lean On Me", *The California Raisins,* A & M Records (R) SP 9505.

CHAPTER 11

Art

NOT LONG AGO, *a farmer in the mid-western United States cleverly designed one of his fields close to a major airport as a still-life art picture. One could not discern much from the ground, but from the air, passengers could see a beautiful bowl of fruit, including oranges, apples and bananas.*

The farmer had outlined the fruits and planted a different crop for each one. For the apples, he planted a cover crop of red clover, which turned from green to a rosy colour when it flowered. For the bananas, he planted mustard, which blossomed as a bright yellow. Other crops were planted to represent the various fruits in the bowl.

Some of the airline passengers who saw this unusual creation may have been inspired by the beauty of the form and colour of the fruit, and they may have reflected upon the bounty of the earth's harvest. Others may have thought of the originality of this form of art and of the imagination of the artist as he planned and executed the many different steps involved in bringing his project to completion.

In a discussion of this project, a group of high-school students responded in a number of different ways. Some thought of the motive of the farmer-artist, who clearly wanted to share freely the product of his mind and his labours. Some compared the large-scale picture with small-scale flower patterns that they had seen in parks and gardens. Some made a link between the bright apples in the field with apples that are displayed in food stores; they are so attractive, yet they are often produced with poisonous insecticides that destroy the natural ecology of the environment. Others were reminded that bananas are often produced on plantations developed by wealthy landowners on land assembled from smaller farms, leaving dispossessed peasants trapped in poverty.

The discussion of this unusual form of art began with its uniqueness, but led to more general questions of bringing joy to the lives of others, the balance of nature and the quality of the environment, and fundamental social justice. In this chapter, we will explore some of the ways in which many different kinds of art, conventional and non-conventional, may contribute to the building of international understanding and peace. We will examine the relationship between peace and art in our environment; the developing of an awareness of values in art; the appreciation of art from different cultures; the relationship between art, creativity and conflict resolution; and, finally, the teaching of art for global perspectives.

Studying Art in the Environment

In virtually every community there are works of art in prominent places for the public to appreciate: statues in squares, gardens and parks; art objects adorning the outside of modern buildings; figures fashioned into the architecture of both old and modern structures. Art is also accessible to the public inside many buildings, particularly in the lobbies of major enterprises and the concourses of airports and railway stations. We often hurry by these works of art routinely, without seeing what they really are, or thinking why they were put there. What purposes do these items of public art serve and in what way may their appreciation be related to education for peace?

Students can easily make a systematic inventory of public art in an area close to their schools or in other places that are easily accessible to them. In fact, art that is "close to home" is often quite intrinsically interesting to young people. Students can draw or photograph items for classification, analysis and appreciation. As a sample study, let us take some art objects that can be found within a radius of one kilometre of Central Station in Montreal.

In a small green space about two blocks south west of the station, beside the Planetarium is a statue of Nicholas Copernicus donated by the Canadian Polish Society and erected on this site in 1967 (see Figure 11–1). Copernicus is seated, holding what appears to be a model of the movements of heavenly bodies in his left hand and gesturing with his right, as though he is instructing others upon the subject. To interpret the statue, one needs to know a little about the man Copernicus and his times. Born in 1473 in Poland, and orphaned at the age of ten, Copernicus was sent by an uncle to the University of Cracow, where he studied Latin, Mathematics and Astronomy. Later on in his career as a university scholar, he undertook further studies in astronomy at several universities in Italy.

At the time in which Copernicus lived, people still believed the teaching of Aristotle that the earth was the centre of the universe; however, Copernicus' observations led him to conclude that the earth and the other planets orbited the sun. His ideas greatly influenced the Italian astronomer Galileo and the German astronomer Kepler, and the system that he worked out remains the basis of modern astronomy to this day. The statue of Copernicus upholds certain universally recognized values: curiosity and the discovery of new knowledge, the value of international collaboration in the pursuit of knowledge, and our indebtedness to scholars from many different cultures around the world.

Three blocks north of the station, on McGill College Avenue, is an unusual and prominent sculpture of a crowd of people (See Figure 11–2). This work, made from stratified polyester resin and painted in a light ochre colour, contrasts starkly with the deep blue background of the building behind it. Entitled "The Illuminated Crowd," it is a reproduction from a smaller original version by artist Raymond Mason.

Close examination of the sculpture shows that the "crowd" is made up of more than thirty men, women and children, and that it is made of four segments that are placed in succeeding levels from the lowest point in the plaza to the highest point, level with the adjacent sidewalk. On the lowest platform are several figures on hands and knees, kneeling, or prostrate, seemingly oppressed and burdened and not comprehending what is going on around them. At the second level are several figures including a hooded, cultish figure forcibly holding a woman with one hand and grasping a knife in the other, as well as other figures that appear to be wounded, reeling with pain or shouting at one another. At the next level are many more figures that reflect different states of mind; some look lost, bewildered or anxious while others are embracing in joviality. Finally, at the fourth level, there are some figures looking forward, obviously awed by what they see; there are others with a look of benign hope and anticipation written upon their faces; and there is one man with an outstretched arm looking earnestly and steadfastly ahead.

Many who observe this sculpture see it as a microcosm of the human condition in our world. They see, at the lower levels, such conditions as hunger, sickness, violence, and death; then fear, oppression, apathy, anxiety and joviality; and, at the most elevated level, interest, illumination and hope. All these conditions are simultaneous. There is nothing in the sculpture to explain the causes of the conditions or the larger circumstances of those who are depicted in the crowd. It is as though the artist is challenging the observer to think profoundly about his, or her, own condition and to ponder, and perhaps to act upon, the actual macrocosmic condition of humankind.

Just a stone's throw away towards the west is the headquarters of the International Civil Aviation Organization, an agency of the United Nations. Even from Sherbrooke Street, the passer-by can see through the huge glass windows on the ground floor a magnificent mural that dominates the lobby of the building. The Swiss artist Hans Erni has drawn upon ancient Greek mythological figures to express some of the hopes and aspirations of humankind.

Represented on the main panel is Daedalus, an architect and designer who worked for King Minos of Crete, and who created for him the famous labyrinth. Feeling that he was a prisoner of the king, and in an effort to escape captivity, Daedalus built wings for himself and for his son, Icarus. Icarus, whose wings melted from the heat of the sun, is not represented in the mural. However, Daedalus is shown escaping from the grips of a monster that haunted the labyrinth, winging his way upwards. The sun is represented by a circular web that emits yellow and red radiations that are both beneficial and deadly.

A second panel to the left shows a profile of Ariadne, the beautiful daughter of King Minos. It was she who gave Theseus a thread that allowed him to find his way out of the maze of pathways. The panel includes a confusion of circular lines that represent both the labyrinth and the thread.

There is a third panel to the right of the main one, which shows a man posing in the classical position of "Man, the Thinker", surrounded by some of the tools of modern tech-

nology. Straight lines shoot upwards, indicating modern exploration of outer space. The man is tenderly touching the face of a woman.

It would be a good exercise to ask students what they (as individuals) see in the panels and what meaning they derive from them. Then they could compare their observations and reflections with one another. It would be interesting, too, to ask them what they think the panels symbolize and to compare their interpretations with the intentions of the artist. The main panel symbolizes more than humankind's endeavour to fly, in that it represents, perhaps more significantly, our attempts to escape from darkness (the labyrinth) to knowledge, wisdom and light (the sun). The second panel has a similar theme in which the thread of Ariadne also symbolizes a way out of ignorance, darkness and despair. The various parts of the third panel remind the viewer of humankind's attachment to the values of love, beauty and truth.

It should never be assumed that public art is beyond the pale of scrutiny and criticism. We should always ask whether the work was indeed fitting for the time at which it was unveiled. Is it fitting for our time? Should every piece of public art be considered as a permanent fixture? What criteria are appropriate for the "permanent" display of public art? The three examples of public art discussed above are intended to illustrate the potential value of such displays in virtually any community to help our young people appreciate art as a means of both personal growth and community development. Art that is on display for public view invariably upholds those beliefs which have been important to the orderly development of our society. Also, it often has universal application in that it represents precisely the same beliefs that can underpin the development of a peaceful world community.

160

Developing an Awareness of Values in Art

The appreciation of a work of art involves attending to its many features including form and composition, use of colours and textures, variety within the work in contrast to its unity, features such as balance and movement, and the symbolic significance of the work as a whole. Art teachers make an important contribution to peace education by developing among their pupils an aesthetic appreciation of different works, particularly an appreciation of the human values represented in them.

Paintings, drawings and other art forms represent values in different ways. Some provide a very clear *statement of values,* such as the landscape paintings of Constable, which convey the beauty of the English countryside, tranquillity, order and stability. Some are more complex in that they represent a *conflict of values.* Rembrandt's etching of "The Prodigal Son" (Clark, 1969: 205) shows a loving father welcoming home his wayward younger son who is barefoot and clothed only in tattered rags. A servant is bringing a new cloak and new shoes. But the etching also shows the older son looking on forbiddingly—resentful and unforgiving at the return of his brother. The dominant value in the work is forgiveness, yet there is clearly an opposing and conflicting force of implacability.

Other works of art portray negative values with the intention that they should evoke within us a strong reaction that, in effect, reinforces the equal and opposite value. A well-known example of this type of portrayal of values is Pablo Picasso's "Guernica" (Canaday, 1959: 485), which depicts the destruction, through bombing, of the Spanish city in 1937. The painting is in black, white and grays and has many fragmented and jagged images.

When we look closely at it, we see a woman agonizing over her dead baby, the severed arm of a warrior still clutching a sword, a woman screaming as she falls through the floor of a burning building, a light flickering on and off. The viewer is filled with revulsion for the horror of death and destruction where there should be the beauty of life and growth.

Art teachers can help their students to identify human values in paintings, drawings and other works by accumulating a bank of pictures that illustrate values clearly as well as other pictures that are more puzzling in regard to the values conveyed. Individual study and group discussion of the pictures can lead to a sharing of perceptions and judgments. Some of the values that are frequently found in art are listed below:

Positive Value	Negative Value
Tranquillity	Turmoil
Orderliness	Chaos
Joyfulness	Sadness
Gentleness	Brutality
Freedom	Constraint
Unity	Fragmentation
Hope	Despair
Passion	Coldness
Gracefulness	Awkwardness
Purity	Impurity
Humility	Pride
Generosity	Meanness
Honesty	Dishonesty
Loyalty	Betrayal
Courage	Timidity
Respectfulness	Discourteousness
Kindness	Cruelty
Love	Hatred
Appreciation	Ingratitude

Children enjoy identifying values in works that are well focussed and relatively uncomplicated. The "Scroll of Ruth", a stained glass window by Eric Wesselow (see Figure 11–3), is an illustration taken from the biblical story of Ruth and Boaz. In that story, Ruth works hard to glean barley from a field after the crop has been harvested. The same evening she helps kinsman Boaz to winnow the barley on the threshing floor. In this depiction we see Ruth and Boaz working together to separate the chaff from the grain. The scene conveys a sense of concentration, devotedness to the task and togetherness. Yet there is also a sense of gentleness, calmness and affection between the participants.

Similar values are found in an 1881 painting of an apple orchard by artist Fred Morgan. In it several children are collecting apples at harvest time. A boy in one of the trees is shaking the branches, while four other members of the family below are holding the corners of a large sheet to catch the falling apples. A little girl, who has gathered windfalls in her skirt, is emptying them into a basket. The whole painting suggests team work and the value of shared purposes and experience.

Making comparisons, as with the works above, can help children to conceptualize values more clearly. The teacher can also use examples to move from the simple to more complex considerations. The painting "Poor Bird" by A. C. King shows a boy and a girl caring for an injured bird, which the girl is holding gently and lovingly in her hand. Another painting with a similar but more powerful theme, Van Gogh's "The Good Samaritan", shows the Samaritan lifting onto his horse an injured man who has been beaten and left to die by highway robbers. The bold brush strokes in Van Gogh's painting sweep towards an empty money chest and then on to the road where there are two previous passers-by who have chosen to ignore the victim. Both of these paintings convey a great sense of com-

passion. The Van Gogh painting, however, has, in addition, the juxtaposition of the value of merciful compassion with that of apathy and cold disregard.

There have been many paintings produced on the theme of parent and child. When we look at the treatment of this theme by artists over the centuries, we can see how the relationship has been interpreted in different epochs. Raphael's "Die Madonna Tempi", painted in the sixteenth century, shows Mary holding the baby Jesus. Her left hand is gently under his legs; her right hand tenderly enfolds him to her breast; her eyes are transfixed upon his head, and their cheeks are delicately snuggled together. On Mary's face there is a look that reflects inner joy and contentment. In Henry Tanner's painting "The Banjo Lesson", which has a theme parallel to that of Raffael's, a father is portrayed with his son. The father is seated in a chair, while his little boy is standing between his legs, his left hand on the struts of the banjo and his right hand picking the strings. The father steadies the instrument by holding it at its extremes. He seems almost to encircle his son, conveying protectiveness, love and patience. Both of these works of art express the wonderful bond of parental love and concern.

Values are ultimately what typify any culture. In the list given above, they have been classified as positive and negative. However, some positive values may be held in creative tension with each other, as in the case of the values of unity and diversity within a culture, both of which may be simultaneously desirable. The international community will build more and more towards a peaceful world society as its members simultaneously cherish differences while at the same time recognizing and upholding those values that are universally shared. Many of the great works of art in

East and West are recognized as masterpieces because they reflect universal human values. Art can, therefore, make a very special contribution to the building of world peace by helping young people to recognize and affirm values in their daily lives that are preconditions to an effective and cohesive world society.

Teaching the Appreciation of Art From Different Cultures

To the ordinary person, art from continents outside our own is often seen as distant and strange, without much meaning for us. That is a normal immediate reaction to objects that are largely beyond our own experience. However, because art frequently upholds values that are important to the culture that produces it, it can be an exceptionally good medium to enrich our understanding of others.

As a non-verbal means of communication, art can convey the landscapes of the country (geography); it can illustrate important events of the past (history); it can depict dramatic events from stories and poems (literature); and it can reveal the values that are cherished by the society (moral education and comparative politics). An illustration of the last may be helpful. During the period of the Cultural Revolution in China (1966–1976), Chinese artists Tuan Hsiao-chin and Ting Shih-chien, produced a painting entitled "On the Way to School" (*Chinese Literature* 1, 1976: 88). It shows a young girl passing through a corn field. She has noticed that the wind has blown down two of the plants. Already she has removed one orange ribbon from her hair and tied up the first plant, and she is in the act of undoing her other ribbon to tie up the second. The picture teaches the idea that personal adornment is not as important as the welfare of the community, reflecting a basic tenet of communist ideology. This picture, together with others in a similar vein, could make very clear, in concrete terms, the model relationship between an individual and society in a country very different from our own.

The link between art and culture is one with which many young people are not familiar, perhaps because of their under-exposure to art. The range of opportunities for incorporating multicultural art into school experiences has received a great deal more attention in recent years. A number of teachers and authors have explored the diversity of art in their own multicultural communities, for example, Grigsby (1991), Branen and Congdon (1994) and Cahan and Kocur (1994). Some have emphasized art as a powerful medium for understanding other nations and cultures, as have Thomas and Morris (1992) and Kaneda (1994); yet others have examined the mutually reinforcing and experience-expanding benefits of both multicultural and intercultural art, as has Schuman (1992). Realizing that art often portrays the values of a culture can be an important step to both conscientization and intercultural understanding.

As an example of using art to promote intercultural understanding, we have selected art in China. China is a complex country with many different ethnic groups and many different artistic traditions in water colours, pottery, sculpture, calligraphy, embroidery, and a vast array of other media. There is, therefore, a need for some delimitation: New Year folk paintings in the Province of Shandong have been selected as an illustration.

During the celebrations of the Chinese New Year, there is a tradition going back to the second century among the farmers of the rural communities to decorate their homes with prints of brightly coloured paintings that remain in place for the following year.

Farmers are both the artist-producers and the consumers of these paintings. Each painting is printed in many copies and so is easily affordable to ordinary people. The paintings reflect the thoughts and feelings of the farmers as well as their aspirations for a better life. The paintings themselves have a central motif that generalizes, romanticizes, or symbolizes the subjects of concern and interest to the artist. Each painting is accompanied by a title or a poem. The style of painting was apparently looked down upon by the ruling classes of the old society, but since the Cultural Revolution, folk painting—or the people's painting, as it is also known—has been encouraged and revived.

Figure 11–4 shows two young people each riding on the back of an enormous fish. Each has an object in his hand, and behind their heads are some large flowers. In the background there is a reservoir with a sluice gate, and pylons to convey hydro-electric power. The picture is embellished with a kingfisher, ducklings and a frog. What meaning does this picture convey?

The picture is entitled, "The Reservoir Is Good". In the Chinese Mandarin language, the word for "fish" is "yu", a homonym for another character meaning wealth or abundance. The fish, therefore, symbolizes the abundance of good things that the construction of the reservoir has brought to the rural community. The flowers in the background are lotuses, which grow from the mud at the bottom of the water. In spite of their origins, the flowers have great beauty and they symbolize purity. They serve to remind us in this painting that a "pure" person may come out of a "corrupt" society. The stem of the lotus is straight and firm; growing upwards, it signifies honesty. In addition, the flower is fragrant: it can be smelled at a distance, just as a person

with a good reputation becomes widely known. One of the young people is holding the root of a lotus plant and the other is holding a lotus seed pod, both nutritious foods that further reinforce the sense of benefit that has come from the reservoir.

The painting in Figure 11–5 is entitled, "Tang Saier: A Woman Leader in the Peasant Uprisings Early in the Ming Dynasty".

This painting shows Tang riding a horse and followed by a crowd of peasants who are rising up against the oppression of their wealthy landlords. Tang carries a number of weapons and is bearing down upon the soldiers of the landlords. She comes with force and fire, and the soldiers with their shields and banners appear to be in disorder and retreat. The theme in this painting is a recurrent one in China. In many of the museums, similar modern paintings, depicting angry uprisings of the peasants against their masters, punctuate the exhibits of historical artifacts. They symbolize the continuing efforts of the Chinese throughout their history to achieve a greater measure of social justice.

While these two examples may help us appreciate, in a small way, Chinese culture, they may also help us to generalize the value of art for intercultural understanding. What is the role that art plays in the culture? (Is it found in homes? At ceremonies? In museums? For public display?) How do we interpret the art and attempt to understand its symbolism? What does the art tell us about the society that produced it? What does the art tell us about similarities of the culture to our own? What does it say about elements in the culture that may have universal appeal or about aspects of the culture that are particular to that society? When we can answer questions of this kind, there can be a greater degree of understanding between the cultures concerned.

FIGURE 11–1 Statue of Copernicus erected in 1967

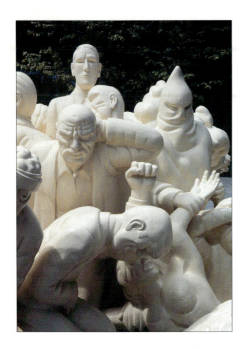

FIGURE 11–2 "The Illuminated Crowd" by Raymond Mason

FIGURE 11–3 "The Scroll of Ruth" by Eric Wesselow

FIGURE 11–4 "The Reservoir is Good"

FIGURE 11–5 Tang Saier: "A Woman Leader in the Peasant
Uprisings Early in the Ming Dynasty"

Art, Creativity and Conflict Resolution

In an essay on the theme of Peace through Art, Eric Wesselow (1986) asserts that everyone is born with artistic potential of some kind. Our artistry may express itself in the design and sewing of a dress, in the layout of a flower garden or in the presentation of a meal on the dining-room table. Unfortunately, for many people, pure artistic expression and creativity are impeded, and the stifling of that activity, Wesselow believes, is related to the problems of our world: "The impediments of negligence and non-participation, passive spectatorship, and, out of these, boredom, dope and violence, all belong to the same circuitry" (1986: 105). If this is the case, then art—as a preoccupying and creative activity in itself, that is valid without having any set purpose—can cause violence to be set aside.

Closely associated with this view is the belief that the creative arts can have therapeutic value for those who participate in them. Children can make puppets that they can then use to act out personal or social problems. Similarly, in painting, there is a strong identification of young artists with the human subjects that they are creating. In fact, the visual image that a child produces may be interpreted as a report of the child's self-perception. Using paint or clay, children can express what they may not be able to put into words. Art work may, in this way, be a medium for children to deal with such problems as loneliness, frustration, fear, and despondency.

Much of the work required of students in our schools is associated with convergent thinking. Intelligence tests have correct responses that have been worked out before a child takes the test. Creativity, on the other hand, stresses divergent thinking. Lowenfeld and Brittain (1982: 73) state: "Divergent ability includes thinking of a great number of different answers, or thinking of different methods or approaches to problems, or thinking of the unusual or novel. Possibly we have given intelligence too narrow a definition, for both intelligence and creativity are part of the cognitive processes." Seen in this light, all of the creative arts may have a special contribution to make in helping young people develop habits of creative thinking, particularly in seeking alternatives to violence in the solution of problems.

In this respect, art has a special role to play in the process of solving problems that extend from the micro to the macro level. An interesting example of this kind of problem solving is discussed by Edmund Feldman (1970: 240). He points out that children are often encouraged in their art fieldwork to go out and to find a beautiful place, which they then draw, or paint, with the object of "capturing" beauty. A quite different problem-solving approach to art would have the children find places that are unappealing, ugly or monotonous and to sketch or photograph such places, reporting back to class. After an analysis of their findings students, through creative and imaginative activity, could paint a picture of the way they would like the place to be. Art then becomes a way of working towards the improvement of our environment.

Artists have long used their work as a means of finding solutions to major problems. A classical example of seeking alternatives to violence is seen in the painting "The Battle of the Romans and the Sabines" by French artist Jacques Louis David, which hangs in the Louvre Museum in Paris (Canaday, 1959: 16). The picture shows a group of Sabine women, with their children, intervening between Roman and Sabine soldiers to try to prevent a

FIGURE 11–6   Example of a response to war toys and nuclear annihilation

bloody carnage. In our day, young people can use art to portray their own solutions to current problems: famine, disease, pollution, militarism and nuclear weapons, racial discrimination, economic disparity, aggression, violence and a host of other problems, both locally and globally. Figure 11–6 shows one example of an artistic response to the problems of war toys and nuclear annihilation.

According to Jonathan Schell (1982), art today is undermined by the threat of nuclear self-extermination. Artists (and writers) have traditionally reached beyond their own lifetimes with their work, and in this sense have communion with the unborn. However, as the future is in doubt for artists in the nuclear world, they subconsciously feel that they no longer can communicate with posterity. Artistic creation has therefore reflected the imperilled condition of the human species. Summarizing the views of art critic Harold Rosenberg, Schell states, "… the meaning of the work [has come] to reside in the act of painting rather than in the finished canvas" (1982: 164). This apparent existentialist view of artistic expression needs to be considered by teachers of art in relation to the creative work of their own students as well as in interpreting the work of some contemporary artists.

Art and Global Perspectives

As noted earlier, it is not surprising that some of the works we encounter in public places look beyond the local and national to deal with the preoccupations of humankind as a whole. Similarly, in the study of values implicit in works of art, we find human qualities that transcend national boundaries. In the art of cultures other than our own, we discover shared experiences and shared meanings.

Some artists have purposely set out to create images that might have global appeal, even if, in most cases, the art has a distinctive, specific cultural style. Many of the works collected at the United Nations headquarters in New York are of this kind. One impressive sculpture donated to the UN by the former Soviet Union is "Let Us Beat Swords into Ploughshares" by Russian artist Evgeniy Vuchetich (1959). Almost 3 metres high, the statue depicts a strong man hammering a heavy steel sword into a plough. In this imposing figure, we see the artistic expression of the prophecy in the book of Isaiah:

> …they shall beat their swords into
> ploughshares,
> and their spears into pruning hooks;
> nation shall not lift up sword against nation,
> neither shall they learn war any more. (2:4)

On the same theme, Picasso's "Colombe de l'avenir" (1962) shows a dove, with an olive branch in its beak, rising above a pile of dismantled weapons of war towards the brilliance of the light of the sun. Implicit in this somewhat abstract sketch is the human yearning for peace and yet also, perhaps, the striving for greater self-knowledge.

Much of the art on widely distributed UNICEF greeting cards is of the same genre. One card, for example, shows an untitled cloth maquette by an anonymous Norwegian artist, depicting a circle of children from different continents of the world, holding hands, seated in a circle, and surrounded by flowers. The picture stresses the values of friendship, equality and unity in a world of beauty.

It is interesting to compare this image with David Jacques' mural, "Internationalism", at the National Education Centre of the Trades Union Congress in Britain. This picture has a globe as its centrepiece. Around the globe are various figures representative of miners, factory workers, teachers, farmers and others. Some of these people are holding hands in friendship while others are working together. The mural portrays several important values: cooperation, education, internationalism, multiculturalism and globalism.

The idea of developing global perspectives in art is one that children themselves can explore from their own experiences and with various media. D'Amico (1994) has developed an activity she calls "Peaceable Murals" in which children paint their own real or imaginary animals and then redraw them into a large mural showing how all these animals live together in a peaceable kingdom. Such an activity involves both independent and cooperative work, and a methodology that, in itself, encourages individual and group creativity.

Sarah Pirtle (1987) cleverly weaves together a story involving a breakdown of friendship between two families in a small town with problems of world disarmament and peace. Reconciliation is attempted through a community exhibit of children's drawings, paintings, posters, origami, poetry and song. In this story, the arts are used constructively to address such global problems as inequality, racial discrimination, violence and militarization.

Summary

The visual arts have enormous potential for building self-esteem, community and global stability. In this chapter, we have explored some of the ways in which young people can realize that potential through the appreciation of art itself and through the exercise of their own potential to make and create. We considered ways in which children can become aware of art around them on a day-to-day basis. We went on to suggest that they develop sensitivities to the values implicit in their own and others' work. We argued in favour of promoting inter-cultural understanding through art and described ways in which art may help to advance peaceful conflict resolution. Finally, we suggested that art can play a significant role in the development of human and global perspectives.

REFERENCES AND SOURCES

Arnold, Alice (1994), "Building Community through Arts Experiences", *Art Education,* 47 (3), May 1994: 47–51.

Arts and Activities (1992), "Drawing from Different Cultures" (Special Issue), *Arts and Activities,* February, 1992.

Branen, Karen and Kristin Congdon (1994), "An Elementary School Celebrates Community Diversity", *Art Education,* Vol 47 (4), July, 1994: 8–12.

Cahan, Susan and Zoya Kocur (1994), "Contemporary Art and Multicultural Education", *Art Education,* 47 (2), March, 1994: 27–33.

Canaday, John (1959), *Mainstreams of Modern Art,* New York: Simon and Schuster.

Chinese Literature, 1, (1976) Peking: Foreign Languages Press.

Clark, Kenneth (1969) *Civilization: A Personal View,* London: British Broadcasting Corporation and John Murray

D'Amico, Elizabeth E. (1994), "Peaceable Murals", *Arts and Activities,* April, 1994: 56–57.

Eisemon, Tom, Lynn Hart and Elkana Ong'esa (1988), *Stories in Stone: An Exhibition of Sculpture from Northern Quebec and Western Kenya,* Montreal: Federation of Cooperatives of Northern Quebec.

Feldman, Edmund Burke (1970), *Becoming Human through Art,* Englewood Cliffs, New Jersey: Prentice-Hall.

Grigsby, Eugene (1991), "Unfolding a Hidden Rainbow of Cultures", *Arts and Activities,* February, 1991: 26–41.

Grigsby, Eugene (1992), "Sources of Multicultural Art Study Materials", *Arts and Activities,* February, 1992: 34–35.

Hatcher, Evelyn Payne (1985), *Art As Culture: An Introduction to the Anthropology of Art,* New York: University Press of America.

Kaneda, Takuya (1994), "Children's Art Activities in Non/Less Industrialized Societies: A Case Study in Nepal", *Art Education,* 47 (1), January, 1994: 20–24.

Kropa, Susan (1994), "Cooperative Learning Via Dinosaurs", *Arts and Activities,* April, 1994: 42–43.

Lowenfeld, Viktor and W. Lambert Brittain (1982), *Creative and Mental Growth,* Seventh Edition, New York: Macmillan.

Murdock, Maureen (1987), *Spinning Inward: Using Guided Imagery with Children for Learning, Creativity and Relaxation,* Boston and London: Shambhala.

Pirtle, Sarah (1987), *An Outbreak of Peace,* Philadelphia: New Society Publishers.

Rigli, Ron (1992), "A.R.T. Exchange", *Arts and Activities,* March, 1992: 40–41.

Schell, Jonathan (1982), *The Fate of the Earth,* New York: Avon.

Schuman, Jo Miles (1992), "Multicultural Art Projects", in Patricia A. Richard-Amato and Marguerite Ann Snow, *The Multicultural Classroom: Readings for Content Area Teachers,* New York: Longman: 349–355.

Sethi, Rajiv (1985), *Aditi: The Living Arts of India,* Washington D.C.: Smithsonian Institution Press.

Smith, Peter (1994), "Multicultural Issues: Dilemmas and Hopes", *Art Education,* 47 (4), July, 1994: 13–17.

Smith, Ralph A. (1986), *Excellence in Art Education,* Reston, Virginia: National Art Education Association.

Steichen, Edward (1983), *The Family of Man,* New York: The Museum of Modern Art.

Thomas, Barbara and Jimmy Oliver Morris (1992), "The Transformative Spirit of African Art", *Arts and Activities,* February, 1992: 24–25.

UNESCO (1969), *The Arts and Man: A world view of the role and functions of the arts in society,* Paris: UNESCO and Englewood Cliffs, N.J., Prentice Hall.

United Nations Bookshop, United Nations, New York, N.Y. 10017. Catalogue of visual materials available upon request.

Wesselow, Eric (1986), "Making or Breaking: Cultural Dimensions of Peace and War," in Paris Arnopoulos (ed.), *Prospects for Peace: An Anthology of Canadian Perspectives on Social Conflict and Peaceful Change,* Montreal: Gamma Institute Press

CHAPTER 12

Towards a Peaceful Future in the Classroom

Graham Pike and David Selby

IN THIS CHAPTER *we offer twenty-six classroom activities for the peace-promoting classroom. The activities are organized under the seven dimensions of broad-based peace education identified in Chapter 3: non-violence, human rights, social justice, world mindedness, ecological balance, meaningful participation and personal peace. Prefatory to the seven sections, however, we offer two activities exploring the nature and meanings of peace.*

The twenty-six activities share at least three broad common characteristics. First, they seek congruence between the "message" (values and content) and "medium" (processes) of peace education through the level of learner participation they invite and the devolution of control they involve. The structural violence of one-way communication between teacher and taught is overturned. Sometimes explicit and sometimes implicit within the activities is a commitment to the experiential, learner-centred, democratic, convivial, participatory and change-oriented classroom within which the teacher's principal, oftentimes only, role is that of facilitator of a learning process.

Second, the activities are interdisciplinary *in nature. They have cross-curricular applicability and often integrate insights, concepts and understandings emanating from different curricular areas. Third, they seek to illuminate the* interconnectedness—*and draw out the conceptual links (sometimes tensions)—between different themes falling under the peace education umbrella.*

Pages marked **P** *may be photocopied for classroom use.*

ACTIVITY 1

Peace is...

Suitable for	Grades 9–12
Time needed	35 minutes
Resources	Four slips of paper for each student; newsprint and markers or crayons for each group of five.
Procedure	Working individually and avoiding discussion, students write four different statements beginning "Peace is" on their slips of paper. The statements should capture their own several understandings of the concept of peace. Groups of five are formed to share and discuss what has been written, and to prepare a mutually acceptable short paragraph definition of peace. The paragraph is written out in large letters on the sheet of newsprint. Graphics (symbols, cartoons, etc.) should be added. Each group presents its work. Discussion of the various contributions (which can be displayed at the front of the class) follows.
Potential	An activity providing a springboard for consideration of the nature of peace through a sharing of perceptions and understandings. A multiplicity of meanings is likely to be aired ranging from peace as absence of war to peace as synonymous with justice and equality to peace as tranquillity, inner calm and centredness.

ACTIVITY 2

Peace Messagematch

Suitable for   Grades 9–12

Time needed   30 minutes

Resources   A piece of a message for each student; an open classroom space; an overhead projection transparency of the complete message collection (or a sheet of the complete set of statements for each group of three students).

Procedure   When the message pieces have been distributed, students move around the room looking for others with whom they can join to complete a message. The total number of messages is given and it is explained that the class will be successful only when everybody is part of a message that makes sense. The task complete, each group reads out its message. If the class number is not a multiple of three, the teacher can join in and/or one student can be given two adjoining pieces from the same set.

A useful way into plenary discussion is to divide the class into mixed-gender or single-sex groups of three with the task of determining a) the most *challenging* statement, b) the most *outrageous* statement, c) the *blandest* statement, d) the most *insightful* statement, and e) the most *inspirational* statement. Decisions can be tabulated on the board and the table used as a basis for class discussion.

Potential   A lively cooperative activity that can be used to prompt reflection and discussion around definitions of peace, the sources and place of war in human society, and the specifics of each message.

Is peace absence of war? Is it absence of injustice? Or both (and, possibly, more)? Is peace a goal to be aimed at or a way of living one's life? Does war come from inside ourselves? Is it a natural part of the human condition? Is it pressed upon us by those in power? Does it come from the way we have organized society and the world? Is there such a thing as a "just" war? Is deterrence and, hence, the maintenance, stockpiling and updating of weapons systems, an effective means of upholding peace? Is it morally defensible?

The single-sex small group discussion alternative is likely to bring out in stark relief gender differences in attitudes towards peace and war.

Source   Sources of messages (in order presented): Mahatma Gandhi, United Nations, Thomas Mann, Vegetius (fourth century A.D.), Martin Luther King, George Bernard Shaw, Mao Tse-tung, Eve Merriam, Mahatma Gandhi, Maria Montessori, unknown, Benito Mussolini, John Lennon, Thomas Hardy, unknown.

P   Peace Messagematch: Messages

There is no / road to peace; / peace is the road.

Wars begin / in the minds / of men.

War is only a cowardly / escape from the / problems of peace.

Let him who / desires peace / prepare for war.

Wars are poor / chisels for carving / out peaceful tomorrows.

Peace is not only / better than war / but infinitely more arduous.

In order to get rid / of the gun it is / necessary to take up the gun.

I dream of giving birth / to a child who will ask, / "mother, what was war?"

Poverty is / the worst / form of violence.

Establishing lasting / peace is the / work of education.

There is no / peace in the world / when there is no peace within.

War is to man what maternity / is to a woman; I / do not believe in perpetual peace.

For we are / saying, give / peace a chance.

War makes rattling / good history / but peace is poor reading.

A just war / is a contradiction / in terms.

Dimension 1: Non-Violence

Knowledge and understanding of non-violence; non-violent conflict resolution; win-win resolutions; overcoming structural violence

---

ACTIVITY 3

The Smarties Game

Suitable for   Grades 3–7

Time needed   10 minutes

Resources   A large box of Smarties.

Procedure   Students are asked to form pairs and to sit at different sides of a table so they can clasp hands for arm wrestling. The teacher holds up the box of Smarties and tells the class that each time their partner's hand touches the table they will win a Smartie, until the box is empty.

Potential   This activity provides an enjoyable springboard for the consideration of cooperation and competition. When the signal to begin is given, some pairs will struggle to force each other's arm down. Others will realize that a cooperative approach, in which each in turn allows the other to press his or her arm to the table, will enable the pair to quickly accumulate a high score. The debriefing should focus on the relative merits of the competitive and cooperative approaches. The dilemma should also be posed as to whether the Smarties should be re-distributed. Are those with the largest totals (gained through cooperation) entirely happy with an uneven distribution?

ACTIVITY 4

Two Mules

Suitable for Grades 3–9

Time needed 1) 10 minutes; 2) 20 minutes

Resources 1) A set of six separate mule pictures for each group of four students;

2) A set of separate pictures for each group of six students.

Procedure 1) Students form groups of four and are handed a shuffled set of mule pictures. They are asked to arrange the pictures in the sequence they think best tells the story of the two mules. Their task is to try to reach consensus on one story but to listen carefully to the different stories proposed should consensus prove impossible. The stories proposed by each group are then recounted to the class and reasons given for the chosen picture sequence. Class discussion follows.

2) Students form groups of six sitting in a circle on chairs or on the floor. Group members are each handed a picture. They are given a minute to look at their picture, permitting nobody else to see it and avoiding talking. At the end of the minute they hide their picture away and, going around the circle, describe their picture to each other. Then, still avoiding looking at the pictures, they discuss and negotiate a sequence or arrangement in which they think the pictures could be placed. As they move close to agreement, they can be asked to place the pictures face down on the table/floor. When this has been accomplished to the group's satisfaction, the group can turn the pictures over, reflect upon their chosen sequence and then renegotiate the arrangement, if deemed necessary.

Potential The story about the two mules, told in the pictures, raises issues surrounding the relative usefulness of competition and cooperation, and non-violent solutions to conflicts.

1) A simple yet highly effective means of promoting logical thought and lateral thinking and developing cooperative, problem-solving, negotiation, consensus-building, discussion and listening skills.

2) An excellent activity for developing/reinforcing a range of skills such as memory, observation, oral description, listening, discussion, negotiation, lateral thinking, consensus-seeking, decision-making, perspective sharing and reflection.

Source 1) Developed from Baker, T., et. al., *Co-operating for a change,* Newcastle upon Tyne Local Education Authority (UK), 1987, 96. (2) Developed from an idea in Fisher, S., & Hicks, D.W., *World studies 8–13. A teacher's handbook,* Edinburgh: Oliver & Boyd, 1985, 142–5.

P

Two Mules

ACTIVITY 5

Ballooning Technology

Suitable for   Grades 7–12

Time needed   5 minutes

Resources   Six hoops of paper of thirty-centimetre diameter, plasticine/masking tape, ninety round balloons, three needles (or thumb tacks).

Procedure   Students form groups of five. Each group is asked to stand by one of the paper hoops (previously fixed at various points to the classroom wall) and is given fifteen balloons and some plasticine/masking tape. The groups are told that the object of the activity is to stick as many fully inflated balloons as possible within the hoop in the three minutes allotted. After a minute or so, the facilitator secretly approaches a single member of three of the groups, offers her a needle and advises that the needle can be used in any way that seems appropriate. In the excitement generated by the activity, the needle is generally used to burst other groups' balloons. Class discussion follows.

Potential   This activity raises questions surrounding the "neutrality" of technology and scientific inventions, and the intentions of those who offer us new technologies. Was the needle a value-free instrument? Or did the needle itself significantly shape subsequent events? Did the facilitator have a clear but unstated agenda in offering needles to students? What were the values implicit in the way(s) in which the needles were used? Did the students have a real choice in deciding what to do? In what ways does the activity mirror the impact new forms of military and civil technology can have upon the future?

ACTIVITY 6

Violence

Suitable for   Grades 9–12

Time needed   40 minutes

Resources   Six slips of paper for each student; a sheet of newsprint, paste stick and marker for each group of five.

Procedure   Students form groups of five and, working individually, are asked to write down examples, six in all, of hurt, harm or injury being done to humans and human well-being of which they have first-hand knowledge or about which they have heard or read. Each example should be written on a separate slip of paper. Two of the examples should be at the *interpersonal* level, two at the *community* or *intercommunity* level, and two at *international* level. The thirty completed slips are pooled. It is explained to the class that violence can be *direct*—i.e., physical violence by one or more persons against one or more others—or *indirect*—i.e., violence, as it were, done to people by social, political, economic and belief systems or through mental or psychological abuse. Examples should be given. Groups are asked to consider each of their thirty slips and to paste them in the appropriate section of the diagram drawn on their sheet of newsprint (see below). Notes and comments can also be added to the diagram if deemed necessary. The completed charts are displayed and reviewed. Class discussion ensues.

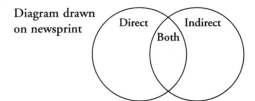

Diagram drawn on newsprint — Direct / Indirect / Both

Potential   A useful means of promoting understanding and critical reflection of the concepts of direct and indirect violence and, by extension, of negative and positive peace. What difficulties did groups experience in placing their examples? What lay behind difficulties encountered? To what extent did groups find that forms of direct and indirect violence were interconnected? Can the two concepts be justifiably extended to human treatment of natural environments and animals? What are a) acceptable and b) effective means of countering and eradicating direct and indirect violence?

ACTIVITY 7

Cat and Mouse Fantasy

Suitable for   Grades 7–12

Time needed   15 minutes

Resources   A quiet open area, preferably carpeted, so that students can lie comfortably on the floor.

Procedure   Students are asked to lie down, find a comfortable position and close their eyes. The following passage, perhaps embroidered with additional detail, is read slowly, but with animation, and with fairly long pauses between sections and after each question.

> Imagine that you are walking out of this room and down a long sidewalk. You come to an old deserted house. Now you are going up the drive, up the porch steps. You try the door and it creaks open. You step inside and look around a dark empty room.
>
> Suddenly you begin to feel a strange sensation in your body. It begins to shudder and tremble. You feel yourself growing smaller and smaller. Now you're only as high as the window sill. You keep shrinking until you look up and see the ceiling very far away, very high. You are only as tall as a book and still growing smaller.
>
> Something else begins to happen. You notice you're changing shape. Your nose is getting longer and longer, and hair is covering your whole body. Now you're down on all fours and you realize that you've changed into a mouse.
>
> Look around the room from your mouse position. You're sitting on one side of the room. Then you see the door move slightly.
>
> In walks a cat. It sits down and looks around very slowly and with great casualness. Then it gets up and calmly begins to wander around the room. You are very, very still. Feel your heart beating. Feel your own breathing. Watch the cat.
>
> Now it sees you and begins to stalk you. Ever so slowly, it comes to you. Then it stops right in front of you and crouches. What are you feeling? What does it look like? What choices do you have right now? What do you decide to do?
>
> Just as the cat moves to leap on you, both of your bodies begin to tremble and shake. You feel yourself being transformed again. This time you are growing larger again. The cat seems to be getting smaller. And changing shape. You see the cat the same size as you, and now smaller.

→

178

The cat is turning into a mouse and you have become a cat. How do you feel being bigger and no longer trapped? How does the mouse look to you? Do you know what the mouse is feeling? What are you feeling? Decide what you're going to do and then do it. What do you feel now?

It is happening again. The changing. You are getting bigger and bigger. Almost your full size. And now you are you again. You walk out the door and back to this building and this room. You open your eyes and look around you.

Potential   Class discussion can first be directed towards *feelings*. How did it feel, for instance, when the cat entered the room, when it began to stalk you, when the cat got smaller, and when you became the cat? The discussion can then move on to *choices*. What did you decide to do when the cat crouched in front of you? What course of action did you decide to take after you had become a cat and the cat had become a mouse? The response elicited from questions about feelings and choices can provide a springboard for discussion of dominance or aggression and submission in interpersonal, inter-group and international relationships. Who are the cats and who are the mice (the powerful and the powerless) in various contexts, interpersonal to global? Is might right? What attitudes, feelings and behaviours do unequal relationships engender in the powerful and powerless? Can students think of occasions in which the cat/mouse metamorphosis has been mirrored in the real world? (Senior students often cite South Africa in response to the last question.) Can they think of cases in which a fundamental change in power relationships is likely to occur in the future? What options are open to you, the mouse, when you become the cat? What options are/were open to the once underprivileged or powerless in cases where they assume/have assumed power? How should the once-powerful be treated?

Source   Wolsk, D., An Experience-centered Curriculum, *UNESCO Educational Studies and Documents*, No. 17, p. 45.

Dimension 2: Human Rights

Liberty-oriented rights; security-oriented rights; basic rights

---

ACTIVITY 8
The Rights of the Child

Suitable for Grades 5–9

Time needed 70 minutes

Resources A sheet of paper and pen for each small group; a sheet of newsprint and marker for each combined group; a copy of *The United Nations Declaration of the Rights of the Child* sheet (see page 183) for each student.

Procedure The class is asked to share ideas about what rights are. If somebody says "I know my rights" or "It's against my rights" what do they mean? Students might need a summary definition of rights such as "something which, in all fairness, you feel that you are entitled to." Then they can be encouraged to volunteer a few examples of rights they think they should have.

Groups of four or five are formed and asked to brainstorm as many rights of the child as they can think of. All ideas are to be accepted. When groups have completed the task (or, in the case of less forthcoming groups, achieved lists of at least ten items), it is explained that in 1959 the United Nations issued a ten-point Declaration of the Rights of the Child. Groups are asked to get together with another group to negotiate and write down their own agreed ten-point declaration. The process may involve rejecting some ideas on the brainstormed lists entirely, collapsing some items together in a more general statement, or simply editing two similar statements so they can stand as one statement. *The final agreed list must contain no more than ten items.*

When the combined group declarations are complete, students are handed a copy of the 1959 Declaration and given the task of comparing and contrasting it with their own work. Are there any important rights that, on reflection, they as a group had overlooked? Are there any important rights that the UN Declaration, now around forty years old, fails to include? Groups are invited to amend their own declaration and/or the UN Declaration in the light of their discussions. Students then move into whole-class session, first to report back on their own declarations, the differences between their own work and that of the UN and any amendments they have made to either declaration, and then to discuss and reflect upon the learnings from the activity.

→

Potential This activity offers a student-centered introduction to human rights in that it limits itself to children's rights and asks class members to first reflect upon what they perceive the rights of children to be. Group declarations will often tend to lay emphasis upon rights at a materialistic and superficial level. The introduction of the UN Declaration often comes as something of a shock with its emphasis upon rights of a more basic nature. Students will probably want to amend their own declaration when the realization dawns that they had been blind to or taken for granted a number of fundamental rights. The ethnocentrism of class perspectives prior to reading the Declaration can be teased out in the final whole-class discussion. (The insights of refugee and other newly arrived children can be very important here.) The final combined group activity may also bring to the surface the point that we continue to identify new rights as time passes. For instance, the UN Declaration (1959) does not mention environmental rights, the rights of children to a voice and to participate, or the right of children to be free from abuse, but there is every chance that the student declaration will—because of the heightened consciousness of environmental and abuse issues and of children's right to be heard in contemporary society and media. At the close of discussion, the class can be informed that a larger, more complex Convention on the Rights of the Child was issued by the UN in 1989. (This is addressed in a number of subsequent activities in this chapter.) The 1959 Declaration, although outdated, is a good way into the subject.

Extension Students revisit their own declaration and the UN 1959 Declaration, having viewed one or more of the excellent UNICEF VHS videos or 16 mm films (see overleaf). Back in their combined groups, they try to draw up the ten-point declaration that the child/children depicted in the film might put together.

→

Videos

- *Beyond Hunger* (1982, 17 minutes, 16 mm/VHS). Children and relief efforts in Somali refugee camps

- *Children of the Sun* (1989, 47 minutes, VHS). Impoverished children and UNICEF projects in Bolivia

- *Ethiopia, Parched Lands and Promises* (1981, 12 minutes, 16 mm). Children facing drought and famine in Ethiopia and UNICEF's relief program

- *Remember Me* (1979, 15 minutes, 16 mm/VHS). The daily lives of seven children in different countries

- *Tarazani of Khartoum* (1989, 10 minutes, VHS). Sudanese children driven from their homes by civil war and forced to turn to life on the streets in Khartoum

- *That's Right* (1989, 15 minutes, VHS). Looks at the lives of two children from Guelph, Ontario, and two from Ghana

- *Who Will Help Paulinho?* (1983, 26 minutes, VHS). Street children in Brazil

These videos are available on *free loan* from UNICEF offices across Canada. Contact UNICEF Canada, 443 Mt. Pleasant Road, Toronto, Ontario M4S 2L8, (tel: 416-482-4444; fax: 416-482-8035) for details of local offices. UNICEF advises booking four weeks in advance.

P

The United Nations Declaration
of the Rights of the Child, 1959

The right to affection, love and understanding

The right to adequate nutrition and medical care

The right to free education

The right to full opportunity for play and recreation

The right to a name and nationality

The right to special care, if handicapped

The right to be among the first to receive relief in times of disaster

The right to be a useful member of society and to develop individual abilities

The right to be brought up in a spirit of peace and universal brotherhood

The right to enjoy these rights, regardless of race, colour, sex, religion, national or social origin.

ACTIVITY 9

Types of Rights

Suitable for   Grades 9–12

Time needed   30 minutes

Resources   A set of rights taken from the UN Declaration of Human Rights (see examples on pages 186–187 for each group of four students, with each right on a separate slip of paper. Sets are placed in separate envelopes. A marker, some masking tape and a large sheet of newsprint for each group.

Procedure   A brief explanation of the nature of basic rights, liberty-oriented rights and security-oriented rights is given (see pages 27–28). Students, working in groups of four, consider each right in turn and decide whether it is a basic, liberty-oriented or security-oriented right. Having come to a decision, they attach it to the appropriate column on their newsprint which has been divided thus:

Basic rights	Civil/political rights	Social/economic rights

If they are undecided or feel that a particular right fits into all columns or no particular column, they either attach it so it overlays the dividing line between the two most suitable columns or omit it altogether. The activity completed, groups report back in plenary session. Discussion follows.

Potential   This activity will raise a number of important discussion points:

The weighting towards civil and political rights. All groups will have a preponderance of statements in the liberty-oriented rights column. They may well ask why. The Declaration of Human Rights was adopted by the then members of the United Nations in 1948 with France, Britain and the USA the most active and influential members. Western democracies placed great emphasis on civil and political rights (e.g., freedom of speech and

→

assembly) whilst communist and developing nations have placed greater emphasis on social and economic rights (e.g., the right to work). The question can be put: "What would a brand new Universal Declaration of Human Rights, hammered out at the UN by western, the remaining communist, and developing nations look like?"

Are some liberty-oriented and security-oriented rights also basic? If a basic right is a right that cannot be taken away whatever the circumstances, how many liberty and security rights might be considered basic? Can some rights be more justifiably taken away than others?

Do groups identify some rights that seem to be both liberty-oriented and security-oriented as defined? Article 26, the right to education, is often raised as a right of this kind. Education, it may be argued is clearly intended to help us secure our social and economic needs but the right to go to school—and the right to choose the kind of school—seem to be civil and political rights.

Which category of rights is most important, liberty-oriented or security-oriented rights? This question will provoke lively discussion and draw out a range of perspectives. The concept of the indivisibility of rights can usefully be introduced here; i.e., that rights are complementary and mutually reinforcing. Security-oriented rights, some argue, are best promoted through the free exercise of liberty-oriented rights and vice versa.

Notes

1. The twenty rights given on pages 186 and 187 are simplified versions of the Articles of the Universal Declaration as devised by a project at Geneva University in support of the World Association for the School as an Instrument of Peace.

2. Numbers in brackets refer to the Article number in the UN Declaration from which the simplified version is taken.

P Types of Rights: Articles of the UN Declaration (1948)

No one has the right to put you in prison or keep you there, or to send you away from your country unjustly or without a reason. (9)	You have the right to work, to choose your work freely and to receive payment for it that allows you and your family to live decently. Men and women should receive the same pay for doing the same work. You have the right to claim unemployment benefit or social security if necessary. You have the right to join a trade union to protect your interests. (23)
You have the right to come and go as you wish in your country. You have the right to leave your country and return to it if you wish. (13)	You have the right to ask to be protected if someone wants to force you to change the way you are, or what you and your family think or write. No one can enter your house without a reason, or say untrue, damaging things about you. (12)
You have the right to social security (a roof over your head, enough money to live on and medical help if you are ill). Also the chance to take part in and enjoy music, art, crafts, sport and anything that helps you develop your personality. (22)	The law is the same for everyone, and it should be applied in the same way for everyone. Laws must never treat people differently just because of race, colour or ways of life. (7)
You have the right to organize or take part in meetings or work together in a peaceful way, but no one can force you to belong to a group. (20)	You have the right to learn. Primary education should be compulsory and free. You should be able to learn a profession or continue your studies as far as you are able. At school you should be taught to develop your talents and to get on with other people, whatever their religion, their race or nationality. Education should help the United Nations in its efforts to bring about and keep peace in the world. Your parents have the right to choose what kind of school you will go to. (26)
You have the right to marry and have a family when you are an adult. There should be nothing to stop you marrying someone from a race, country or religion that is different from your own. Men and women have equal rights in marriage. No one can force you to marry. The government of your country should protect your family. (16)	

→

P

You have the right to a decent standard of living and to be helped if you cannot work because there is no work, or because you are ill or too old, or because your wife or husband is dead or for any other reason beyond your control. Mothers and children deserve special care. All children have the same rights, whether their parents are married or not. (25)	You have the right to own something yourself or share it with other people. No one can take it away from you without reason. (17)
	You have the right to rest and leisure, to work reasonable hours and to take regular paid holidays. (24)
You have the right to think and to express your thoughts freely. No one should stop you from having your own views, or from getting or giving information and ideas from or to other people, no matter where they live, through books, newspapers, radio, television or other means. (19)	You have the right to take an active part in your country's affairs by belonging to the government or by voting for politicians of your choice. You have the right to work in local government. The government shall be elected freely by all people. Elections shall be held regularly and everyone's vote is equal. (21)
You should be considered innocent until it can be proved that you are guilty, and you have the right to defend yourself against any charge at a public trial. You should not be punished for something you did before a new law was made that now forbids it. (11)	You have the right to join in cultural activity and to share in the better life that scientific progress makes possible. Anything you invent, write or produce should be protected and you should be able to benefit from it. (27)
No one has the right to make you a slave and you cannot make anyone your slave. (4)	You have the right to life, and to live in freedom and safety. (3)
You have the right to make up your own mind, to follow your conscience and to choose your religion freely; you can change your religion, teach it to others, and practise it as you wish, either alone or with other people. (18)	No one has the right to torture you, or to treat or punish you in a cruel way, and you cannot torture anyone. (Torture means to act in a way that hurts someone purposefully and severely in body or mind, when someone in authority or power wants to punish, frighten or force someone to confess.) (5)

ACTIVITY 10
Rights Balloon Game

Suitable for Grades 6–12

Time needed 20 minutes

Resources Each student requires a student chart (see page 189) and a class chart (page 190).

Procedure Students are asked to imagine that they are on their own, gently drifting in a hot-air balloon. On board are ten rights. Each weighs two kilos. Suddenly the balloon begins to lose height. To stop their descent, they must throw a right overboard. The balloon then levels out for a while before beginning to lose height again. Another right must be jettisoned. The process continues until they have only one right left. Students are asked to read the list carefully and think about which rights they are prepared to surrender and which they want to keep as long as possible. They then make their decisions—without discussion—by putting a 1 against the first right to be thrown overboard, a 2 against the second and so on. The right that remains at the end is numbered 10. The teacher then makes a class chart so that everybody can see the priority given to each right by the class as a whole. Discussion follows.

Potential This activity can raise some questions about the relative importance of the different rights we claim and the idea of basic rights. Which rights do we consider more important than others? Why? Are some rights so important to our well-being and essential humanity that we should never surrender them? Which can be—and are—sometimes surrendered? Under what circumstances? Can students suggest any rights that are even more important than the ones on the list, especially those they kept until last?

Variation Having made their own decisions (filling in the first column of the class chart), students move freely around the room questioning nine others and entering their scores on the same chart. This approach encourages a great deal of interaction and can be less time-consuming and repetitive than attempting to produce a profile of the whole class. Students can then be asked to analyze and reflect upon results they have collected prior to plenary discussion.

→

P

Rights Balloon Game: Student Chart

❏ The right to my own bedroom

❏ The right to clean air to breathe

❏ The right to pocket money

❏ The right to love and affection

❏ The right not to be bossed around

❏ The right to be different

❏ The right to holidays away from home each year

❏ The right to food and water

❏ The right to time for play

❏ The right to be listened to

P

Rights Balloon Game: Class Chart

	1	2	3	4	5	6	7	8	9	10
Bedroom										
Clean air										
Pocket money										
Love and affection										
Not bossed around										
Be different										
Holidays										
Food and water										
Time for play										
Be listened to										

ACTIVITY 11

The Oppression Game

Suitable for   Grades 10–12

Time needed   30 minutes

Resources
- A large open space, preferably cleared of furniture except for four "oppressors" desks and chairs at one end of the room, two "suppliers" desks and chairs at the other (see below).
- A set of role cards (see pages 194–203), one for each participant. One hundred "tokens" made by cutting sheets of plain paper into eight, with each token numbered 1–4 in the top right-hand corner (twenty-five of each number). About twenty of these should have "Defective" written across them.
- Ten sheets of plain paper and two pens or pencils.
- Four pairs of scissors; two pieces of string, each 100 cm; one party hat; one eye patch.

Oppression Game Setting

"Suppliers" desks and chairs

On each desk are: one pen/pencil, five sheets of paper, half the tokens (shuffled)

String, hat and eyepatch in centre of room

"Oppressors" desks (numbered 1–4) and chairs

On each desk is one pair of scissors

Procedure   On entering the room set out as shown above, students are given (or can randomly select) a role card. Participants have a few minutes to read and digest their role, to obtain and attach any props as demanded by their role card and then to take up positions in the room as requested. If there are disabled students in the class, they could be given "able-bodied" roles.

The activity proceeds, without interference from the facilitator, for 15–20 minutes. The facilitator should then give a suitable "reward" to the "oppressed worker" who has collected the most paper. Before discussion, participants may need some spontaneous "letting off steam" activity (e.g., shouting, hugging, jumping about) to free themselves from role.

→

Potential   A powerful and effective means of creating an oppressive structure and attendant feelings: oppression, domination, submission, discrimination, prejudice, etc. Initial discussion of the activity will probably be most productive
if it concentrates on emotions. What feelings did you experience during the
activity? Did these feelings change as the activity progressed? What attitudes
did you have towards people playing other roles? It may be useful at this
stage to brainstorm participants' emotions and record them on the chalk-
board or overhead projector.

Many of the participants were physically or socially "disabled" in some
way. What experience did they have as a result of these disabilities? What was
the attitude of other participants towards them? Such a discussion can then
broaden into consideration of people in our society coping with disabilities,
and our attitudes towards them. There is also deliberate, built-in discrimination against male participants in *The Oppression Game,* a feature that
might go unnoticed unless focused upon. One way of doing this would be
to draw up a simple "satisfaction graph" as shown below, asking each participant to record his or her overall level of satisfaction/dissatisfaction with the
experience.

Satisfaction Graph

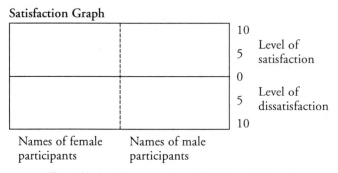

Names of female   Names of male
participants   participants

Participants will undoubtedly want to talk about "what happened" or
"what I did". The facilitator should note during the activity which participants fail to keep their role and those who rebel or are aggressive. A "rebel-
lion" by a group of "oppressed workers" is a common occurrence if the activity is allowed to continue for long enough. Discussion should also focus
upon why other participants *didn't* rebel, and the role of, and attitudes
towards, the "police". What individual rights did participants feel they
enjoyed or were denied? Were these rights, or rights denials, justified? What
could the "oppressed workers" do about the rights denials?

The "defective" tokens are a surprise element, as none of the participants
has been told about them or what to do with them. What action, if any, was
taken on account of a "defective" token?   →

If it does not happen naturally, discussion should be steered towards relating the participants' feelings and experiences during this activity to real-life situations. As role cards do not give a title (facilitators should avoid using words like "oppressed workers", "oppressor", "supplier", "police", etc.), nor specify a situation, it is interesting to ask participants if the activity reminds them of any real-life situations they have experienced or know about. Responses such as "factory", "social insurance office", "immigration control", etc. are common, but so is "school"—a revelation that may lead to fascinating insights into the education system as viewed by students.

The Oppression Game can give participants an understanding of what it feels like to be oppressed, or an oppressor, and the kind of actions that result from such feelings. As it can give rise to strong emotional responses, it should be used with a well-affirmed group, and is probably not suitable below upper secondary level.

Source Based on *The Oppression Game* by Martha Evans and Alan Tuttle, in Coover, V. et al., *Resource Manual for a Living Revolution* (Philadelphia, New Society Publishers, 1981).

Role Cards The following role cards are designed for twenty participants. For twenty-one to thirty participants, increase the number of "oppressed workers", add an extra "police officer" and another "supplier". For groups of less than 20 participants, only one "supplier" can be used, with two or three "oppressors". The number of "oppressed workers" should account for at least 60 percent of total participants. "Disabilities" can be varied or deleted, as required.

Role Cards

P

You have to do everything with your right wrist connected to your right ankle by a piece of string.

When told to do so, go and stand in line in the centre of the room, facing the two desks. Do not talk. When your turn comes, go to one of the desks, where you will be asked to do something. If you do it correctly, you will be given a token; take this to one of the four desks at the other end of the room. The number on your token tells you which desk. Before handing over your token you must bow three times. You are not allowed to say anything.

You will be given a small piece of paper in return, which you can keep. Go back to the centre of the room and wait in line until your turn comes round again. You should try to collect enough pieces of paper to make up the equivalent size of one token. DO NOT SHOW THIS CARD TO ANYONE ELSE.

You have to do everything with your eyes always focused on the ground in front of you.

When told to do so, go and stand in line in the centre of the room, facing the two desks. Do not talk. When your turn comes, go to one of the desks, where you will be asked to do something. If you do it correctly, you will be given a token; take this to one of the four desks at the other end of the room. The number on your token tells you which desk. Before handing over your token you must bow three times. You are not allowed to say anything.

You will be given a small piece of paper in return, which you can keep. Go back to the centre of the room and wait in line until your turn comes round again. You should try to collect enough pieces of paper to make up the equivalent size of one token. DO NOT SHOW THIS CARD TO ANYONE ELSE.

→

P

You have to do everything with your hands tied behind your back.

When told to do so, go and stand in line in the centre of the room, facing the two desks. Do not talk. When your turn comes, go to one of the desks, where you will be asked to do something. If you do it correctly, you will be given a token; take this to one of the four desks at the other end of the room. The number on your token tells you which desk. Before handing over your token you must bow three times. You are not allowed to say anything.

You will be given a small piece of paper in return, which you can keep. Go back to the centre of the room and wait in line until your turn comes round again. You should try to collect enough pieces of paper to make up the equivalent size of one token. DO NOT SHOW THIS CARD TO ANYONE ELSE.

You have to do everything without speaking.

When told to do so, go and stand in line in the centre of the room, facing the two desks. When your turn comes, go to one of the desks where you will be asked to do something. If you do it correctly, you will be given a token; take this to one of the four desks at the other end of the room. The number on your token tells you which desk. Before handing over your token you must bow three times.

You will be given a small piece of paper in return, which you can keep. Go back to the centre of the room and wait in line until your turn comes round again. You should try to collect enough pieces of paper to make up the equivalent size of one token. DO NOT SHOW THIS CARD TO ANYONE ELSE.

→

P

You have to wear an eye patch all the time.

When told to do so, go and stand in line in the centre of the room, facing the two desks. Do not talk. When your turn comes, go to one of the desks, where you will be asked to do something. If you do it correctly, you will be given a token; take this to one of the four desks at the other end of the room. The number on your token tells you which desk. Before handing over your token you must bow three times. You are not allowed to say anything.

You will be given a small piece of paper in return, which you can keep. Go back to the centre of the room and wait in line until your turn comes round again. You should try to collect enough pieces of paper to make up the equivalent size of one token. DO NOT SHOW THIS CARD TO ANYONE ELSE.

When told to do so, go and stand in line in the centre of the room, facing the two desks. Do not talk. When your turn comes, go to one of the desks, where you will be asked to do something. If you do it correctly, you will be given a token; take this to one of the four desks at the other end of the room. The number on your token tells you which desk. Before handing over your token you must bow three times. You are not allowed to say anything.

You will be given a small piece of paper in return, which you can keep. Go back to the centre of the room and wait in line until your turn comes round again. If you collect more paper than anyone else, you will be rewarded. DO NOT SHOW THIS CARD TO ANYONE ELSE.

→

P

You have to wear a hat all the time.

When told to do so, go and stand in line in the centre of the room, facing the two desks. Do not talk. When your turn comes, go to one of the desks, where you will be asked to do something. If you do it correctly, you will be given a token; take this to one of the four desks at the other end of the room. The number on your token tells you which desk. Before handing over your token you must bow three times. You are not allowed to say anything.

You will be given a small piece of paper in return, which you can keep. Go back to the centre of the room and wait in line until your turn comes round again. You should try to collect enough pieces of paper to make up the equivalent size of one token. DO NOT SHOW THIS CARD TO ANYONE ELSE.

When told to do so, go and stand in line in the centre of the room, facing the two desks. Do not talk. When your turn comes, go to one of the desks, where you will be asked to do something. If you do it correctly, you will be given a token; take this to one of the four desks at the other end of the room. The number on your token tells you which desk. Before handing over your token you must bow three times. You are not allowed to say anything.

You will be given a small piece of paper in return, which you can keep. Go back to the centre of the room and wait in line until your turn comes round again. If you collect more paper than anyone else, you will be rewarded. DO NOT SHOW THIS CARD TO ANYONE ELSE.

→

P

When told to do so, go and stand in line in the centre of the room, facing the two desks. Do not talk. When your turn comes, go to one of the desks, where you will be asked to do something. If you do it correctly, you will be given a token; take this to one of the four desks at the other end of the room. The number on your token tells you which desk. Before handing over your token you must bow three times. You are not allowed to say anything.

You will be given a small piece of paper in return, which you can keep. Go back to the centre of the room and wait in line until your turn comes round again. If you collect more paper than anyone else, you will be rewarded. DO NOT SHOW THIS CARD TO ANYONE ELSE.

When told to do so, go and stand in line in the centre of the room, facing the two desks. Do not talk. When your turn comes, go to one of the desks, where you will be asked to do something. If you do it correctly, you will be given a token; take this to one of the four desks at the other end of the room. The number on your token tells you which desk. Before handing over your token you must bow three times. You are not allowed to say anything.

You will be given a small piece of paper in return, which you can keep. Go back to the centre of the room and wait in line until your turn comes round again. If you collect more paper than anyone else, you will be rewarded. DO NOT SHOW THIS CARD TO ANYONE ELSE.

→

P

When told to do so, go and stand in line in the centre of the room, facing the two desks. Do not talk. When your turn comes, go to one of the desks, where you will be asked to do something. If you do it correctly, you will be given a token; take this to one of the four desks at the other end of the room. The number on your token tells you which desk. Before handing over your token you must bow three times. You are not allowed to say anything.

You will be given a small piece of paper in return, which you can keep. Go back to the centre of the room and wait in line until your turn comes round again. If you collect more paper than anyone else, you will be rewarded. DO NOT SHOW THIS CARD TO ANYONE ELSE.

When told to do so, go and stand in line in the centre of the room, facing the two desks. Do not talk. When your turn comes, go to one of the desks, where you will be asked to do something. If you do it correctly, you will be given a token; take this to one of the four desks at the other end of the room. The number on your token tells you which desk. Before handing over your token you must bow three times. You are not allowed to say anything.

You will be given a small piece of paper in return, which you can keep. Go back to the centre of the room and wait in line until your turn comes round again. If you collect more paper than anyone else, you will be rewarded. DO NOT SHOW THIS CARD TO ANYONE ELSE.

→

P

Go and sit behind one of the four desks at one end of the room. When a person approaches you, s/he must bow three times before handing over a token. Take the token, cut off a small piece (about one eighth of the token) and hand it back, keeping the larger piece for yourself; be mean, particularly to males. Tell the person to work harder. Collect as many tokens as you can. DO NOT SHOW THIS CARD TO ANYONE ELSE.

Go and sit behind one of the four desks at one end of the room. When a person approaches you, s/he must bow three times before handing over a token. Take the token, cut off a small piece (about one quarter of the token) and hand it back, keeping the larger piece for yourself; you can be generous sometimes, but never to males. Encourage the person to work harder. Collect as many tokens as you can. DO NOT SHOW THIS CARD TO ANYONE ELSE.

→

Go and sit behind one of the four desks at one end of the room. When a person approaches you, s/he must bow three times before handing over a token. Take the token, cut off a small piece (about one eighth of the token) and hand it back, keeping the larger piece for yourself; be mean, particularly to males. Tell the person to work harder. Collect as many tokens as you can. DO NOT SHOW THIS CARD TO ANYONE ELSE.

Go and sit behind one of the four desks at one end of the room. When a person approaches you, s/he must bow three times before handing over a token. Take the token, cut off a small piece (about one quarter of the token) and hand it back, keeping the larger piece for yourself; you can be generous sometimes, but never to males. Encourage the person to work harder. Collect as many tokens as you can. DO NOT SHOW THIS CARD TO ANYONE ELSE.

→

P

Go and sit behind one of the two desks at one end of the room; on each desk is a pile of tokens. When a person approaches your desk, ask her/him to do something, e.g.,

Touch her/his toes five times.

Spell "syntax" or "parallel".

Count up to one hundred in fives.

Draw a picture of a horse.

Make the actions of a windmill.

Make up some of your own, too. When the task has been done to your satisfaction, give the person a token. Be harsh: don't let her/him get away with not doing the task well. Be particularly harsh on males. You can give two chances, but if the task is still not completed satisfactorily, send the person back to the centre without a token. DO NOT SHOW THIS CARD TO ANYONE ELSE.

Go and sit behind one of the two desks at one end of the room; on each desk is a pile of tokens. When a person approaches your desk, ask her/him to do something, e.g.,

Touch her/his toes five times.

Spell "syntax" or "parallel".

Count up to one hundred in fives.

Draw a picture of a horse.

Make the actions of a windmill.

Make up some of your own, too. When the task has been done to your satisfaction, give the person a token. Be lenient: just satisfy yourself that the person is doing the task to the best of her/his ability. Do not be too lenient, however, with males. You can give two chances, but if the task is still not completed satisfactorily, send the person back to the centre without a token. DO NOT SHOW THIS CARD TO ANYONE ELSE.

→

You must ensure that everyone acts according to the rules. Do not tolerate any disobedience or you may lose control. Points to watch out for:

People standing in the centre of the room:

1. They must always wear/do whatever they have been told to on their role cards.
2. They must wait quietly in line until their turn comes.
3. They must do whatever is asked of them when they approach one of the two desks; do not allow any arguments.
4. Before presenting their token at one of the four desks (the one corresponding to the number on the token), they must bow three times, and are not allowed to speak.

People sitting behind desks:

These people may need your protection: be prepared at all times to help them.
DO NOT SHOW THIS CARD TO ANYONE ELSE.

You must ensure that everyone acts according to the rules. Do not tolerate any disobedience or you may lose control. Points to watch out for:

People standing in the centre of the room:

1. They must always wear/do whatever they have been told to on their role cards.
2. They must wait quietly in line until their turn comes.
3. They must do whatever is asked of them when they approach one of the two desks; do not allow any arguments.
4. Before presenting their token at one of the four desks (the one corresponding to the number on the token), they must bow three times, and are not allowed to speak.

People sitting behind desks:

These people may need your protection: be prepared at all times to help them.
DO NOT SHOW THIS CARD TO ANYONE ELSE.

Dimension 3: Social Justice

Structural violence; unequal distribution of wealth; systemic discrimination; racism; sexism

---

ACTIVITY 12
Trading Game

Suitable for   Grades 7–12

Time needed   60 minutes

Resources   Plain paper, pencils, scissors, rulers, compasses; chart displaying correct shapes and values (see below); chart displaying resource prices (see below); units of currency (slips of paper with numbers, in denominations of 5 and 10).

Procedure   Before students enter, the classroom is set out as follows: six to eight desks (one desk for every four students in the class) are set out in the centre of the room, each containing "raw materials" in different quantities. For example:

Desk 1:   2 sheets of paper; 5 currency units

Desk 2:   4 sheets of paper, 1 pair of scissors; 10 currency units

Desk 3:   2 sheets of paper, 1 pair of scissors, 1 ruler; 20 currency units

Desk 4:   1 sheet of paper, 2 pairs of scissors, 1 pair of compasses; 50 currency units

Desk 5:   6 sheets of paper, 2 pairs of scissors, 1 pair of compasses, 1 ruler; 80 currency units

Desk 6:   6 sheets of paper, 2 pairs of scissors, 3 rulers; 100 currency units.

(The quantities can vary, according to availability of resources; it is important, however, to have an unequal distribution between the desks). A limited supply of extra resources should be kept at the "bank" (operated by the teacher) for purchase at fixed prices (see chart).

The charts below are placed at the front of the class, so that they are visible from all desks.

Groups of four students are assigned to each desk. They are told that their task is to make any of the shapes, to the *exact* measurements as displayed on the chart (see page 206), and to sell them to the "bank" in exchange for currency units (the number by each shape indicates its value). The teacher

→

204

has the right to refuse to buy any shapes that are not to the exact specifications. Additional resources can be purchased, for the amount indicated, from the bank; trading of resources between groups can also take place at a price to be arranged by the groups concerned. The game should be allowed to proceed without interruption from the teacher for a fixed period of time or until all the available resources have been used. At the end, groups count up their units of currency and the "winners" are declared. Discussion follows.

Potential This activity is likely to generate a strong sense of injustice among the least-resourced groups as the accumulative impact of the unequal distribution of resources becomes evident. This emotional energy can be tapped at the beginning of the debriefing by first concentrating upon the students' *feelings*. The vocabulary they use to describe their feelings—of both "winners" and "losers"—can be written up on the board. Once feelings have been explored, students should be asked to reflect upon whether or not this activity is a realistic simulation of any situation they know. Examples from within their own society are likely to be given. Statistics about global wealth distribution and the operations of multinational corporations can be introduced at this stage. Students can be asked to consider how the trading system in this activity could be made fairer, and what parallels there might be in the wider world. What are the advantages and disadvantages of "free trade" agreements, such as NAFTA, for both powerful and not-so-powerful member states? What role can individual consumers play in creating more just and equitable trading systems?

Source Based on *The Trading Game*, Christian Aid.

→

Market Prices and Product Specifications

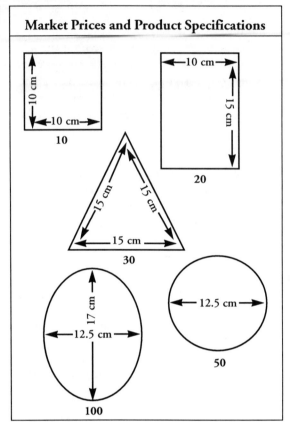

Resource Prices	
Paper, per sheet	5
Scissors, per pair	15
Ruler, each	15
Compasses, per pair	50

ACTIVITY 13

Recalling Injustice

Suitable for   Grades 9–12

Time needed   30 minutes

Procedure   Students form groups of six and then divide into pairs. One partner is nominated "A", the other "B". The activity begins with a few minutes' silence in which everybody is asked to recall occasions when they have felt unjustly treated. "A" students are then asked to recount those incidents they have recalled (and wish to recount) to their partner. "B" listens actively, contributing only encouraging words and prompting questions if need be. After five minutes, "B" recounts her incidents while "A" listens. The group of six then reforms. The students are asked to take on the story or stories of their partner as their own and retell them, in turn, to the group, using the "I" first-person form. When groups have completed the task, the facilitator asks the class to brainstorm the emotions they felt when treated unjustly. These words are recorded on the board or overhead projector.

Potential   This is a powerful introductory activity to work on discrimination, involving the exercise of listening, memory and oral skills. The recounting and sharing of instances of injustice create a context in which participants tend to respond sensitively and empathetically to injustice done to others. Teachers often follow the activity with film or video material of racial or gender injustice. At points in the ensuing discussion attention can be drawn to the results of the brainstorming. This activity should only be attempted with a well-affirmed group. If the group is particularly well-affirmed, the activity can be repeated with a recounting of occasions when students feel they have treated others unfairly or unjustly.

ACTIVITY 14

The Power Flower

Suitable for   Grades 7–12

Time needed   60 minutes

Resources   A "Power Flower" sheet ("Power Flower (1)" for Grades 7–10; "Power Flower (2)" for grades 11–13) for each participant; a centre circle of eight chairs and an outer circle containing one chair for each participant.

Procedure   Working individually and avoiding discussion, participants complete the "Power Flower" sheet by writing in details that describe themselves under each petal heading. The task complete, eight volunteers for a goldfish-bowl discussion are required. The volunteers take seats in the centre circle and, in turn, make an initial statement clarifying whether they regard themselves as relatively powerful or powerless people and identifying the sources/causes of their powerfulness/powerlessness. The eight then engage in discussion around their statements. Sufficient time having elapsed (ten to fifteen minutes), the facilitator invites participants sitting in the outer circle to tap a member of the inner circle on the shoulder, as and when they wish, as a signal that they want to take their place in the discussion. Participants can join the inner circle on more than one occasion. On their first visit to the inner circle, they can be invited to make a brief initial statement about their relative powerfulness/powerlessness and its sources or causes. Whole group discussion follows at an appropriate point.

Potential   An activity likely to raise a range of issues concerning the possession and exercise of power in society. From what sources is power particularly derived? Are there particular constellations of sources that especially lend themselves to the possession and exercise of power and influence? Are there particular combinations of sources that tend to determine who are the powerless? Are there factors determining one's relative powerfulness/powerlessness that are missing from the flower? Have the sources of power shifted in any way during the last hundred years? Are they likely to shift in the future? What means are used by the powerful to retain their power? What can the powerless do to effect a redistribution of power? What responsibilities should come with the possession and exercise of power and influence?

   The activity can also be used as a springboard for the exploration of particular forms of discrimination and marginalization in society (for instance, ageism, racism, sexism).

→

If attempted as a professional development activity, teachers can also be asked to reflect on their relative powerfulness/powerlessness and on the nature of the power they possess and exercise. From what sources is that power derived? Are some teachers more powerful than others? How has that come about? Why were the teachers represented in the group successful in obtaining the position of relative power and influence that comes with being a teacher? Who are/were the people unable to aspire to any such position?

Follow-up 1. As a post-activity written assignment, students are asked to reflect upon whether they felt powerful or powerless during the goldfish-bowl discussion and to describe people who do appear powerful in such situations. With the agreement of the students concerned and with anonymity maintained, extracts of the assignments are typed out and become the stimulus for further small and large group discussion.

2. Participants pool the words they used to complete, for instance, the "ethnic background", "race", "social class" or "ability/disability" petals. Working in small groups, they discuss whether the phrases and terms used are meaningful, appropriate, accurate and/or likely to cause offence to particular groups. Reporting back and discussion in plenary session follows.

Variation Participants begin by filling in three "Power Flower" sheets; one for themselves, one for an imaginary person possessing a lot of power and one for an imaginary person possessing very little power. Before the goldfish-bowl discussion begins, they share their work in small groups, reflecting upon which imaginary person they approximate to most closely.

Source After an idea adapted by Meri Macleod and Susan Walker of the International Centre, Queen's University, Kingston, Ontario, from Lee, E., *Letters to Marcia: A teacher's guide to anti-racist education*, Toronto, Cross Cultural Communication Centre, 1985. *Follow-up 1* and *Variation 1* devised by the 1994-5 Grade 7 team at Westmount Public School, London, Ontario (Anne Marie Fitzgerald, Jackie Fitzsimmons, Steve Rathbar).

Power Flower (1)

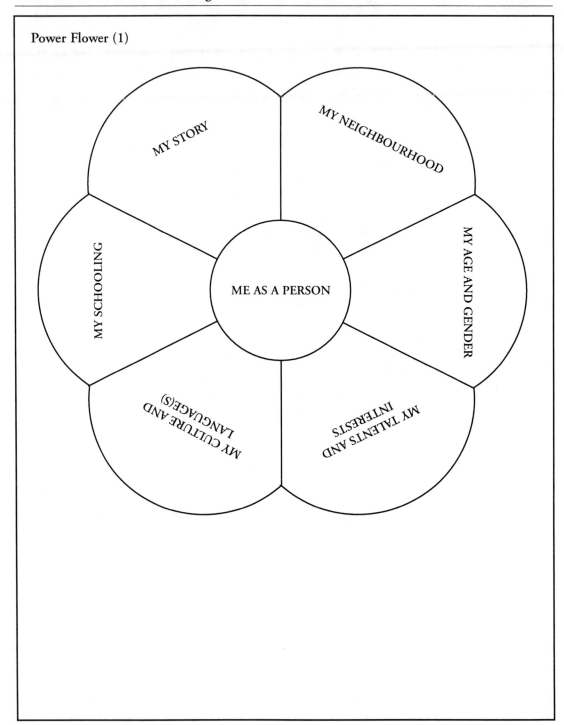

Power Flower (2)

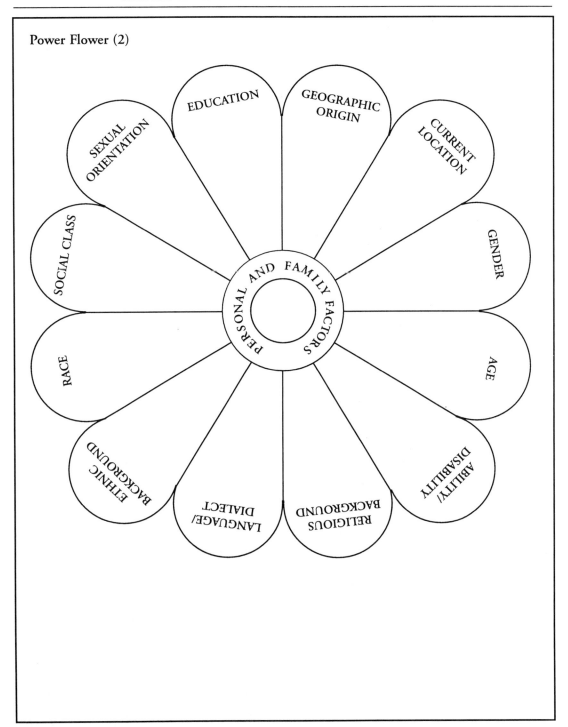

Dimension 4: Worldmindedness

Viewing the world from the perspectives of other cultures; interconnectedness of local and global

---

ACTIVITY 15
Wit and Wisdom

Suitable for   Grades 7–12

Time needed   60 minutes

Resources   A set of badges (at least one per student) inscribed with proverbs (see pages 214–215). A sheet of newsprint and two markers of different colours for each group of four students.

Procedure   *Stage 1.* Working in groups of four, students brainstorm as many proverbs as they can think of, writing them on newsprint with one of the markers. They then discuss the basic value(s) or moral(s) that underpin the proverbs and write these next to each proverb, using the second marker (see example below). Plenary discussion follows, focussing on the use and impact of proverbs in the students' childhood and upbringing.

Proverb	Value(s)/Moral(s)
Don't cry over spilt milk	Be practical; don't worry unnecessarily
Too many cooks spoil the broth	Don't interfere in others' affairs
A stitch in time saves nine	Think ahead

Stage 2. Students individually select, or are given, a badge to wear. After initial reflection on the meaning of their own proverb, they try to form pairs or groups of people whose proverbs have the same or similar underlying values or morals. Any remaining individuals should be encouraged to join the most appropriate pair/group. After discussing the various proverbs, each pair/group selects one as the basis for a short dramatic sketch that conveys its underlying message. The sketches are presented to the rest of the students who have to guess what the proverb might be. Plenary discussion follows.

Potential   A light-hearted exploration of the function and significance of proverbs in the students' own and other cultures. Discussion could include an analysis of the similarities/differences between proverbs (and their underlying meanings) in various cultures; matching proverbs from other cultures with those derived from *Stage 1*; and an assessment of the appropriateness of selected

→

proverbs as suitable moral guidelines for the twenty-first century (including the language used).

Follow-up   Many opportunities exist for further creative work. Students can illustrate the meanings of selected proverbs through creative writing (i.e., turning the proverb into a fable) or in cartoon form. They can also try to invent new proverbs that portray values they feel will be significant for life in the twenty-first century, e.g.,

—encourage people to embrace new information technology;

—encourage boys to be gentle and caring/girls to be assertive;

—warn of the dangers of environmental destruction;

—warn of the dangers of nationalism/sectarianism.

Ⓟ Wit and Wisdom: Proverbs

Nobody cries who has not been pinched. *Kenya*

An old crow does not croak for nothing. *Russia*

You cannot hold onto two cows at the same time. *Burkino Faso*

A man cannot whistle and drink at the same time. *Denmark*

Do not hold a leopard's tail, but if you hold it, don't let go. *Ethiopia*

If you have to kill a snake, kill it once and for all. *Japan*

He who is starving hates him who is eating. *Gabon*

When one eats and others look on, there is likely to be a fight. *Turkey*

In multitude there is strength. *Nigeria*

United we stand, divided we fall. *United States*

A bad brother is far better than no brother. *Swahili, East Africa*

Blood is thicker than water. *Norway*

The wise child is spoken to in proverbs, not in simple language. *Ghana*

The wise child listens to his elders. *Italy*

Unless you fill up the crack, you will have to build a new wall. *Ewe, West Africa*

A stitch in time saves nine. *Holland*

Fair speech turns elephants away from the garden path. *Swahili, East Africa*

Gentle words open iron gates. *Bulgaria*

Time passes on but sayings remain. *India/Sri Lanka*

Learn proverbs well and good speech will come naturally. *China*

→

A rotten trade does not produce fruits, and empty words have no value. *China*

Together, people can move mountains; firewood bunched together can produce higher flames. *China*

Pain in the finger affects the whole body. *Philippines*

One who does not know how to dance blames the flooring. *Burma*

A pumpkin thief is known by his shoulder. *Sri Lanka*

The hardest rock erodes in water. *Philippines*

Repairing the cow-shed after the cow is lost. *Republic of Korea*

A sparrow does not skim over a rice mill. *Republic of Korea*

Constant grinding can turn even iron into a needle. *China*

Where elephants fight, the seeds get hurt. *Tanzania*

Unity among the small makes the lion lie down hungry. *Swahili, East Africa*

By trying often, the monkey learns to jump from the tree. *Zaire*

We must all hang together or we'll all hang separately. *United States*

Better a slip of the foot than of the tongue. *France*

He who looks not before, finds himself behind. *France*

Begin in time to finish without hurrying. *Germany*

He conquers who sticks in the saddle. *Italy*

Where there are too many cooks the soup will be salty. *Italy*

Truth and oil always come to the surface. *Spain*

The wise man does not hang his knowledge on a hook. *Spain*

ACTIVITY 16
Going Dotty

Suitable for   Grades 3–12

Time needed 5 minutes

Resources   Small, self-adhesive coloured dots, in at least four colours, one for each participant. An open classroom space so that students can move about freely.

Procedure   Students form a circle, close their eyes and remain silent. Each participant has a coloured dot stuck on his or her forehead. The different colours should be spread among the class so that neighbouring students do not have the same colour, but there should be an approximately equal number of each colour. Students then open their eyes and try to form groups of the same-coloured dots without speaking, pointing at colours, looking for reflections or peeling off the dot.

Potential   A simple exercise with a variety of possible uses. It establishes very quickly the need for cooperation among individuals in order to solve a group task; there is a degree of affirmation in bringing individuals together through a short, enjoyable problem-solving exercise; it heightens the importance of non-verbal communication and raises issues surrounding trust. At a conceptual level, the exercise provides an illustration of the concepts of interdependence and identity. Nobody can fulfill the task set save through mutual dependence and trust. Everybody's sense of identity (understanding of their dot colour) is dependent upon everybody else. This activity, therefore, can provide an effective springboard into work on interconnectedness and citizenship. At a practical level, the activity can be used as an enjoyable means of organizing students into random groups for further work.

Variations   The activity model described here has multiple classroom uses. In science it has been used to reinforce students' understanding of body parts. A large outline of the human body is chalked on the floor. Students, with eyes closed, have a sticky label, with the name of a body part written on it, stuck to their backs. Avoiding speaking, they help each other take up the appropriate juxtaposition within the body outline. They then have to guess the part they represent. In geography the activity has been used similarly to develop locational knowledge of the cities, towns, rivers, mountains and other key features of a country using a chalked country outline. Students can be encouraged to use body sculptures to good effect in both the above

→

suggestions (e.g., lying on the floor with body curled to represent intestines or the meandering of a river). In math the activity can be employed to practise fractions or decimals; for instance, students have a decimal number placed on their back and in silence must form groups of five in which the sum total of the numbers equals, say, 2.5. In language arts, students can be asked to form groups in which the word(s) and/or punctuation mark stuck on their back forms part of a grammatically correct sentence. *In all these variations, nobody has completed the task until all classmates have been placed.* Acquisition or reinforcement of knowledge is, thus, combined with the practise of non-verbal and cooperative skills.

ACTIVITY 17

Globingo!

Suitable for   Grades 4–12

Time needed   20 minutes

Resources   A "Globingo!" handout for each student; open classroom space so that participants can move freely about.

Procedure   Students spread out and are given copies of the handout (see page 219). The purpose of the exercise is for each student to fill in as many squares as possible by obtaining information from other students. It should be emphasized that the name of the country and the name of the student should be written in the appropriate square. A particular student's name should only appear once on a sheet so as to encourage the maximum possible interaction amongst the group. Each time a row of four squares—horizontal, vertical or diagonal—has been completed, a student should call out "Globingo!" The students should go on to attempt more rows (ten are possible). It is important to encourage students to actively ask questions of each other rather than passively swapping sheets.

Potential   This is an excellent starter activity for work on global interconnectedness and interdependence. Students will probably make some surprising discoveries about their classmates, too! One way into follow-up discussion is first to ask about those surprises. After exploratory discussion, the class can be encouraged to explain and categorize the types of global connections they found during the activity (e.g., trading connections, media connections, connections brought about by the movement of peoples).

Extensions   A useful follow-up is to pin a large world map to a bulletin board and ask the students to locate the countries identified during "Globingo!" The squares in each student's handout can be cut up and pinned to the country (repetitive squares being laid aside). The coloured pins are then connected by cotton to a pin identifying the school's location. The final product will show "the world in our class". Discussion questions might include: Do we seem to be particularly connected with certain parts of the world? If so, can we suggest why? What would happen to life as we know it if all these connections disappeared?

Source   Derived from Johnson, J. and Benegar, J., *Global Issues in the Intermediate Classroom,* Boulder, Colorado: Social Science Education Consortium, 1981.

P

Globingo!

Find someone who:

A   has travelled to another country

B   has a pen pal in another country

C   is learning a language other than English or French

D   has a relative in another country

E   has helped a visitor from another country

F   enjoys a music group from another country

G   is wearing something that was made in another country

H   enjoys eating foods from another country

I   has given to a charity that helps people in another country

J   has a family car that was made in another country

K   has talked to someone who has lived in another country

L   lives in a home where more than one language is spoken

M   saw a story about another country in the newspaper recently

N   learned something about another country on TV recently

O   owns a TV or other appliance made in another country

P   has a parent or other relative who was born in another country

A	B	C	D
name	name	name	name
country	country	country	country
E	F	G	H
name	name	name	name
country	country	country	country
I	J	K	L
name	name	name	name
country	country	country	country
M	N	O	P
name	name	name	name
country	country	country	country

Dimension 5: Ecological Balance

Global environmental problems, e.g., global warming, deforestation; linking environmental to other global themes, e.g., development, human rights

---

ACTIVITY 18

Fruits of the Forest

Suitable for   Grades 7–12

Time needed   40 minutes

Resources   One set of "Fruits of the Forest" cards (see page 222) and one strip of paper (made by cutting newsprint lengthways into three) for each pair; glue sticks; extra set of cards and paper strip for each group of six.

Procedure   Working initially in pairs, students read through and discuss the twelve "Fruits of the Forest" cards which describe some common uses of the world's forests and forest products. Pairs then try to agree upon where each card should be placed on the paper strip which represents a continuum from "totally acceptable use" at one end to "totally unacceptable use" at the other. When agreement is reached, the cards are glued down in position. Individually, students decide at what point they would "draw the line" (i.e., between "acceptable" and "not acceptable") and mark that point with an initialled pencil line. Three pairs then join together to explain and justify their card placing before trying to negotiate a consensus placing for the group of six, using a fresh set of cards and paper strip. Finally, each student can again mark where he or she would "draw the line", having listened to the arguments of others.

Potential   An activity that promotes awareness of some major uses of forest products and encourages reflection upon the complex issues generated by their use. Although this is a consensus-seeking activity, to stimulate maximum discussion and sharing of perspectives individuals are still encouraged to state their own value position in terms of where they would "draw the line" between acceptable and non-acceptable uses. In follow-up discussion it should be pointed out that all of these activities are, to varying degrees, depleting the world's forests or interfering with their complex ecosystems. The concept of "sustainable use" might be introduced here, along with discussion about practical steps (e.g., recycling paper, not buying tropical hardwoods or rare

→

animal and bird species) that students can take to help safeguard the remaining forests. Further discussion and follow-up work could focus on the question of who benefits from the extraction of these forest products. Drug companies and food manufacturers have made millions of dollars from such products; many developing nations are now demanding a realistic return for their valuable resources.

P # Fruits of the Forest Cards

Firewood One third of the world's people rely on firewood for heating and cooking. In the poorest countries of the world, most wood collected is used for fuel.	**Food** Many common foods, including coffee, bananas, cocoa and rice, originated in the rainforest. Genes from these wild plants are still required to make new strains which are resistant to disease.
Cattle Large areas of rainforest are cleared so that cattle can be grazed. Much of the resulting beef is used for making hamburgers in wealthy countries.	**Skins** The skins of wild cats from the rainforest, such as the jaguar and the ocelot, are used to make expensive fur coats. An ocelot coat is made from ten skins.
Medicines Extracts of many forest plants are used as the basis of modern drugs. Quinine (from the bark of the *cinchona* tree) is widely used to treat malaria and extracts from the *rosy periwinkle* are effective cancer treatments.	**Hardwood** Prized hardwoods, like mahogany, teak and cedar, are used to make quality furniture, window frames, boats and musical instruments.
Paper The world uses an enormous quantity of wood pulp to make paper—an estimated 4 billion trees are cut each year for paper. One bumper issue of the *New York Times* is the end product of 400 hectares of forest.	**Mining** Many important minerals, such as gold, iron-ore, tin and aluminum, have been found in rainforest areas. Mining causes extensive damage to the land.
Medical Research Drug companies are studying thousands of rainforest plant species used in medicines by Aboriginal peoples. Some of these may contain cures for diseases like cancer.	**Electricity** Over thirty hydro-electric dams are planned in the Amazon basin by flooding huge areas of rainforest. Much of the electricity produced will be used by local industry.
Pets Rainforest birds, such as parrots and macaws, are sold and kept in cages in western countries. Iguanas are popular house pets, too.	**Transport** Mining, logging and other forest industries require the construction of road and rail networks through thousands of kilometres of rainforest.

ACTIVITY 19

Big Bad Wolves?

Suitable for   Grades 7–12

Time needed   40 minutes

Resources   Sheet of newsprint, two markers and a set of statements about wolves (see page 225) for each group of three or four students.

Procedure   The teacher first leads a class brainstorming session of ideas, associations, idioms and sayings stimulated by the word "wolf". All suggestions are written up on the board or overhead projection transparency. Groups then form. Using the newsprint and markers provided, their first task is to divide the class responses into positive and negative images and to discuss and write down where they think the images of the wolf may have come from. A set of statements is then given to each group to promote further discussion. With which statements (or sentiments within statements) do they agree? With which do they disagree? Who do they think might have made such statements? Class discussion follows.

Potential   A useful activity for exploring stereotyping in attitudes towards a much-maligned animal. Discussion is likely to focus upon why people tend to have a negative image of the wolf. What characteristics of wolves might generate fear and misunderstanding in humans? Which people might most feel their interest to be threatened by the wolf? Who might believe their interests to be best served by perpetuating fear and misunderstanding? How is the negative image of the wolf passed on to fresh generations? Is the image fair? Why do some people see the wolf in a very different way? What effect has the negative image of the wolf upon wolf populations?

Extensions   1. The class watches a film exploring the reality of wolf behaviour and social interaction prior to further group and plenary discussion. Suitable films for elementary use include: *Never Cry Wolf*, Disney Education Productions, 1983, 30 mins.; *Where Timber Wolves Call*, Wombat 1977, 25 mins.; *Wolf Pack*, Canadian Wildlife Service, Ottawa, 1976, 20 mins.; *Wolves*, Owl TV Productions, no. 37, Toronto, 1990; *Wolves*, Rainbow Educational Video, New York, 1990, 10 mins. Suitable films for the secondary classroom include: *Death of a Legend*, National Film Board of Canada, 1971, 49 mins.; *The Wolf Saga*, BBC, 1990, 29 mins.; *Wolf*, ABC News Productions, New York, 1977, 22 mins.; *Wolves*, National Audobon Society, USA, 1988, 60 mins.; *Wolves and the Wolfman*, MGM, CA, 1971, 52 mins.

→

2. The negative images of wolves brainstormed by the class are apportioned among groups. Each group undertakes project collection or library research to find out if their selection of images is fair. Groups report back in plenary session.

3. Each group undertakes a cooperative re-writing of a children's story in which wolves feature, but from the wolf's point of view. Stories might include "Little Red Riding Hood" (see "The Maligned Wolf", page 226, as an example), "The Three Little Pigs" and "The Wolf and the Seven Goats" (Grimm). Old and new versions of the stories are tried out on younger children and their respective effects assessed. The class goes on to read and reflect upon a selection of contemporary pro-wolf stories for children.

4. Groups sift through collections of children's traditional fables, stories, songs and nursery rhymes for examples of creatures being portrayed as villains (e.g., "Little Miss Muffet") or of animals being uncritically and complacently depicted as victims of cruelty and violence (e.g., "Three Blind Mice", "Ding Dong Bell"). Examples are written up or summarized on sheets of newsprint in a marker of one colour and the students' general and specific criticisms of the text written in a marker of a second colour. In addition, students can re-write pro-animal versions of offending items. Group work is shared and the effect of negative and "victim" depictions of animals on children's attitudes discussed. Letters of criticism with regard to newly published anti-animal literature can be sent to the publishers concerned.

Some pro-wolf books for children:

• Jon Scieszka, *The True Story of the 3 Little Pigs!*, New York, Viking, 1989. Told from the wolf's point of view.

• Celia Godkin, *Wolf Island*, Markham, Ontario, Fitzhenry & Whiteside, 1993. Set on an island in Northern Ontario and based on an actual event. Chronicles what happens when the highest link in the food chain is removed.

• Farley Mowat, *Never Cry Wolf*, Toronto, Seal Books, McClelland-Bantam Inc., 1968. True story of life amongst the Arctic wolves.

P

Big Bad Wolves?: Statements

Wolves are responsible for the cold-blooded slaughter of huge numbers of defenceless sheep and other livestock. They are cruel and cunning animals. They are the criminal exploiters of nature; vermin deserving to be eradicated.

Wolves have been found to act as an important "natural safety valve" on populations of deer, moose, rabbits and other animals. They weed out the weaker members of the population, thus preventing overcrowding and allowing the stronger, fitter animals to flourish.

The Great Spirit is within the wolf as it is within all things. The wolf is the voice of the wilderness and it is part of the pattern of nature that connects us all. If we destroy the wolf, we destroy ourselves.

I wanted to give something of my past to my grandson. So I took him into the woods, to a quiet spot. Seated at my feet he listened as I told him of the powers that were given to each creature. He moved not a muscle as I explained how the woods had always provided us with food, homes, comfort, and religion. He was awed when I related to him how the wolf became our guardian, and when I told him that I would sing the sacred wolf song over him, he was overjoyed. When I had ended, it was as if the whole world listened with us to hear the wolf's reply. We waited a long time but none came. All of a sudden I realized why no wolves had heard my sacred song. There were none left! My heart filled with tears. I could no longer give my grandson faith in the past, our past.

P

The Maligned Wolf

The forest was my home. I lived there and I cared about it. I tried to keep it neat and clean.

Then one sunny day, while I was cleaning up some garbage a camper had left behind, I heard footsteps. I leaped behind a tree and saw a rather plain little girl coming down the trail carrying a basket. I was suspicious of this little girl right away because she was dressed funny—all in red, and her head covered up so it seemed like she didn't want people to know who she was. Naturally, I stopped to check her out. I asked who she was, where she was going, where she had come from, and all that. She gave me a song and dance about going to her grandmother's house with a basket of lunch. She appeared to be a basically honest person, but she was in my forest and she certainly looked suspicious with that strange get-up of hers. So I decided to teach her just how serious it is to prance through the forest unannounced and dressed funny.

I let her go on her way, but I ran ahead to her grandmother's house. When I saw that nice old woman, I explained my problem, and she agreed that her granddaughter needed to learn a lesson, all right. The old woman agreed to stay out of sight until I called her. Actually, she hid under the bed.

When the girl arrived, I invited her into the bedroom where I was in bed, dressed like the grandmother. The girl came in all rosy-cheeked and said something nasty about my big ears. I've been insulted before so I made the best of it by suggesting that my big ears would help me to hear better. Now, what I meant was that I liked her and wanted to pay close attention to what she was saying. But she makes another insulting crack about my bulging eyes. Now you can see how I was beginning to feel about this girl who put on such a nice front, but was apparently a very nasty person. Still I've made it a policy to turn the other cheek, so I told her that my big eyes helped me to see her better.

Her next insult really got to me. I've got this problem with having big teeth. And that little girl made an insulting crack about them. I know that I should have had better control, but I leaped up from that bed and growled that my teeth would help me to eat her better.

Now, let's face it, no wolf would ever eat a little girl—everyone knows that—but that crazy girl started running around the house screaming—me chasing her to calm her down. I'd taken off the grandmother's clothes, but that only seemed to make it worse. And all of a sudden the door came crashing open and a big lumberjack is standing there with his axe. I looked at him and it became clear that I was in trouble. There was an open window behind me and out I went.

I'd like to say that was the end of it. But that grandmother character never did tell my side of the story. Before long the word got around that I was a mean nasty guy. Everybody started avoiding me. I don't know about that little girl with the funny red outfit, but I didn't live happily ever after.

By Leif Fearn, San Diego, California

ACTIVITY 20

Woolly Thinking

Suitable for Grades 9–12

Time needed 45 minutes

Resources For a class of thirty students: ten sheets of newsprint, ten sets of labels (three per set and each set of a different colour), thirty pins, scrap paper and ten balls of wool of colours to match the labels.

A large open space in the classroom is required so that the following arrangement is possible:

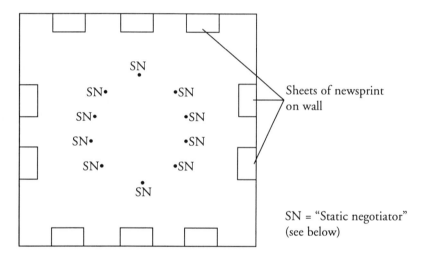

SN = "Static negotiator" (see below)

The ten chosen topics should be written up at the top of the newsprint, one on each sheet. Topics could be: The Arms Build-up, Environmental Pollution, Unemployment, Third World Under-development, Terrorism /Freedom Fighting, Human Rights Violations, Nationalism, Natural Resource Depletion, Malnutrition, Urbanization. The topics should also be written on the set of labels.

Procedure Students choose one of the ten topics by standing next to a particular sheet of newsprint. There should be no more than three students per group. Each student should wear a label identifying him or her as representing that particular topic. Groups first brainstorm the issues surrounding their topic

→

using the scrap paper provided. They then appoint a "static negotiator" and two "mobile negotiators". The static negotiators should take up position in a circle and tie the ends of their balls of wool around their waists. Their role is to stay in one position but to join in negotiations with any of the mobile negotiators of the nine other groups. The role of the mobile negotiator is to go out and negotiate connections, links or relationships between topics. Each time a connection between two topics has been discussed and agreed, the two balls of wool are passed across the circle and looped around the waists of the static negotiators of the two groups concerned. It is important that the wool is kept taut and that the ball is brought back to the static negotiator from whom it started each time. It is also very important that the thinking behind each agreement is recorded by mobile negotiators of both groups on their respective sheets of newsprint. As the activity continues, a spider's web of connections between the ten issues will be produced; the web will probably be so closely woven that mobile negotiators will have to crawl underneath in pursuit of their task.

Potential The web of different coloured wools offers a potent visual symbol of the interlocking/systemic nature of contemporary global issues. Throughout the discussion it is helpful to keep the web intact. This can be done by asking static negotiators to sit down where they have been standing. Class members can be encouraged to describe the negotiations in which they were involved and to reflect upon the connections made during the activity. Discussion of the absence of connections can also be very productive. *Woolly Thinking* is an ideal activity for exploring relationships among themes on which students have already undertaken some background work.

Variations The themes or topics chosen are, of course, open to considerable variation. The activity can be used in elementary or intermediate science to explore interdependencies within an ecosystem; in first or second languages at various grades to examine relationships among different characters in a story or novel (each team representing a character); in world religions courses at senior level to identify commonalities among different world religions studied.

To focus more directly on ecological balance, the following ten topics could be used. Rainforests; Oceans; Polar Icepacks; Atmosphere; Rivers and Streams; Mountain Ranges; Deserts; Prairie Grasslands; Swamps and Marshlands; Lakes and Ponds.

Dimension 6: Meaningful Participation

Reducing alienation through democratizing decision making and grassroots involvement

---

ACTIVITY 21

Where Do We Draw the (Action) Line?

Suitable for   Grades 10–12

Time needed 45 minutes

Resources   For each pair: a paste stick, a marker, a set of twelve action statements (page 230) and a long strip of paper.

Procedure   Working in pairs, half the class organize the statements on an acceptable-unacceptable continuum, following the procedure described on page 220. Partners decide at which point along the continuum they would draw the line between actions that are acceptable and unacceptable. They mark the point with an initialled line (a double line if they can reach consensus). The other half of the class, also working in pairs, organize the statements on an effective-ineffective continuum drawing the line between actions considered effective and ineffective. Pairs that have undertaken the activity using the different criteria are then brought together to discuss, compare and contrast the results.

Potential   The activity, and subsequent plenary discussion, will help clarify individual attitudes towards different forms of social action while, at the same time, alerting students to a range of conflicting viewpoints and perspectives. The statements cover a wide spectrum of action possibilities from direct action involving violence to property, to non-violent direct action of varying levels of risk and intensity, to action using well-established channels of persuasion within a democratic society. A range of important issues are there to be aired in plenary session. Which action strategies are felt to be most effective? What is meant by "effective"? For what reasons do individuals rule out certain forms of action? Does everybody agree? If not, why not? To what extent does the choice of form of action depend on the severity of the injustice/oppression perceived? To what extent is it reasonable to resort to forms of action that might be considered more "extreme" upon the transparent failure of other channels of persuasion to halt the perceived injustice/oppression or to highlight a problem? Is direct action involving a threat to person or property ever justifiable? Is it congruent with the values that motivated the action in the first place? What would students say to the people described in the twelve statements if they could be present in class?

→

P   Where Do We Draw the (Action) Line?

Sit-down Protest Opponents of nuclear power mount a peaceful sit-down protest across the entrance to a nuclear power station.	**Slogans** Opponents of the international arms trade daub an armaments factory with slogans and put glue in the locks.
Lobby A representative group from organizations concerned about the decline in Canada's aid to developing countries visits federal parliament to meet MPs to press their case.	**Petition Drive** Members of anti-immigration groups combine to obtain signatures for a petition calling upon the federal government to severely restrict immigration into Canada.
Letters A network of people opposed to entertainment involving performing animals write letters of protest to the local MPP or MLA, to councillors, and to local radio and newspapers on hearing that a circus is coming to town.	**Walk-out** University students shout down, and walk out of, a lecture in which the professor questions whether sexual harassment is as common as the figures suggest.
Break-In Opponents of scientific research involving animals break into a laboratory and release beagles intended for use in experiments.	**Bomb Hoax** A person opposed to abortion phones a hoax bomb call to an abortion clinic causing the clinic to close for the day.
Stunt Opponents of a factory that is polluting a local lake undertake a hazardous climb up the factory's tallest chimney to hang a banner.	**Picketing** Opponents of a very oppressive foreign government mount a regular picket outside a store selling goods from that country, leafletting people entering the shop, engaging them in discussion about human rights denials and requesting them not to enter.
Personal Change An individual contributes to environmental protection by making environmentally friendly lifestyle and purchasing decisions.	**Demonstration** Opponents of welfare cuts stage a demonstration outside the provincial parliament, break through the police cordon and temporarily occupy part of the building.

P

ACTIVITY 22
Children's Hearings

Suitable for   Grades 7–12

Time needed   Occasional periods of time over several weeks.

Resources   Postcards and sheets of paper.

Procedure   By means of an assembly or through an orchestrated series of individual lessons, students are introduced to the Norwegian-inspired Voice of the Children International Campaign and the concept of Children's Hearings. Following the meeting of the World Commission on Environment and Development, held in Bergen, Norway, in May 1990, ten Norwegian children were given the opportunity to put their hopes, fears, demands and visions for the world's future to their country's leaders at a Children's Hearing. The hearing, which received widespread media coverage in Norway, was the culmination of a process that had started with letters to schools inviting students to send postcards conveying their thoughts and feelings about the state of the world's environment and world development. Some 6000 postcards were received. An editing group clustered the cards under a number of headings and drew up a Children's Appeal reflecting the children's opinions and using the children's own words. At the hearing, the ten selected children put questions to a panel including the Norwegian prime minister, Gro Harlem Brundtland, and other national figures. The Norwegian Children's Ombudsman chaired the hearing and ensured that questions were answered without evasion. After the hearing, the Appeal was presented to the media, non-governmental organizations and schools. Looking back on the event, Gro Harlem Brundtland wrote:

> I believe this was an important event—for the children who were invited to take part in the political process at a very high level, for the political leadership who had to face the challenges from the children taking part, and for the children and grown-ups in the audience who became part of the process. We need engaged, informed, active young people. We need young people who believe they can be part of the process, who have enough faith and enough self-confidence to fight for their future and the future of the world.

The Voice of the Children International Campaign is now promoting children's hearings at school, local, regional, national and global levels. (A global children's hearing was held in Rio de Janeiro during the Earth Summit in June 1992; see page 236.)

→

Students are also alerted to the fact that Article 12 of the United Nations Convention on the Rights of the Child lays down that each child has the right to be heard in all matters affecting him or her. It is emphasized that it is important for children to be heard, and that it is just as important for adults to be told in the children's own words what they are concerned about: their hopes, fears, visions and demands for the future.

Students are encouraged to take part in a children's hearing process in the school itself, which will establish open channels of communication between themselves and adult society and representative decision makers. To begin the process they are asked to do two things: firstly, to prepare a postcard (or letter, poster, drawing or poem) expressing their ideas, concerns, questions and demands about vital issues such as the state of the environment, human rights, world peace, the treatment of animals, world development, unemployment, poverty and hunger; secondly, to elect a student committee to organize the hearing (a male and female representative from each year would produce a committee of reasonable size). The committee would have the right to coopt teachers to serve in an advisory and supportive capacity.

The committee's initial task is to encourage students to send in postcards, etc., and to collect and synthesize the views expressed therein, the aim being to produce a concise, frank, document—a Children's Appeal—of no more than a few typed pages, summarizing students' concerns. During this process, the interest of the whole student body can be maintained by regularly producing a news sheet and by committee members occasionally reporting back to class or year groups.

The Children's Appeal should provide the basis for the school-based children's hearing. The student committee sets a date and invites parents, local politicians, local clergy, trade union and media representatives and other decision/opinion makers to join a panel (of six to eight members) to respond to children's views and questions. The committee also invites applications from students who would like to represent the views of the student body and to actually address the panel (applicants should explain which major world issues they are particularly concerned about and should say why they would be a good choice for the children's panel). The committee's task is to choose about ten to twelve students for the lead role in the hearing. Those chosen should be representative of the student body in terms of age, gender and ethnicity and should have shown themselves, through their postcards and their overall contribution to school and local life, to be genuinely concerned about environment, development, human rights and peace issues. The choice of the student panel should be completed in sufficient time for chosen students to be able to brief themselves and carefully plan the content and sequencing

→

of their questions or stateof their questions or statements (using the Children's Appeal as their framework).

An invitation to the hearing, together with a copy of the Children's Appeal, should be sent to all students and their parents and the event should be widely publicized in the community. The media (local radio, press and television) should be invited. An exhibition of students' postcards, etc., should be displayed in the hall where the hearing is to take place.

A sympathetic, well-qualified mediator or ombudsperson should be invited to the hearing to chair the event firmly and to ensure that the questions and concerns raised by the students are directly addressed by the grown-ups without evasion (the person chosen should have time to talk to the students in advance). In addition, a few experts on global issues can be asked along to clarify factual matters as and when called upon (they should be briefed about the questions to be put beforehand). It is also a good idea to include in the program some student-initiated musical or dramatic entertainment relevant to the event.

At appropriate moments during the hearing the mediator should encourage contributions from children in the audience (but not from adults, as their role, on this occasion, is to listen). It is a good idea to end the hearing by having one or more of the children read the *Children's Appeal* to the audience.

Encouragement should be given to the media to interview members of the students' committee and participating students; also to take photographs of the exhibition.

Potential A demanding yet potentially hugely effective process offering students the opportunity to speak their minds to the adult world and to decision makers and opinion formers. Involvement in such a process, even if it leads to no immediate solid changes, can build in students a conviction that their collective actions can help create a better world. This feeling of empowerment is the most important objective in organizing a school-based children's hearing; hence, the more the process is controlled by students the better. The event should be made known to the Secretariat of the Voice of the Children International Campaign (attn. Kristin Eskeland, c/o Norwegian People's Aid, P.O. Box 8844, Youngstorget, N-0028 Oslo 1, Norway) and documentation (e.g., a copy of the *Children's Appeal* and newspaper cuttings) forwarded. Students could then be sure that their views would also be noted internationally.

It is recommended that the hearing should become an annual school event, providing students with the opportunity to put their views to local leaders and to hold them to account for promises made at previous hearings that remain unfulfilled.

→

Source   Voice of the Children International Campaign.

The process itself is the real goal, to give children the opportunity to act, to speak their minds to the grown-up world. Whether their concerns are poverty, hunger, lack of housing or clean water, or worries about depletion of the ozone layer and the destruction of the rainforests, *the aim is to establish channels of communication between children and the adult society, between children and the decision makers.* Even if the grown-ups are unwilling or unable to take the children's views into account, the process, the involvement and activities of the children have a value in themselves. No one can guarantee that politicians and other decision makers will take the children's viewpoints really seriously or that they are willing or able to take their opinions into account when final decisions are being made. But children's voices should be heard as well as the voices of other parts of society.

Children today are worried, often angry. They blame the adults for the problems, and rightly so. They get a lot of depressing information about the state of the world, they realize that their own future is at stake. A continued flow of information about environmental degradation, about poverty, hunger, war; coupled with a feeling that there is nothing they can do about it, no one is interested in their ideas, might lead to new generations of youngsters with no hope. They might turn into an aggressive group who would use any means to produce a change, or—much worse, a gang of frustrated, lethargic youngsters with no direction. As adults, they are likely to have very little faith in their own ability to play an active role in the democratic process.

The campaign Voice of the Children wants to prevent this from happening by giving active, knowledgeable kids a chance to speak their minds to the people in charge, by speaking TRUTH TO POWER.

Voice of the Children International Campaign

Additional Resources

- Environment Canada, *What we can do for our environment. Hundreds of things to do now,* 1991. A compilation of good ideas for more environmentally friendly lifestyles and action projects. Available free from Inquiry Centre, Environment Canada, 351 St. Joseph Boulevard, Hull, Quebec, K1A 0H3, Canada.

→

- *HSUS student action guide*, Humane Society of the United States (Youth Education Division, 67 Salem Road, East Haddam, CT 06423-0320), 1991. Excellent eight-page newspaper-format guide, full of ideas for school-based animal and environmental protection projects.• James, B., *The young person's action guide to animal rights*, Virago, 1992. An A to Z of animal rights and welfare issues. At the end of every topic are answers to the important question: What can you do? Highly recommended.

- Levinson, R., *Spring clean your planet*, Beaver, 1987. A book of easy-to-follow scientific experiments about pollution, designed to enable students to make informed decisions about what action to take to help clean up the planet.

- Lewis, B., *The kid's guide to social action*, Minneapolis: Free Spirit Publishing, 1991. Subtitled *How to solve the social problems you choose—and turn creative thinking into positive action*, this is an indispensable guide to young people's social action that should be in every school library.

- Silver, D., and Vallely, B., *The young person's guide to saving the planet*, Virago, 1990. Over one hundred environmental issues presented in an A to Z format. Each topic ends with a "What can you do?" section.

Chidren's Appeal to World Leaders, Rio de Janeiro, June 1992

WE WANT TO INHERIT A CLEAN EARTH. We would like everybody to understand that the Earth is like a beautiful garden in which no one has the right to destroy anything. We would like our grandchildren to know: What is a tree, a fish, a dog. Leave us trees to climb in.

ECOLOGY IS NOT JUST TREES, ANIMALS AND RIVERS; IT IS ALSO HUNGER AND THE HOMELESS. We should all help our brothers and sisters who have been abandoned on the streets. Eliminate poverty. We want you to understand that all excessive consumption affects developing countries most.

WE WANT CHILDREN'S RIGHTS TO BE RESPECTED ALL OVER THE WORLD. No child should be imprisoned or beaten, no child should die of hunger or from diseases that could easily be prevented. All children have a right to have parents.

WE WANT EVERY GIRL AND BOY IN THE WORLD TO GET AN EDUCATION FOR A BETTER START IN LIFE. WE WANT TO SEE ILLITERACY WIPED OUT. It is our future and we want to have a say in it. We want to be educated in such a way that we get the courage to speak our minds. We want a world without discrimination.

WE WANT VERY STRICT LAWS AGAINST DESTROYING NATURE. Anybody polluting the environment should have to pay large fines. Stop producing materials that harm the ozone layer or it will be broken and the sun's rays will burn us. Stop global warming, reduce CO_2 emissions. Cut the use of fossil fuels, use sun and wind power. Instead of drilling for more oil, use energy less wastefully.

WE WANT YOU TO STOP USING NUCLEAR POWER. End nuclear testing in our oceans and seas. We demand the removal of all nuclear power stations.

WE DON'T WANT OUR CITIES TO BE RUINED BY CARS. We don't want to be sick from exhaust fumes. We want you to make cars that don't pollute. Public transportation should be better, cheaper and more efficient than private cars. Make it easier for us all to use our bicycles.

WE DON'T WANT OUR WORLD TO DROWN IN RUBBISH. NOBODY SHOULD BE ALLOWED TO DUMP THEIR RUBBISH IN OTHER COUNTRIES. Stop littering, make less waste. We don't need all the packaging materials.

WE WOULD LIKE ALL THINGS TO BE RECYCLED. Make it easier for people to recycle their rubbish. Stop producing disposables.

→

PLEASE, LEADERS OF THE WORLD, GIVE US CLEAN DRINKING WATER. Without water there is no life. Too many children are drinking clayish water from shallow wells, pipe-borne water is still a luxury. Too many children spend hours walking a long way to find water.

WE FEAR THAT WHEN WE GROW UP THERE WILL BE NO FISH IN THE OCEAN. We want you to stop oil spills in the oceans, to stop factories from releasing their sewage and waste into rivers and lakes. The sea cannot absorb poison without being harmed.

ANIMALS HAVE AS MUCH RIGHT TO LIVE ON THIS EARTH AS WE DO. Protect endangered animals, stop buying products made from rare animals. People should be able to do without real fur coats, crocodile leather or jewelry from ivory. Ban animal testing for cosmetics, ban killing animals for sport.

WE WANT MORE DONE TO SAVE WHAT IS LEFT OF THE NATIVE FORESTS. The rainforests are home to many people and animals. We want indigenous peoples to be able to live by their own rules. Don't cut down all the native trees because the birds need homes, just like all the children in the world.

WE ARE AFRAID OF BEING SWEPT OFF THE FACE OF OUR COUNTRY BY THE APPROACHING DESERT. Stop bush-burning and overgrazing that is killing our trees and hurting our grassland vegetation. We want canals to be built alongside the main rivers to prevent flooding. Stop building large dams against people's wishes.

ALL HAVE A RIGHT TO LIVE IN PEACE. The money spent on military armaments should be spent on saving the planet. Instead of making bombs, improve the standard of living in the world.

THE EARTH IS A SINGLE COUNTRY, AND ALL PEOPLE ARE ITS CITIZENS. We have to share this planet, so don't be selfish. We want food to be shared so that everyone has enough. We want clean water and a home for all people. We are worried about pollution, war and children starving, while others don't appreciate the food they get. We are afraid that the world will soon belong only to the rich.

THIS EARTH IS MORE VALUABLE THAN ALL THE MONEY IN THE WORLD. WE WANT ALL COUNTRIES TO WORK TOGETHER TO PROTECT IT.

Dimension 7: Personal Peace

Inner harmony; peaceful interpersonal relations; recovery of values of compassion, loyalty, self-restraint, reverence, collective interest

ACTIVITY 23

Inner Warmth

Suitable for Grades 4–12

Time needed 20 minutes

Resources A sheet of paper and pen/pencil for each student.

Procedure Working on their own, students are asked to write down as many things as they can think of that make them feel warm inside. Their ideas should be spread all over their sheet of paper. They are asked to:

- draw a rectangle around every item that requires money in order to experience it;

- draw a triangle around every item that does not involve the company of others;

- draw a circle around every item that involves the company of, and interaction or sharing with, others.

It is pointed out that some items might require the drawing of more than one shape. Groups of six are formed and students asked to share and discuss their findings. What shape was used most often? By what shape(s) do items that students treasure the most tend to be enclosed? What does this suggest about us individually and us as human beings? Did any items fit neither a rectangle, nor a triangle, nor a circle? Why? Has anything been learned that will make the group rethink and adjust how they relate to others? Plenary discussion follows.

Potential A useful activity for promoting self- and group esteem, an appreciation of what others value, empathy and sensitivity towards other people.

ACTIVITY 24

Developing Empathy Through Storytelling

Suitable for Grades 1–12

Time needed 20 minutes per session following an initial 60-minute symbol production and story preparation session.

Resources Paper, felt pens, scissors

Procedure In the first session students devise their own personal logo, symbol or totem. A large version is posted on the classroom wall and a number of smaller versions made. Students also prepare a story of a person or event that changed and/or significantly influenced their life and/or engendered strong emotion in them personally. A random sequence of storytelling is determined for future sessions with the teacher included as one of the storytellers. (Prior to the first storytelling session, the teacher prepares his or her own symbol copies and story.)

At each subsequent session, the storyteller of the day places a pile of his or her symbols in the circle before beginning the story. If a listener identifies with an aspect of the story, the storyteller quietly retrieves one of the symbols. (Some listeners may want to hear all the story before they can connect with it.) When the story is finished, those with symbols describe the connections they made with what has been told. At the end of the session, they stick the symbol they have acquired on their own large-version symbol on the classroom wall.

Potential This ongoing activity creates empathy between members of the class. The tangible acknowledgment of connection helps all the group recognize commonalities of life experiences and emotions. As students stick more and more small symbols to their own large-version symbol, they will realize how much they have in common with other members of the class. The storytelling is, thus, an esteem-building, bonding and, hence, empowering process.

Source An activity devised by four Ontario teachers: Veronica Church, Maple Grove School, Lanark; Lois Kuebler, Moira Secondary School, Belleville; John Martyn, Peterborough, Victoria, Northumberland & Newcastle RCSS Board; Jim Rule, London School Board.

ACTIVITY 25

Mini Despair and Empowerment Exercise

Suitable for   Grades 9–12

Time needed   Minimum of one hour

Resources   Class seated in circle, well spread out; small pieces of paper or card—four per student (12 cm x 7 cm file cards are suitable); pencils; board or flip-chart.

Procedure

1. The sequence and rationale is explained (see below):

   Stage A: "Thinking the unthinkable…"

   Stage B: "It won't happen because…"

   Stage C: "A hopeful future…"

   Stage D: "From ideas to action…"

2. Four cards and a pencil are given to each student. It is explained that the cards are not to be written on until instructions to do so are given, and that names should NOT be written on the cards at any stage.

3. **Stage A** *Instruction.* Students are told that, on the first card, they should write down one or two sentences beginning something like:

   "The thing what worries me most about the future is…"

       or

   "What scares me most about the world is…"

       or

   "What frightens me most is…"

       or

   "The thing I prefer not to think about happening is…"

   It is probably best at this stage not to give any examples, but simply to say that the sentences can be about anything the students wish.

   Three to four minutes are given for writing. The first cards are collected, shuffled and given out again.

   Each student in the circle reads the card he or she has, without comment. All sentences should be accepted without comment.

→

4. **Stage B** *Instruction.* Students are told that, on their second card, they should write several sentences, beginning:

"There won't be a nuclear war because…"

or

"The problems of famine and hunger will be solved because…"

Some help may be needed by way of suggestions, to encourage the idea that any sentence is acceptable. Humorous sentences should be encouraged, for example:

"There won't be a nuclear war because I'll be the next prime minister and won't let it happen"

or

"…because the Easter Bunny will be world ruler".

As before, three or four minutes are allowed to write, collect, shuffle, give out, and read round, again without comment.

5. **Stage C** *Instruction.* Students should use the third card to complete the sentence:

"The world will be a better place in fifteen years' time because…"

As before, three or four minutes are allowed to write, etc. (It may be helpful each time to collect the previous set of cards while the next sentences are being written.)

6. **Stage D** *Instruction.* The group is asked to brainstorm as many ideas as possible about:

"Things I can do to make the world a better and a safer place for ALL human beings."

As with all brainstorming, any ideas are acceptable; there should be no comments or discussion; as many ideas as possible are gathered. The ideas should be written up on the board or a flip-chart. It may be helpful to have two students do the writing to keep up with the flow of ideas.

7. In groups of three, the ideas brainstormed are considered, students being asked to identify those which "YOU could actually do something about".

Potential The purpose is to encourage students to share their anxieties about the future, and so discover that most of their unspoken worries are shared by others. The encouragement of humour in Stages B and C allows for the release from possible despair that is brought about by shared laughter, leading to the development of possible positive and practical strategies, and the empowerment that this can bring.

→

Variations   Where a group's listening skills are well developed, students work in pairs instead of using cards for Stages A, B, and C, but the facilitator should make sure sufficient time is allowed for each partner to complete the sentences in turn. There is no need for the large-group sharing at the end of each of these stages, if this is done.

Sources   Sandy Parker, Ackworth School, Pontefract, based on ideas from *Despair and Personal Power in the Nuclear Age* by Joanna Macy, New Society Publishers, 1983, and from Diana Whitmore at the Findhorn Foundation's "Peace Within" workshop, January 1984.

ACTIVITY 26

Four Hands on Clay

Suitable for   Grades 5–12

Time needed   30 minutes

Resources   A block of clay about 20 cm x 20 cm x 20 cm for each two participants. The clay should be soft enough for moulding but not too wet. A table and two chairs for each two participants arranged so that participants face each other across the table; the tables so arranged that individuals can be led, eyes shut, between them. Blindfolds (optional). Soothing or relaxing music (optional).

Procedure   Students stand around the walls of the room or, if possible, outside the room in which the tables are set up. It is explained that the activity involves working in pairs and modelling something out of clay; also, that it can be a very profound experience for those who keep to two basic rules, namely, eyes should be kept shut throughout and no one should reveal his or her identity by laughing or talking.

It is particularly important with this activity to indicate that participation is optional; students opting not to model can play a most useful part as observers and rapporteurs. Those intending to take part should be advised to remove watches, bracelets and rings and to roll up their sleeves.

With eyes shut and avoiding talk and laughter, participants are led carefully and protectively to chairs. Once in place, they are asked to fold their arms and wait silently until everybody is seated. During this period, and throughout the activity, soothing music can be played. The facilitator may wish to bear a variety of factors in mind in creating pairings. The problem of uneven numbers can be handled by putting three students together in one group.

With everyone in position, the facilitator goes to each pair in turn, brings their hands together on the clay and says: "With your four hands working together on the clay, make one model." The pairs will usually be finished in fifteen to twenty minutes, at which point they can be asked to open their eyes. An excited and spontaneous sharing of experiences and feelings normally follows. Allow five or so minutes for this before attempting plenary discussion.

Potential   Students are also usually keen to share their experiences and feelings with the class as a whole. How did they feel being led with eyes shut? Did they trust

→

the facilitator? What feelings did they have during the decision period about what to model, during the modelling and when things seemed to be going well or badly? What pleasures or frustrations did they encounter in reaction to their unknown partner, from not talking or seeing, from the music that was being played?

Out of this sharing, a number of key areas for further discussion will probably emerge:

Non-verbal communication. Did pairs communicate in deciding what model to make, if so, how? Later on, were feelings about what was happening communicated; if so, how? Were communications clearly understood by the other partner, etc?

Decision making. How was the decision reached as to what to make? Was it a joint decision? Did one partner in some way take the initiative? Which kinds of initiative-taking proved acceptable, which did not? How did participants react to what they felt was a dominating partner, etc?

Gender issues. Were many guessing who their partner was? Why? Was it important to know whether the partner was male or female? Did participants, in fact, decide whether their partner was male or female? On what evidence did they make the decision? Was that evidence, on reflection, reasonable evidence, etc?

Touch. Were participants comfortable touching another person's hands? Did it become more or less comfortable or uncomfortable once they had decided in their minds whether a partner was female or male, etc? (This area can usefully lead into consideration of tactile and non-tactile cultures.)

This is an excellent unit for filming with a video camera but only if the group is highly affirmed. The playback can be a powerful emotional experience and sections can be replayed to facilitate deeper exploration of the issues raised above.

PART 3

Implementing Education for Peace in Schools

CHAPTER 13

The Ethos of the School

WHEN I THINK BACK to my school days in England during the Second World War, I remember workers mixing cement to build air-raid shelters that were constructed close to the doors at each end of our rectangular, four-roomed building. When the shelters were completed, student prefects were posted at all times by the head teacher at the front of the school. The prefects rang a hand bell as an alarm whenever they saw approaching enemy aircraft, so that we could quickly exit to the shelters. Sometimes these emergencies were combined with gas-mask drills so that we could get accustomed to fitting and wearing our masks in the event of a gas attack.

Gardening became a compulsory part of our curriculum. We were encouraged to grow vegetables at school and to have a productive garden at home, so that we could do our part to help the country be more self-sufficient at a time when merchant navy ships were being torpedoed by enemy submarines. The knowledge that food was scarce was reinforced at school lunches: we were not allowed to waste precious food by leaving anything on our plates.

Current events often crept into our classroom work. Sometimes our written compositions reflected experiences in air raids, observations of troop manoeuvres or of military hardware hidden under camouflage along country lanes. Similarly, our art work occasionally expressed what we saw on the land and in the air of a country at war.

At recess, besides playing the usual games, we traded cigarette cards, which had profiles of friendly and enemy fighter and bomber aircraft. Most of my classmates became quite expert in aircraft identification. Sometimes we unloaded from our pockets pieces of shrapnel collected from bomb craters on the way to school or fragments from a recently-downed pilotless plane, as valued artifacts of our time.

The school had two major continuing projects in which everybody was urged to participate. One was the collection of aluminum foil, to be used in military aircraft construction or to be dropped in thin strips by aircraft as a means of confusing enemy radar. The other activity was the purchase of saving stamps and certificates (government war bonds) to assist in the financing of the war.

It is quite revealing, when these experiences are recalled now, to see how the school responded to the conditions of war and contributed in its own way to the national war effort. As a result of ministerial policy, and of conscious decisions by the school administration itself, the physical plant was altered; the curriculum modified; and informal school projects noticeably changed.[1]

When we consider the school as an organic institution, even if only very briefly, as in this example, we realize that its character and quality of life are very much bound up with the people who are part of it and with the society of which it is a part. The ethos, or climate, of the school is formed by the students and staff, by school traditions, and by influences from the community and from society at large. Rather than being static, it is almost always constantly in flux, as students and staff change and as outside influences—both wanted and unwanted—intrude upon the life of the school. In this chapter we will explore some of the dimensions of school life, with a view to helping teachers and administrators assess their school activities in relation to peace education, and as a basis for the development of the school as a peace-building institution. We will consider first the cultural identity of school; second, the values underpinning school life; third, the formal curriculum; and fourth, the informal life of the school.

---

[1] Adapted from Smith (1987).

The Cultural Identity of the School

Each school has a unique and particular identity. That identity is shaped by the *student population* with all the features and characteristics of its constituent groups. It is shaped by the *staff, the administration and representatives of the community* who bring philosophical and value choices and qualities of leadership to the development of the school. It is determined by the *subject matter* of the formal courses of study, which may be prescribed by educational authorities or, in more decentralized systems of education, developed locally. In addition, it is determined by the *physical structure* of the school and its environment, both immediate and distant. As described by Schwab (1973), the quality of education in a school is the sum total of these four "commonplaces" and the interactions among and between them.

The school is an exceedingly complex community. Each learner brings to it his or her own individual experiences of human living. Those experiences vary enormously with regard to the elements of peace-building that have been highlighted throughout this book: experiences of justice and injustice, non-violence and violence, participation and alienation, environmental sustainability and despoliation, wholeness and fragmentation, and the like. Any on-going assessment of the cultural identity of the school involves some general, and in some cases specific, understanding of peaceful and "unpeaceful" circumstances in the lives and relationships of students and staff, among groups and group relationships, and in the dynamics of the day-to-day life of the school as an institution.

The culture of the school is always changing. Change occurs partly because of conscious decisions to change educational practice, but also because the cultural lifestyles of individuals and groups both within and outside the school are changing—and changing in relationship with each other. Morin (1989) points out that individual life itself is both an open and a closed system. Individual identity is imprinted in our genes and we preserve this identity by regenerating ourselves: the cells of our bodies are continually being destroyed and renewed, so much so that every five years our bodies are completely replaced, yet we remain the same person. But each living being is also open to the environment from which it gathers resources and information. The self feeds on the non-self to simultaneously preserve and renew its individuality. In a similar way, Morin states, the cultural life of an institution or a people can pursue, at the same time, both a closed-door and an open-door policy. Within a closed circuit, cultural life perpetuates itself, yet at the same time it is renewed and developed in a circuit open to external cultural influences. The processes of cultural exclusion and cross-fertilization happen together.

This kind of dialectical relationship between cultures has important implications for peace education. It suggests that each person has the possibility of many cultural identities: a personal culture (or lifestyle or quality of life), a family culture, a school culture, an ethnic culture, an occupational culture, a national culture, a continental culture, a world culture, and so on. It suggests also that the very development of polycentric identities is part of the process of positive peace. Young people whose cultural identities do not transcend any unit beyond the gang may easily be swept into street violence; those whose cultural identities do not exceed the nation can easily be led into international warfare. The school, therefore, has the responsibility of developing school culture that is in dialogue with other cultures. It also has a role in helping students to acquire other cultural identities that are in a dialectical relationship with one another.

Morin concludes that all cultures are ultimately rooted in the human condition, which requires that we open our doors to the modern world: our many cultures the world over should "preserve their specific, original features, but also be strong enough to remain open, assimilate extraneous elements and accept a principle of evolution and transformation" (p. 34). The development of a school culture based on inclusive cultural identities involves the concomitant sharing and transformation of values.

Peace Values Underpinning School Life

It can be argued that the principal function of those who manage and administer schools is to identify and uphold the central values of the institution. In their book *In Search of Excellence*, Peters and Waterman (1984) found that the most successful corporations were value-driven. Their leaders were ones who were concerned with the promotion and protection of values and with the development of a distinctive identity for the institution. Hodgkinson and Jackson (1986) make a similar claim for schools, stating that school leaders and policy makers need to be committed to chosen values. They state that peace education, in its essence, is values education that occurs "in all the extra- and intra-school curricula, overt and hidden", in which children participate.

In some instances, the central values of a school may be quite apparent, especially in the case of specialized schools that have a distinctive focus. International schools may emphasize the values of multiculturalism, wholeness and globalism; art schools, creativity and self-expression; technical and occupational schools, utilitarianism and practicality; progressive schools, freedom, self-development and self-regulation. In some schools, however, the values—especially as they relate to peace-making and peace-building—may not be well articulated. The chapters in Part II of this book have all referred to the teaching of values, and have included explanations of the way in which certain values contribute to the building of peace. We may now ask, Which of these same values can be upheld by the school, underpinning institution-wide activities, serving as the basis for decision-making, and reinforcing the teaching of values in classroom settings?

Figure 13–1 shows that there are a number of elaborated clusters of values that correspond to the conceptions of peace outlined in Chapter 2. They include, first, the value of learning itself, and learning how to learn, since indifference to learning presents a barrier to understanding ourselves and our planet. The kind of learning that includes openness, critical thinking and resourcefulness develops problem-solving abilities that so urgently need to be brought to bear upon contemporary issues in our personal lives and in the lives of the larger communities of which we are members.

The second value is the search for wholeness, which includes reaching out to one another in every scale of human living from small families to the world community. The value of wholeness requires the building of dialectical relationships among different cultures and appreciating the totality of the human condition, or the unity of humankind. When cultures at all levels selectively integrate elements from each other, they contribute to the process of building positive peace.

FIGURE 13–1 Peace values and school life

1. Learning ↔ Incognizance Curiosity ↔ Closed-mindedness Activeness ↔ Passiveness Logic ↔ Irrationality Reflectiveness ↔ Vacancy Creativity ↔ Uninventiveness	**2. Wholeness ↔ Fragmentation** Compassion ↔ Indifference Generosity ↔ Meanness Harmony ↔ Divisiveness Integration ↔ Separation Loyalty ↔ Infidelity
3. Participation ↔ Alienation Openness ↔ Secretiveness Respectfulness ↔ Indignity Conscientization ↔ Powerlessness Enfranchisement ↔ Subjugation Freedom ↔ Oppression	**4. Non-Violence ↔ Violence** Encouragement ↔ Coercion Cooperation ↔ Discordance Tolerance ↔ Intolerance Friendship ↔ Belligerence Forgiveness ↔ Retaliation
5. Justice ↔ Injustice Honesty ↔ Dishonesty Truthfulness ↔ Falseness Equality ↔ Discrimination Impartiality ↔ Bias Lawfulness ↔ Unlawfulness	**6. Ecological Balance ↔ Despoliation** Conservation ↔ Wastefulness Interdependence ↔ Independence Sustainability ↔ Exhaustion Stewardship ↔ Exploitation Constraint ↔ Indulgence

A third cluster of values centres on participation, which is associated with the personal empowerment of individuals to govern their own lives and to contribute openly and freely to the building and governance of the many social groupings and communities in which they live.

The fourth value of non-violence involves the search for alternatives to the use of physical force and (especially in schools) psychological violence and degradation as means of resolving conflicts. Within this cluster are allied values that help to minimize the resort to violence.

The fifth value involves the commitment to justice for all in the school setting and in all those social groupings external to the school, including world society. Unless the school is perceived to be a just society by those who live and work in it, the moral power of the institution to teach other values is seriously undermined.

The sixth peace value that needs to be exemplified in the school is ecological balance. Policies and practices of the school should, as far as possible, be consistent with environmental sustainability, since despoliation of the environment is one of major threats to planetary stability and insecurity.

Several brief observations may be made on these value clusters. The six values can be considered as "meta-values", providing focus and organization for a number of other significant peace values. The subsidiary values associated with them are not intended to be inclusive, but rather suggestive of values that support the meta-values. The meta-values are not hierarchical, since all need to be pursued simultaneously. It may be further noted that there is a certain resonance between all the positive values and between all the negative values. Positive peace in a school is the process of moving in gradual progress from negative values towards positive ones.

The Formal Curriculum

Since various courses of study have been discussed in detail in Part II, formal curriculum will not be dealt with at length here. However, an overview of the common themes in the courses of study will be given, as there need not be, and perhaps should not be, a firm boundary between the formal curriculum and the more informal life of the school. What happens in the classroom can often be effectively integrated into school-wide projects which, in turn, may have important links to the community and to the school's international relationships. Besides the teaching of *values* as a common theme in the curriculum, we have emphasized *cooperative learning, peaceful conflict resolution, multicultural education* and *global perspectives*.

Cooperative Learning

As we have seen, especially in the discussion of second-language learning, mathematics and science, cooperative learning is a promising practice for peace education because it involves students working together towards common goals, undertaking complementary allocated tasks, sharing resources and receiving joint rewards. Such learning finds expression in peer tutoring, team learning and group projects. Summarizing research on cooperative learning, Hilke (1990) found that replacing highly competitive learning with a supportive learning environment produces an increase in academic achievement, larger networks of friendship across racial lines and with students who have learning disabilities, and greater growth in self-esteem for individual students. In the large school setting, cooperative learning can be encouraged in such activities as the preparation of the school yearbook, the production of a weekly television program for broadcast to the community, or the informal learning that goes on in noon-hour or after-school clubs.

Peaceful Conflict Resolution

We have seen ways in which students can deepen their understanding of conflict and its resolution through such subjects as art, literature, and history. Consideration has been given to the development of skills in analyzing sources of conflict, in understanding the ways in which conflicts can be escalated or defused, in using divergent thinking for generating alternative solutions to conflicts and in evaluating the consequences of various alternatives. These understandings and skills can then become part of classroom behaviour and, just as importantly, can be linked to creative ways of resolving disputes within the school, as in the use of peer mediation and other non-confrontational, non-violent responses to conflict (Shepherd, 1994; Cutrona and Guerin, 1994). Students, counsellors, teachers, administrators and support staff can all play, in the various forums of school life, a significant role in developing a school ethos in which peaceful conflict resolution is an integral part. The constructive management of tensions between individuals and groups over problems or issues that arise during the school year leads to the healthy growth of the institution.

Multicultural Education

A deep appreciation of cultures in other lands as well as the variety of cultures represented in the community can be built into the curriculum, as we have seen in subjects as diverse as music, mathematics and geography. Students can experience delight in their encounters with other peoples, gaining insights into cultural features that are, on the one hand, universal and, on the other, unique. Classrooms that use such practices as heterogeneous groupings and inter-group education help to develop tolerance, trust, and enduring friendships across cultural lines. Multicultural education needs also to be developed on a school-wide basis (Ghosh, 1996). School twinning and school exchanges that include person-to-person relationships open new windows on the world; art displays that manifest the lifestyles of other cultures enable us to see ways of living through the eyes of others; guest speakers from the community and visitors from abroad enrich the life and culture of the school.

Global Perspectives

Another theme that has run through a study of curriculum is the development of perspectives, particularly of global perspectives. In the study of art, for instance, we examined universal human values; in literature, writing that conveys our sense of kinship with the human community as a whole; and in history, the development and interconnectedness of political and economic systems and the growth of world society. The school, as an institution, can play an important role in helping students to acquire perspectives—local, regional, national and global—beyond the classroom. Opportunities exist in many facets of school life: in the themes and topics dealt with in school assemblies, in the content and emphases of the yearbook, in school-wide projects to raise funds for those stricken by natural disasters or trapped by the actions of others into the cycle of ignorance, poverty and disease.

• • •

In conclusion, we can say that the formal curriculum makes its most significant contribution to the building of a peaceful school ethos when students are helped to understand the wholeness of their lives. The process of integration occurs when teachers correlate their work across the disciplines and students make connections across subject lines. It happens when students have opportunities to work cooperatively with peers or with students at other grade levels. It occurs when classroom work is connected to school-wide activities. It occurs when teachers are seen to work together as models of collaboration and cooperative learning. It happens when the work of the school is linked to the people and activities of the community. It becomes greater when classes and schools reach out to the larger world.

The Informal Life of the School

The life of the school "outside the classroom" goes on with the formal curriculum, ideally interacting with that curriculum. It provides important opportunities for students and staff together to reflect upon and reshape the culture of the institution. School activities of every kind can be driven by the underlying values consonant with peace-building. In cases where the school population—or large parts of it—come together to recognize and celebrate the achievements of individuals and groups, values that are important to the school can be publicly upheld. In this section, using the values criteria discussed earlier, we will consider some of the possibilities inherent in these activities. The following is a working checklist designed to help schools undertake a critical review of the quality of school life.

The School Building and Its Resources

Like any building, the school as a physical structure, its learning resources and the surroundings themselves all provide messages of some kind to students and visitors.

THE SCHOOL BUILDING   Does the school building itself convey the message that it is a place of learning, and a place where young people enjoy learning? Does it convey that it values learning within and beyond the physical limits of the building? Does the school display a motto? Would someone from outer space recognize the purpose of the institution? Would an outsider obtain the impression that this is a "peaceful" school?

SCHOOL ART   Are there any pictures on corridor, library, cafeteria, stair-well walls? Any stained glass, ceramics, sculptures or other art to beautify the school? If so, does the art convey values that the school is a creative, expressive, peace-building community?

ROTATING EXHIBITS   Does the school have places for rotating exhibits of interesting books, documents, crafts, photographs, stamps, coins, artifacts? Are there any exhibits that advance inter-cultural education or contribute positively to the ambiance of the school?

SCHOOL DISPLAYS   To what extent does the school display student work? Are there opportunities for the display of student art, social studies projects, photography or materials that manifest the school's valuing of a peaceful world? Do students have a sense of "ownership" of their school through participation and involvement in displays?

RESOURCE CENTRES   Does the school have small learning centres associated with particular departments? Are such centres an invitation to learn? To learn independently? To learn cooperatively? Do the materials (books, maps, globes, cassettes, computer programs) help students to acquire a variety of perspectives?

SCHOOL LIBRARY   Is peace education a factor in the policy that guides the collection of magazines, books, audio and video tapes and computer software? Does the library contain bound copies of exemplary student writing? Does it value local and national publications yet also create a climate of internationalism?

SCHOOL GROUNDS   Do the surroundings of the school indicate that the staff and students are collectively concerned about the environment? Have there been any attempts to beautify the school externally through landscaping, gardens, art, or trees? What impressions or messages do the school grounds give to visitors, passers-by and students?

The School as Community

The ethos of the school is established, in part, by the values implicit in activities that bring staff and students together in ways other than classroom learning.

SCHOOL ASSEMBLIES   Is the assembly used as a way of developing shared experiences, shared values and shared expectations at the institutional level? Does it help to develop an informed awareness of local, national and world affairs? Does it invite wide student and staff participation? Does it convey peace values as the ones that underpin school life?

SPECIAL DAYS   Does the school take the opportunity to observe, or celebrate, special days: Human Rights Day, United Nations Day, Remembrance Day, Earth Day? Does it help to develop respect for differences by celebrating, or developing an understanding of, the holy days and festive holidays of different religious and ethnic groups?

SCHOOL PROJECTS Does the school respond to humanitarian appeals for help locally, nationally or internationally? Are such projects used to help students understand more broadly and more critically the problems of community and world development? Do they raise issues of building social and economic justice?

SPORT Does the sports program of the school invite widespread participation, or is there a tendency for the school to be preoccupied with a sports elite? Is aggression and violence in sports discouraged or condoned? Are sports programs highly competitive or are they primarily designed for fitness, personal enjoyment and the development of team spirit?

SCHOOL DRAMA Do drama classes or the drama club present plays for the rest of the school? Do these plays provide an insight into conflict and provoke thought about acceptable and unacceptable ways of dealing with it? Are analyses and reviews of school drama that take into account the handling of conflict reported in school newspapers or yearbooks?

CLUBS Does the school encourage the voluntary formation of clubs to extend pupil learning in current affairs, world issues, planetary ecology, the arts, or second languages? To what extent are students encouraged to participate across grade levels?

SCHOOL FUNCTIONS How representative of the diversity of the student body is the committee that organizes functions such as school dances or other gatherings? Over the year as a whole, do the functions represent a wide range of ethnic cultures and backgrounds? Do functions help to cultivate a sense of togetherness and school identity?

BULLETINS AND NEWSPAPERS Does the school publish bulletins or newspapers, either regularly or occasionally, to reflect its quality of life? Is the publication controlled democratically so that students learn about crucial issues in journalism? Is the publication an effective means of communication for all groups? Are writers made aware of problems of bias? Are they encouraged to use a critically reflective approach to journalism? Does the publication contribute effectively to the building of peaceful school culture?

SCHOOL YEARBOOK What attempts are made to enable all students to feel that this is their yearbook? Does the yearbook reflect school highlights of the year, major accomplishments or developments, the contemporary concerns and hopes of students? Does it include student poetry, writing, drawings and photographs that deal with substantive matters of peace? Is it both a souvenir of good times and a thoughtful reflection of student values and concerns?

STUDENT COUNCIL What role or mandate does the Student Council have in contributing to school life? Does it have an advisory role to the principal? Does it have real and significant input into the life of the school? Does it give students a sense of responsibility and enfranchisement?

The School in the Community

There are many ways in which the school can develop meaningful relationships with the community. When the school interacts with groups outside, its culture is essentially in dialogue with the cultures of the community. It both benefits and is benefitted by this cultural engagement.

COMMUNITY SERVICE Is there a separation between the school and its community, or does the school reach out in service to help build a larger sense of community? Does it encourage activities such as reading to the blind, entertaining in hospitals, doing errands for shut-ins and working for public-spirited voluntary organizations?

SCHOOL-BUSINESS PARTNERSHIPS Does the school behave as a "self-sufficient" institution, or does it forge links with businesses in the community? Are there any work-study programs? Does the school seek the cooperation of manufacturers and service industries to organize educational visits for students?

FIELD STUDIES Do teachers feel bound to "cover the course" using limited resources in the school, or do they use the environment to complement and extend learning, and to cultivate a wider sense of community? Do they use resources such as the landscape, museums, art galleries and libraries?

HOME AND SCHOOL Does the school minimize contact with parents, or does it forge strong links between parents and teachers, home and school? Does it invite input from parents into the governance of the school and into the formulation of educational policy? Does it seek the talents and resources of parents to enrich the life of the school?

SCIENCE AND HISTORY FAIRS Are the products and instruments of learning in such subjects as science and history shared only with other students, or are they shared with parents and other community members such as journalists, politicians, business leaders and community organizations?

MEDIA Does the school issue any press releases of special interest to local media? Does it share information about its activities, especially those involving the community? Does it ever use resources such as community chan-

nels on cable television? Is the school linked to a computer network such as Schoolnet or the Internet?

CONCERTS To what extent do school choirs, bands and other musical groups share the pleasure of their music with parents and other members of the community? Does the school reach out to provide occasional entertainment in seniors' homes, children's hospitals or shopping centres?

GRADUATION EXERCISES Is the occasion of graduation used to commend individuals and groups for their achievements and contributions to school life? Is it used by all those who actively participate to uphold peace values as being central to school life? Is it used to support and strengthen the relationship between school and society?

HOMECOMING Does the school encourage its graduates to attend class reunions? Do reunions help the school to understand how it has changed and how it is changing as an institution? In what ways can current students and graduates benefit each other and help to bond the school to the community?

The School in the World

While much global learning goes on in classrooms, the school as an institution can also develop important links to the world, further helping students to extend their knowledge and expand their perspectives.

STUDENT AND TEACHER EXCHANGES Does the school arrange short-term exchanges with students in other countries and use such exchanges as a means of building bridges between cultures? Are teachers encouraged to exchange positions with counterparts elsewhere as a means of expanding their experience and horizons?

SCHOOL TWINNING Is the school twinned with one, or more, schools overseas? To what extent does the school exchange art, music, project work and learning materials with its counterparts? How much is the link used as a means of understanding another people and their cultural values?

COMPUTER LINKS Has the school explored the exchange of electronic mail with networks of schools in other countries? Are there any cooperative ventures between networked schools, such as joint publications by students who write and edit their work through electronic mail?

PEN FRIENDS Does the school encourage students to have pen friends in different parts of the world? In what ways does the school help develop communication and trust on a person-to-person basis? Are students helped to explore ways in which writing may be mutually beneficial in such areas as second-language learning, geography, science, home economics and sports and pastimes?

INTERNATIONAL PROJECTS Does the school have any international projects through organizations such as Oxfam, UNICEF or World Vision as an extension of international development education? Are any opportunities opened for students to provide tangible, personalized help to specific individuals or communities overseas?

ORGANIZATIONAL NETWORKS Do members of the teaching staff belong to any international organizations that promote education for peace, such as the Canadian Peace Educators' Network, the World Education Fellowship, or the World Council for Curriculum and Instruction? Is the school affiliated with the UNESCO Associated Schools Project, with the World Association for the School as an Instrument of Peace or any other similar organization?

This checklist identifies some of the ways in which the informal life of the school can add significantly to its educational goals for peace. It can be used as a basis for assessment, recognizing that each school is unique and will be in a position to devise its own combination of activities and create methods of its own. It underlines that learning "outside" the classroom can advance the social maturity of students by helping them develop larger cultural identities and personalities integrated to function in a variety of cultural settings.

Summary

This chapter has examined the relationship between the ethos of the school and the development of peace education. We explored the cultural identity of the school and the relationship of that culture to others within and beyond the community. We then considered clusters of value alternatives and the directions of value changes that need to be considered as elements central to the culture of the school concerned with positive peace. A brief retrospective was given of the peace education themes previously discussed in the chapters on the formal curriculum of the school. These themes were also considered as being equally relevant to the informal educational activities of the school. The chapter concluded by presenting a checklist of informal learning opportunities in school and the ways in which they can contribute to the development of peace education.

REFERENCES AND SOURCES

Alladin, Ibrahim (1989), "Teaching for Global Awareness", *The ATA Magazine,* May/June, 1989: 6–11.

Anderson, C. S. (1982), "The Search for School Climate: a review of research", *Review of Educational Research,* 52: 368–420.

Brenes-Castro, Abelardo, ed. (1991), *Seeking the True Meaning of Peace,* San José, Costa Rica: University for Peace Press.

Brown, George I., Mark Phillips and Stewart Shapiro (1976), *Confluent Education,* Bloomington, Indiana: Phi Delta Kappa Educational Foundation.

Carson, Terrance (1991), *The International Classroom,* World Council for Curriculum and Instruction Forum, 5(1): 49–56.

Cutrona, Cheryl and Diane Guerin (1994), "Confronting Conflict Peacefully: Peer Mediation in Schools", *Educational Horizons,* Winter 1994: 95–104.

Ghosh, Ratna (1996), *Redefining Multicultural Education,* Toronto: Harcourt Brace Canada.

Hammond, Merryl and Rob Collins (1993), *One World, One Earth: Educating Children for Social Responsibility,* Gabriola Island, B.C.: New Society Publishers.

Hilke, Eileen Veronica (1990), *Cooperative Learning,* Bloomington, Indiana: Phi Delta Kappa Educational Foundation.

Hodgkinson, Christopher E. and John J. Jackson (1986), "Peace Education: A Sophisticated Approach", *Education Canada,* Winter, 1986: 44–49.

McHarris, Ian (1988), *Peace Education,* London: McFarland and Company.

Mitchell, Morris R. (1967), *World Education: Revolutionary Concept,* New York: Pageant Press.

Morin, Edgar (1989), "Cultural Identity in a Global Culture", *Forum,* Council of Europe, February, 1989: 33–34.

Nenova, Yordanka, Anelia Kanova and Julia Angelova (1992), *Continuing Challenges to Human Rights and Peace,* Rousse, Bulgaria: Pimat.

Oakes, Jeannie (1985), *Keeping Track: How Schools Structure Inequality,* New Haven: Yale University Press.

Peters, Thomas J. and Robert H. Waterman (1984), *In Search of Excellence,* New York, Warner.

Reardon, Betty (1988), *Comprehensive Peace Education: Educating for Global Responsibility,* New York: Teachers College Press.

Rutter, Michael (1979), *Fifteen-Thousand Hours: Secondary schools and their effects on children,* Cambridge, Massachusetts: Harvard University Press.

Sapon-Shevin Mara and Nancy Schniedewind (1990), "Selling Cooperative Learning Without Selling It Short", *Educational Leadership,* December 1989/January 1990: 63–65.

Schwab, Joseph J. (1973), "The Practical 3: Translation into Curriculum", *School Review,* August 1973: 501–522.

Shepherd, Kathleen (1994), "Stemming Conflict Through Peer Mediation", *School Administrator,* April 1994: 14–17.

Smith, David C. (1986), "The Development of Values for a World Society" in Paris Arnopoulos (ed.), *Prospects for Peace: An anthology of perspectives on social conflict and peaceful change,* Montreal: Gamma Institute.

Smith, David C. (1987), "Peace Education and the Ethos of the School", *The McGill Journal of Education,* 22 (3), Fall 1987: 307–316.

Strivens, Janet (1986), "Values and the Social Organization of Schooling", in Peter Tomlinson and Margret Quinton, *Values Across the Curriculum,* London: The Falmer Press.

Changing the Culture of the School

IN SEPTEMBER 1970, *Steve Ramsankar became principal of the Alex Taylor Community School, located in the tough inner core of the city of Edmonton. At that time, the neighbourhood around the school was a depressed area of shabby apartments, derelict town-housing, smudgy taverns and sleazy hotels. The community was beset by problems of unemployment, drug dealing, prostitution and petty theft. The frequent presence of police signified a troubled community in which some groups exploited others, where human relationships had become fragmented, and where life had become stressful as a result of poverty and desperation.*

Inevitably, many of the tensions and problems of the inner city were reflected in the community's school. Children often arrived at school hungry. Some were embarrassed by their dirty clothes; others came in worn-out clothing or dressed inadequately for the cold weather. Moreover, the children frequently came with psychological problems. Many bore emotional scars inflicted by the alcoholism of their parents or the separation of their families. Some bullied younger pupils or vandalized school property. The divisiveness and disintegration of the community seriously affected the quality of school life and the quality of learning.

Principal Ramsankar saw his primary role as providing leadership in building love and trust among students and teachers within the school. He recognized, however, that if the school was to try to meet the special needs of the pupils, it could not work in isolation; it had to work closely with the families of the neighbourhood. For this reason, the principal conceived of the school as a welcoming place for the whole community.

He began by providing breakfast to children who came to school hungry. The costs were paid entirely by himself and private donors, until the Alberta government subsidized the program. Used clothing was distributed to children in need, and the school board installed showers, as well as washing and drying machines so that youngsters could clean their clothes at school. A program of day care was opened for pre-schoolers, enabling unemployed single parents to work and provide better conditions for themselves and their children. The destitute elderly were invited to the school once a week for a free lunch and a time together where they gave each other mutual support and encouragement. English classes were provided for immigrant adults whose children were often struggling with English as their second language at school. During the summer months, a recreation program was introduced for all children and parents in the downtown core.

Support for the school and its programs has been promoted through the building of a network of relationships with the community. Local business leaders have contributed financially to school programs and promoted various cultural activities, including a celebration of the Chinese New Year with a parade, music and dancing. War veterans associated with the Canadian Legion participated in the observance of Remembrance Day. Local and provincial politicians were involved in a variety of celebrations and festivities through the school year. High-school students sponsored a Halloween Party for the children at Alex Taylor, and students from colleges and universities helped with summer recreational and educational programs. The police, whose role had once been limited to the search and arrest of thieves and drug dealers, came to present safety pro-

grams and to participate in games and sports with the youngsters. The building of these and other bonds with the community have helped to transform the school into a place of joyful activity and to promote a spirit of change and renewal in homes and businesses of the surrounding area.

The cultural values of the school and the community have changed. Children who, at one time, had little self-worth have gained self-esteem. At school, the one-time atmosphere of apathy and alienation has given way to a sense of love and trust. The pupils greet teachers, custodian and principal with hugs, and exude a sense of joy in learning. The community, too, has gradually been transformed: legitimate businesses have prospered and the neighbourhood has developed a new-found sense of worth and solidarity. Many of the frustrations and deep divisions within the school and its surroundings have disappeared. The process of re-integration guided by new values has been producing a more peaceful community.

As a brief sample study, the Alex Taylor Community School illustrates well the process by which an institution can educate for a more peaceful future. But what is the process by which a school can change its directions of development? How can schools themselves become more internally integrated institutions? By what process can the school and the community draw more closely together? How can the school and the community build a sense of identity that takes into consideration their international and global links? In this chapter, we will first consider a framework for examining the contexts of change in school culture and then go on to examine the process of such change.

The Contexts of Change

In thinking about the role of the school in educating for a more peaceful future, it is necessary to recall that the school has the function of building its own climate and culture while still playing a part in the development of polycentric identities, as discussed in the previous chapter. A consideration of the on-going process of the transformation of the school for peace needs to be seen within the context of cultural development and identity-building in this larger sense. Figure 14–1 summarizes the contextual relationships of school development and other spheres of development with which, in a sense, it is co-dependent.

FIGURE 14–1 Some contexts of school development

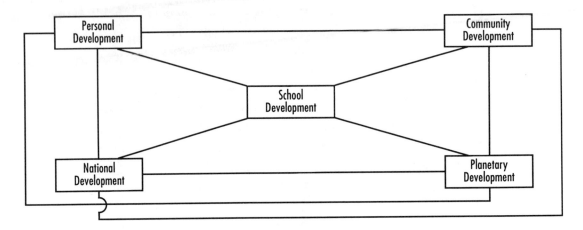

Personal Development

The personal, inner development of students and staff can be thought of as one of the co-dependent functions of school development. The idea of personal peace was described as an important dimension of peace education in Chapter 2, and we have seen that a number of school subjects—particularly music, art, literature and religious studies—can contribute to personal peace. But what do we mean by personal peace?

Some writers have argued that the process of peace-building must begin with the integration of the self. Eastham (1992) has written that Western intellectual tradition has tended to create an adversarial relationship between the sciences (nature), the humanities (humankind) and religion (spirit), and that the re-integration of these three dimensions in the human person is a requirement for peace-building in the external world. Similarly, in his study of peace education, Hicks (1988) describes the need for a paradigm shift from fragmentary thinking to ecological, systemic and holistic thinking at the personal, political

and planetary levels. The growth of personal peace lies in the individual's establishment of larger and larger connections, in dissolving the "us versus them" mentality, and in constantly seeking coherence and integrity in one's worldview. In the sense that personal peace involves learning to live with paradox and always seeking an enlargement of understanding, it is the process of finding wisdom.

Community Development

The story of the Alex Taylor Community School illustrates well the way in which school development needs to go hand-in-hand with community development. The school's activities reach into the community and the community develops links to the school for the betterment of all. To their detriment and that of the community, many schools have been relatively isolated from their surroundings. There is a need for reconnection and integration to provide students with a wider encounter with people, places and problems and to give them new experiences and wider associations.

The involvement of the school with the community's development needs to be inspired and guided by values consonant with those underpinning school life, as discussed in the previous chapter. The values include openness to learning, participation, friendship, sustainability, justice and wholeness. In striving for such values, the school and community will tend to work towards a common goal: the building of peace in a larger totality.

A striving for community development can involve authentic and significant academic learning when it embraces all aspects of community life: the political (the making and implementation of by-laws and policies, the resolution of issues such as rezoning of land and community renewal, etc.); the economic (community businesses, taxation, employment, budgets. etc.); the physical (buildings, roads, parks, and other features of the landscape); and the social (social facilities, social services, community celebrations, etc.). It is the interplay among these factors that creates the fabric of community living. Lipka et al. (1985) point out that service projects should ideally arise from real community needs.

In a comprehensive review of research and theory in school-based community studies, Conrad and Hedin (1991) found that there was convincing evidence that students who engaged in community service projects benefited in a number of ways. They found that students who participated in political and social action in the school and in the wider community became more open-minded and acquired significantly more skill in problem solving than students in comparison groups. Such students gained in self-esteem, had lower levels of alienation, and advanced in their sense of personal and social responsibility. They also had more favourable attitudes towards adults and towards the organizations and people with whom they worked. The connection between school and community development appears strongly to support the kinds of value orientations necessary for more harmonious community living.

National Development

Historically, more attention has been given to national development in relation to education than to either community or planetary development. In fact, modern movements for compulsory primary and secondary education in nearly all countries have gained impulse primarily from the need for national development. Most countries have issued major periodic reports that shape, or reshape, educational policy in relationship to their social, cultural, economic and political goals.

At any stage in the growth of their identity, nations have invariably seen education as an important means of achieving national solidarity. Increasingly, nations have become "learning societies", valuing education. They have developed institutions to improve the management of conflict, valuing non-violence. They have often worked, achieving varying degrees of success, at building more effective democratic governments, valuing participation. Most have made some progress towards human rights and responsibilities, valuing justice. They have frequently worked hard at improving internal transportation and communications, valuing integration and unity. And more recently, they have, for the most part, acknowledged responsibility for the environmental support of future generations, valuing sustainability.

The relationship between national and educational development is a vital one. Where the educational system is perceived simply as an instrument of national development, without a critical function and critical perspective, national development can be arrested. Nations that deny human rights, perpetuate elitism or use violence against sectors of the population are, in some respects, at war with themselves. If their abuses are sufficiently extreme, they may be at war with other nations as well.

A great deal can obviously be done through school development to enhance national development towards ends that are consonant with peace. Strategies include, for instance, changes in courses of study and in curriculum that help in nation-building, and the development of school-wide activities that enhance participation in the nation's affairs, that develop cross-country friendship and trust, that promote unity in diversity, and that otherwise support peace values in a national context.

Planetary Development

In the twentieth century we have become aware of the many world problems that threaten international peace and security: significant inequalities in the consumption of resources over the globe; the installation of elitist or repressive governments in many nations; the abridgement of human rights and other injustices; the existence of structural violence and institutionalized use of force; and environmental catastrophes that imperil human life. These problems are not separate crises, but as many analysts have concluded (Myers, 1984; Barnaby, 1988; Hicks, 1988), they are different facets of a single world crisis. They are systemic problems in the sense that they are all inter-related.

Planetary development needs to take into account the organic relationship between these problems. Modern scholarship has helped us to understand more completely the nature of the problems and their global connectedness. As a result, global and universally human perspectives have been treated as an important part of learning throughout this book. Developing a conciousness of human oneness is, in itself, a process that enhances planetary development.

World development requires the emergence of responsible and just government at the global and at other levels—government that invites participation and consultation, that always works towards the building of consensus and towards strengthening international law for a cohesive and stable world society. Considerable progress has been made in the organization of regional economic and political cooperation and even cooperation at the global level through the United Nations and its agencies. However, the improvement of these systems to reflect more equal participation and influence at the world level is imperative to development.

For many decades, the world was preoccupied by the East-West ideological split and was divided fundamentally on the question of the redistribution of wealth. The differences between East and West have now faded behind the comparison between North and South. The global economic system—in which the rich nations have become richer and the poor, poorer—has been evolving into the greatest source of international tension. Planetary development requires a commitment to justice in finding ways to redistribute wealth at the global level.

The elimination of various forms of violence is equally essential. The global economic system is a form structural violence, as are imperialism, racism and sexism. Structures of dominance are only gradually being dismantled and transformed into relationships based upon equity. Physical violence at the global level, once a norm for resolving international disputes, is now less acceptable as a legitimate form of conflict resolution, and is being replaced by the gradual institutionalization of non-violent means of settling disputes.

Planetary development must also be consistent with the principle of sustainability. Earlier indigenous societies generally recognized their dependence upon the land, water and air, and held these resources sacred. Modern urban civilizations, however, have lost their communion with nature. In consequence, the environment upon which they depend is deteriorating through deforestation, erosion, desertification and pollution. World society must aim at reestablishing contact with the natural environment and achieving a sustainable relationship with all of our planetary resources.

In the context of planetary development, schools face an enormous challenge in responding creatively to the changing circumstances of the globe. Part II of this book dealt with ways in which the curriculum can be adapted to contribute to global development. The larger life of the school, too, can enrich the international experiences of students, enhance their awareness of world issues and, as evident in the discussion of school ethos, provide authentic opportunities for positive action at the global level.

The school is a living institution. It changes and develops in a variety of contexts, all of which are important and all of which the school needs to recognize. The relationship between the school and those contexts is a dynamic one, with the school both shaping and being shaped by its total environment. If school development is guided by values that promote peace in all of these contexts, it can be a bright beacon in the lives of its students and of every individual with whom it is networked.

The Process of Change

The desire to change a school into a more peaceful environment can arise from a number of sources. It can arise from a crisis in the life of the school (as in the case of the injury or death of a student resulting from gang rivalry); it can arise from concerns expressed by students, staff or parents (with regard to drug or alcohol abuse, poor academic achievement among sectors of the school population and the like); it can happen as a consequence of careful observation, reading and reflective thinking; it can occur as a result of discussions and a shared vision of what the school can become. Whatever the spur to change, the development of the school as a just and peaceful community, as a place of optimal learning for all, as an institution networked to the real world for the construction of peace, requires the building of consensus, especially among teachers and preferably among all who are touched by the activities of the school. The transformation of school culture is an ongoing process; yet there may be some goals that are short-term (such as improving relationships among different ethnic groups within the school) and some that are longer-term goals (such as the elimination of structures of dominance within the school or community). In this section we will consider the process of change by examining each of the following aspects: taking stock of the quality of school life; planning for change; sharing responsibility for change; making decisions about change; and evaluating change on an on-going basis.

Taking Stock of School Life

To some extent, the procedure for changing the culture of the school depends upon the initial motives of the institution and its leaders. If the desire for change is relatively unhurried, the school and its community can go through a process of collective reflection upon the mission of the school and the place of peace education in that mission. There can be an assessment of the strengths and areas in need of development. For this purpose, the kind of checklist suggested in Chapter 13 (pp. 254–257), may be used to consider the school as a whole. From the results of such a self-examination, a profile can be drawn of the degree to which peace education is infused into the life of the school. The profile can be used as a point of departure for deciding which areas may need to be strengthened or developed.

If the desire for change develops from a specific crisis, or from the identification of major problems or concerns, there may be a need for a relatively swift analysis of the problems, some necessary consultation, the development of recommendations, and prompt action. Professional literature in recent years has identified a number of relatively common problems concerning the need for a greater commitment to such values as learning, equality, integration, and justice. For example, Oakes (1985, 1992) has studied the way in which the tracking, or separation, of students by ability results in the legitimization of inequality, and has suggested new ways of providing for the special needs of children in heterogeneous groupings. Knapp and Shields (1990) review ways of providing for more challenging content and more effective instruction in teaching the children of poverty, who are most at risk of school failure. Kehoe and Hébert (1992) have devised a very practical approach to assessing the multicultural needs of the school and the community and ways of providing greater equality of opportunity to children from diverse cultural backgrounds.

The process of taking stock of school life is essentially one of self-examination; however, on occasion, some schools may invite an external evaluator, or a visiting team, to review the school, conduct interviews with students and staff, and make recommendations for school development in accordance with peace values. While external evaluators may have the advantage of greater objectivity, they lack the depth of knowledge which the community has of itself. External evaluation, therefore, is acceptable as a supplemental perception of the school rather than a self-sufficient assessment. Further, if new goals are to be identified and change achieved, then those who are centrally involved need to participate in the process from the beginning.

Sharing Responsibility for Change

When the school is conceived as being a true community of learners, each participant recognizes that he or she gives and shares in the planning and growth of every other person. In this context, educational change is more likely to be authentic when administrators, teachers, parents and students play some part in the process of bringing about change. Change will be less effective when it is seen as the enactment of policies and directives from a central authority. Moreover, educational change brought about in a democratic manner is consistent with the peace value of participation. There is a need for a sense of ownership of proposed changes by those who are instrumental in bringing them about, and that includes all people who are associated in some way with the school.

Administrators can exercise a great deal of influence upon the school's culture and climate by setting the formal and informal agendas for change (Richardson, 1988). Principals, vice-principals and department heads can take leadership by upholding peace values for the school as a whole and, in the day-to-day life of the school, modelling cooperative behaviour, respect for cultural and racial diversity, peaceful conflict resolution, and appreciation of multiple perspectives. More and more, however, it is recognized that the administration of a school needs to undergo development itself, and that it can share some aspects of leadership to great advantage with other members of the school and the community (Meadows, 1990; Conley and Bacharach, 1990).

Most changes towards the development of a more peaceful school culture require a great deal of effort, adjustment and reorientation on the part of teachers and other members of staff. The teachers themselves may, indeed, often be initiators of change and, therefore, need to accept that they have a role in persuading colleagues in their schools and professional organizations of the need for value shifts or greater commitment to peace values. They also need to be open to proposals for change made by colleagues and, where differences exist, to encourage a climate of open discussion (as opposed to secretiveness and backbiting), so that conflicts can be worked out in an atmosphere of respect and trust. Teachers must be convinced that any proposed changes are in the interest of their students, and they must appropriate any change for themselves (Richardson, 1988). Along with teachers, school nurses, secretaries, counsellors, librarians and custodians can all contribute effectively in special ways; for example, nobody in the school is more aware of acts of vandalism than the school custodian.

Students are only rarely included in discussions of educational change and reform, yet they have valuable perspectives that can contribute to the effective redirection of a school.

Wells (1987) makes the point that students should be asked to imagine what a peaceful society (school, community, nation, world) could be like, as a step towards their understanding that a peaceful future is largely the result of human choice. Writing on the insightfulness of student perspectives, Phelan et al. (1992) report that students are very much aware of, and sensitive to, the overall ambience of their schools, including mechanisms for student input into decision-making, their perceptions of safety or violence, and the collective messages conveyed by the school as an institution. Significantly, they tend to be very much aware, too, of groups within the school, the amount of tension among them and the fluidity with which it is possible to move among groups. Students are an important source of information about the school, and they can learn to share some responsibility for peaceful change during their school experience.

Much attention has traditionally been given to the support role that parents can play in learning and to the improvement of communications between home and school, both of which have an important relationship to peace education. More recently there have been studies of other ways of expanding parental involvement in school development. Epstein (1987, 1988) for instance, has found that parents can be important resource persons for school activities and can participate in school and school-district decision-making. Such an emphasis draws upon the strengths of families, on the kinds of experiences they have that can enrich the academic life of the school, and on the solidarity that can be built between the school and the community.

Responsibility for change can also be shared with other members of the community, as was so well illustrated in the case study of the Alex Taylor Community School. There is an old

African saying, "The whole village educates the child." Members of cultural organizations and voluntary associations, business people, police, college and university students, staff and others can be partners in helping the school to become a more peaceful community and in increasing the longer-term influence of the school as an important agent in transforming society.

Making Decisions to Effect Change

The process of making decisions about change in the school can involve a collective approach by all the schools in a board or district (Richardson, 1988: 239) or it can focus primarily on the individual school (Marsh et al., 1990). Our focus here will be on school-based development, and will be suggestive rather than prescriptive. In general, it is recommended that the work of school development be coordinated through a policy committee representing the different constituencies of the school and community. After some preliminary planning, the committee can organize a series of work groups, or task forces, to undertake the more detailed work of consultation and consensus-building and to oversee the implementation of decisions for action. It is advisable, however, for each school to choose the kind of systems approach to change that suits its special character and needs.

A policy committee, or school-improvement committee, will normally be composed of teachers and other staff members, students, administrators, parents and, possibly, community representatives. Its role is essentially as a steering and coordinating committee concerned with the improvement and peaceful development of the school. The committee may be confronted with a series of questions relating to school climate: Does the ambiance of the school foster excellence in all-round achievement? How can we develop the school as a just community? How can we improve the integration of the school with our community? How can the school contribute to the strengthening of national development? In what ways might the school improve education for world development and peace? The committee might conduct an assessment of the quality of school life (Howard et al., 1987) or it might make use of data or evaluative profiles of the school that are already available.

When the committee knows something of the strengths and deficiencies of the school, it can use the assessment as a point of departure for thinking about development. A profile of the school might also provide a base line from which later appraisals of progress can be made. If we suppose, for example, that the committee finds the school strong in school-community relationships and in contributions to national development, but weak in its global or world orientation, it could do some brainstorming of ways in which these weak aspects of school life could be improved. Figure 14–2 illustrates the mapping of ideas that could emerge from such a brainstorming session.

The committee might find that the ideas generated can be grouped into coherent clusters and that the clusters suggest specific lines of development. If we start at the top and move clockwise, we find that Figure 14–2 suggests a number of such themes for strengthening world perspectives. They include school activities, the physical environment, learning resources, school communications and school-wide projects. Upon further discussion, the committee might find that some items need to be reclassified, or that others overlap several categories. It might wish to use these groupings, or revised ones, as a basis for organizing a number of project teams to explore each aspect further.

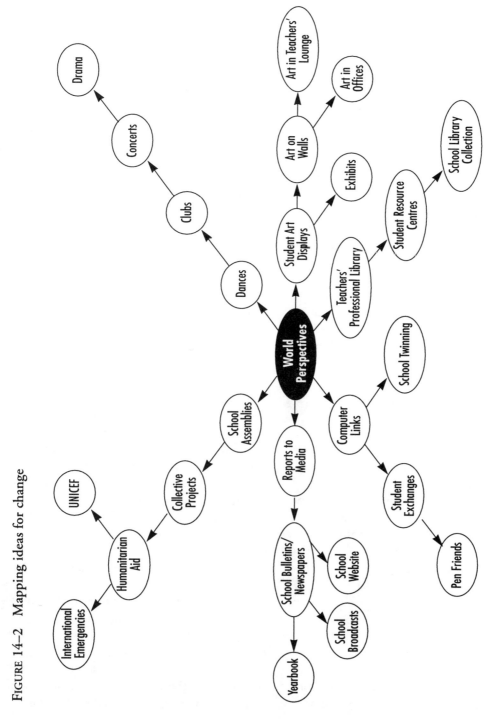

FIGURE 14–2 Mapping ideas for change

The policy committee can then organize an appropriate number of project teams to be composed mainly of teachers invited to participate on the basis of their talents and interests. Each team will have the task of exploring the topic in greater detail, consulting with the school community, building consensus and reporting back in periodic dialogue with the policy team (Marsh et al., 1990). A project team can benefit from reading professional literature, from visiting other schools that model activities for world perspectives, and from inviting members of the school community generally to share their observations and thoughts on promising school practice. The teams may wish to use meetings, seminars and forums as means of generating ideas and building consensus. Any of these formats will help to maximize school and community participation.

School development activities of this type almost inevitably produce some conflicting ideas about growth and change. Conflicts like these can be used by the peace-building school as opportunities to add to the experience of constructive conflict resolution. Deepening understanding of the processes of de-escalating conflict, developing role convergence and improving communication can lead to important growth in positive peace within the school (Doll, 1986; Steinberg, 1989; Achoka, 1990; Isherwood and Achoka, 1992). Further, there can be a process of checks and balances between the project teams and the policy committee. The project teams are normally required to produce brief reports to the policy committee, and to work within its parameters and budget.

The project teams themselves may be given responsibility for implementing recommendations. For example, a team working with learning resources, after agreeing upon priorities with the policy committee, might develop a world studies resource centre within, or outside, the library. It could include books, computer programs and networks, video cassettes, audio tapes and slides dealing with international and global themes. On the one hand, the team could encourage and monitor the use of the centre by students at different levels and in different subject areas, and on the other, it could negotiate the building of learning resources in other areas that are seen as emerging priorities. The policy committee has the function of coordinating the total effort so that cultural change occurs as a coherent and integrated process. Through continuing formative assessment and on-going dialogue, the school would aim to engage in self-sustaining change.

Evaluating Changes in School Culture

As we say in Chapter 13, the heart of the ethos, or culture, of a school lies in the kinds of values that prevail in the life of the institution. In assessing cultural change, we are concerned ultimately with shifts in value orientations over a period of time. Values and value changes are not measurable directly, but are manifested primarily through school policies, administrative practice, school norms and the attitudinal and behavioural changes of individuals. If we wish to study changes in school culture, it is necessary initially to gather baseline data, and then to collect corresponding data over a period of time that can be subjected to longitudinal analysis (Howard et al., 1987). New initiatives to change the climate and culture of the school may take at least two or three years, since new leadership actions and the work of project teams make only gradual impact upon the totality of the life of the school.

Who evaluates changes in school culture? In a strictly authoritarian structure, evaluation would be carried out by the administration of the school or by an external group. If, however, the school is aiming to be a genuine learning community that values participation, all parts of the school will be implicated in the process. Assessment of change, coordinated by the policy committee, will involve as many of the constituencies as possible. The school will tend to seek a balance between self-evaluation, the evaluation of different parts of school life by the various constituencies and assessment of the school as a whole. Evaluation would, in consequence, require a synthesis of conclusions to be drawn from quantitative *and* qualitative data.

The precise data that a given school collects for evaluation will depend upon the particular character of its development. Marsh et al. (1990) recommend that the evaluation of school-based development should be decentralized, but that the "performance indicators" used should be carefully chosen to ensure the validity of the exercise. Some examples of baseline data that would reflect changes in school climate with regard to conflict resolution, participation in school life, growth of community and enlargement of perspectives are as follows:

Students:
• Incidents of vandalism
• Cases of violence in sports activities
• Discipline referrals to the principal's office
• Rate of participation in community service projects
• Attendance at meetings of school clubs such as a UNESCO club, an international affairs club, etc.
• Use of learning resource centres
• Voter turn-out in school elections
• Number of students having pen friends abroad
• Number of contributors to humanitarian projects

Teachers:
• Memberships in local, national and international organizations
• Journal entries regarding classroom conflict
• Systematic observations of teaching by colleagues
• Interviews regarding change undertaken by colleagues
• Establishment of school websites devoted to international understanding

Parents:
• Contributions to school policy development
• Support of school activities related to peace education
• Attitudes towards school development
• Observations concerning changes in their children's interests and perspectives

Administrators:
• Peace education initiatives
• Response to project team/policy committee recommendations
• Pattern of resource allocation
• Administrative links to the local community
• Journal of conflict resolution in the school
• Administrative support of international networking

It has been emphasized that efforts to change the culture of the school, to develop peace-making and peace-building as an integral part of school life, is a shared responsibility. Since evaluation is part of the process of change, on-going evaluation is also a shared responsibility: assessments by students, teachers, parents, administrators and community members all help the school to evolve. The data gathered can enable the participants to evaluate the success of specific projects and to determine, by implication, whether school culture is changing in terms of incremental, or even significant, shifts in values. On the basis of evaluation, existing projects can be consolidated, priorities can be re-ordered, resources can be re-directed, restructuring and regrouping can occur, new projects can be created. The effect upon the collective life of the school of individual efforts for peaceful development is greater than the sum of the parts, and there is abundant evidence to show that a positive school climate has a beneficial effect upon individual "performance". Personal peace, good group relationships, and institutional peace are interdependent with each other.

Summary

This final chapter began with a brief case study of the way in which an "unpeaceful" school was transformed, over a period of time, into a more peaceful institution. The case study was used, in part, to raise a number of significant questions about institutional change, and especially to highlight that school development occurs within the context of the personal and individual development of its members, the organic development of the community, and development at the national and planetary levels.

The chapter then provided some guidelines for school improvement consonant with principles of peace education. Emphasis was placed upon the idea of cultural transformation in a school and the values inherent in the peace-making and peace-building process: openness, reflectiveness, participation, cooperation, creativity, integrity and wholeness. The suggested steps included taking stock of a school's strengths, problems and goals; sharing widely the responsibility for change; exploring solutions freely and creatively; building consensus and making decisions on a democratic basis; and evaluating goals and progress as a continuing and on-going process. It is within this framework that the everyday life of the school in classrooms, hallways, laboratories, gymnasia, libraries, playing fields and in the community beyond may be lived as a more wholesome, peaceful and joyful experience.

REFERENCES AND SOURCES

Achoka, Judith (1990), "Conflict Resolution: The Need for Virtuosity", *Education Canada*, 30 (1): 43–46.

Berger, Michael (1974), *Violence in the Schools: Causes and Remedies*, Bloomington, Indiana: Phi Delta Kappa Educational Foundation.

Boyte, Harry C. (1991), "Community Service and Civic Education", *Phi Delta Kappan*, June, 1991: 765–767.

Carson, Terrance (1987), "Curriculum research and implementation of peace education", *Canadian Journal of Peace Education and Research*, 19(3): 29–40.

Conley, Sharon C. and Samuel B. Bacharach (1990), "From School-Site Management to Participatory School-Site Management", *Phi Delta Kappan*, 71 (7), March 1990: 539–534.

Conrad, Dan and Diane Hedin (1991), "School-Based Community Service: What We Know from Research and Theory", *Phi Delta Kappan*, June, 1991: 743–749.

Doll, Ronald C. (1986), *Curriculum Improvement: Decision-Making and Process*, Toronto: Allyn and Bacon.

Eastham, Scott (1992), "How Is Wisdom Communicated? Prologue to Peace Studies", *Interculture*, XXV (2), Issue No.115, Spring 1992: 3–33.

Epstein, Joyce L. (1987), "What Principals Should Know About Parent Involvement", *Principal,* 66: 6–9.

Epstein, Joyce L. (1988), "How Do We Improve Programs of Parent Involvement?" *Educational Horizons,* 66: 58–59.

Gay, Geneva (1990), "Achieving Educational Equality Through Curriculum Desegregation", *Phi Delta Kappan,* 72 (1): 56–62.

Gregory, Thomas B. and Gerald R. Smith (1987), *High Schools as Communities: The Small School Reconsidered,* Bloomington, Indiana: Phi Delta Kappa Educational Foundation.

Hawkins, Donald E. and Dennis A. Vinton (1973), *The Environmental Classroom,* Englewood Cliffs, New Jersey: Prentice Hall.

Hicks, David (1988), "Changing Paradigms" in *Education for Peace: Issues, Principles and Practice in the Classroom,* London: Routledge.

Hodgkinson, Harold (1991), "School Reform Versus Reality", *Phi Delta Kappan,* 73 (1), September, 1991: 8–16.

Howard, Eugene, Bruce Howell and Edward Brainard (1987), *Handbook for Conducting School Climate Improvement Projects,* Bloomington, Indiana: Phi Delta Kappa Foundation.

Isherwood, Geoffrey B. and Judith Achoka (1992), "Conflict and the Principalship: Quebec English secondary schools circa 1990", *Education Canada,* 32 (1), Spring 1992.

Kehoe, John and Yvonne M Hébert, (1992), *A Handbook for Enhancing the Multicultural Climate of the School,* Vancouver: Western Education Development Group, Faculty of Education, University of British Columbia.

Knapp, Michael S. and Patrick M. Shields (1990), "Reconceiving Academic Instruction for Children of Poverty", *Phi Delta Kappan,* 71 (10), June 1990.

Kretovics, Joseph, Kathleen Farber and William Armaline (1991), "Reform from the Bottom Up: Empowering Teachers to Transform Schools", *Phi Delta Kappan,* 73 (4), December, 1991: 295–299.

Lipka, Richard P., James A. Beane and Brian E. O'Connell (1985), *Community Service Projects: Citizenship in Action,* Bloomington, Indiana: Phi Delta Kappa Foundation.

London, Samuel B. and Stephen W. Stile (1982), *The School's Role in the Prevention of Child Abuse,* Bloomington, Indiana: Phi Delta Kappa Educational Foundation.

Marsh, Colin, Christopher Day, Lynne Hannay and Gail McCutcheon (1990), *Reconceptualizing School-Based Curriculum Development,* London: The Falmer Press.

Meadows, B. J. (1990), "The Rewards and Risks of Shared Leadership", *Phi Delta Kappan,* 71 (7), March 1990: 545–548.

Melamed, Lanie and Rosemary Sullivan (1987), "Guides for Peacemakers: Improving Discussions and Group Meetings", *Peace Education News,* 2, Summer/Fall 1987.

Meyers, Norman (1984), *Gaia: An Atlas of Planet Management,* New York: Doubleday.

Oakes, Jeannie (1985), *Keeping Track: How Schools Structure Inequality,* New Haven, Yale University Press.

Oakes, Jeannie and Martin Lipton (1992), "Detracking Schools: Early Lessons from the Field", *Phi Delta Kappan,* 73 (6), February, 1992: 448–454.

Peace Education Resource Centre (1992), *Children and Peacemaking,* Toronto: Peace Education Resource Centre.

Phelan, Patricia, Ann Locke Davidson, and Hanh Thanh Cao (1992), "Speaking Up: Students' Perspectives on School", *Phi Delta Kappan,* 73 (9), May 1992: 695–704,

Pierson, Ruth Roach (1987), *Women and Peace: Theoretical, Historical and Practical Perspectives,* London: Croom-Helm.

Richardson, Robin (1988), "Changing the Curriculum", in David Hicks (ed.), *Education for Peace,* London: Routledge.

Sergiovanni, Thomas J. (1993), *Building Community in Schools,* San Francisco: Jossey-Bass.

Steinberg, Adria, Editor (1989), "Talking It Out: Students Mediate Disputes", *The Harvard Education Letter,* 5 (1), January/February 1989: 4–5.

Tyrwhitt, Janice (1987), "A Loving Principal", *Readers Digest,* August, 1987: 80–84.

U.S. Committee for UNICEF (1985), *Joy Through the World: Holiday celebrations of feasting and giving around the world,* New York: Dodd, Mead and Company.

Wells, Margaret (1987), "Teaching for Peace in the Secondary School" in Ruth Roach Pierson (ed.), *Women and Peace: Theoretical, Practical and Historical Perspectives,* London, Croom-Helm: 215–223.

World Confederation of UNESCO Clubs and Associations (1987), *Yes we can... together! UNESCO Clubs and Associations, UNESCO Associated Schools Project,* Paris: UNESCO.

Wynne, Edward A. (1990), *Planning and Conducting Better School Ceremonies,* Bloomington, Indiana: Phi Delta Kappa Educational Foundation.

INDEX